Ain't Gonna Study War
No More

Ain't Gonna Study War No More

Biblical Ambiguity
and the Abolition of War

Albert Curry Winn

Westminster/John Knox Press
Louisville, Kentucky

Scripture quotations from the Revised Standard Version of the Bible are copyrighted 1946, 1952, © 1971, 1973 by the Division of Christian Education of the National Council of the Churches of Christ in the U.S.A. and are used by permission.

Scripture quotations from the New Revised Standard Version of the Bible are copyright © 1989 by the Division of Christian Education of the National Council of the Churches of Christ in the U.S.A., and are used by permission.

Book design by Drew Stevens

First edition

Published by Westminster/John Knox Press
Louisville, Kentucky

This book is printed on recycled acid-free paper that meets the American National Standards Institute Z39.48 standard. ∞

PRINTED IN THE UNITED STATES OF AMERICA

9 8 7 6 5 4 3 2 1

Library of Congress Cataloging-in-Publication Data

Winn, Albert Curry, 1921–
     Ain't gonna study war no more : biblical ambiguity and the abolition of war / Albert Curry Winn.
          p.   cm.
     Includes bibliographical references and index.
     ISBN 0-664-25207-9 (recycled alk. paper)

     1. War—Biblical teaching.   2. Peace—Biblical teaching.   3. War—Religious aspects—Christianity.   4. Peace—Religious aspects—Christianity.   I. Title.
BS680.W2W56   1993
261.8′73′09015—dc20
                                                                            92-33997

For James, Bruce, and Randolph,
three who did the right thing

Contents

Foreword

Anybody who knows Al Winn will know to expect a book on peace that is honest, trenchant, evocative, and energizing. And that is exactly what this book is. The thing about Al Winn is that he cares so much and knows so much—rare combination! He cares so much because there resonates in his body the deepest passions of Christian faith for justice, peace, and human welfare. And those passions regularly drive him to public action that is risk-taking and future-creating. He knows so much because he is an informed, disciplined scholar who works the classic sources, and who thinks with judiciousness about the present crisis. This book, as a result, is a rich, well-documented resource.

The outcome of that caring and knowing is a book that will force rethinking and that will summon to reperception and to faithful action. Winn is honest about the ambiguity of the Bible on his topic, but equally unambiguous about the requirement of the gospel in our particular moment of discernment and obedience. His book is a courageous, poignant contribution to the missional crisis now facing the church. Winn understands about the match between means and ends, and understands that peaceful ends require peaceable means. The message, rooted deep in this man of peace, offers the best of evangelical faith in an accessible, inescapable way.

Walter Brueggemann

Columbia Theological Seminary

Preface

This book is a tract for the times. It is written for Christians who love the Bible and acknowledge its authority for faith and life. It faces openly the fact that the Bible is ambiguous about many great moral issues, such as slavery, the place of women, and war and peace. That is to say that people on either side of the argument can quote considerable selections of scripture that seem clearly to support their side.

For Christians in the peace movement to work with a "mini-canon" of beloved peace passages, totally ignoring the war passages, and for the advocates of peace through strength to work with the war passages and ignore the peace passages gets us nowhere. Someone needs to present as plainly and honestly as possible both sides of the ambiguity and to work through them to a position that is faithful to the central thrust of scripture and to the Lord of scripture. Until we can do that, millions of Christians will be "nowhere" on one of the most critical issues of our time.

I first sensed the ambiguity of the Bible regarding war and peace as a child, listening to my father and mother quote scripture to each other in their ongoing debate about this issue. It figured heavily in my approval as a candidate for the ministry: the chairman of the committee, a veteran of World War I, was disturbed because I refused to embrace completely the warmaking side of the ambiguity. I agonized with it as I faced my own participation in World War II.

As the reality of the nuclear threat has come home to me and I have been caught up in the peace movement, the biblical ambiguity has continued to haunt me. I have been driven to grapple with this problem in lectures at Presbyterian School of Christian Education, Louisville Presbyterian Theological Seminary, Davidson College, and elsewhere. Finally I have been driven to put my struggle into this book. My purpose here is to meet the biblical ambiguity head on and to see if in spite of it, and indeed because of it, there is a scriptural basis for working for the abolition of war, for joining in the chorus of "Ain't Gonna Study War No More."

I am indebted to many books; I have tried to acknowledge them in the Notes. I owe a special debt to Walter Brueggemann, who patiently read the manuscript while on leave at Cambridge and promptly sent a multitude of helpful suggestions back across the Atlantic. Portions of an early draft were read to a small World Peacemakers group that met weekly at six-thirty A.M. and included Walter and Clare Baldwin, Salome Betts, Beverly Blomgren, Dick Ellis, Barbara Gifford, Elaine Green, and others. Many of their suggestions helped to shape what is here. A special word of thanks goes to Gilbert Gragg, who persistently suggested the title. None of the above is responsible for the imperfections that remain.

An early draft resembled an anthology, because I wanted to assemble a large number of the relevant passages on both sides and let them speak for themselves. Readers and editors have persuaded me to reduce the number of passages quoted, but a considerable bulk of scripture quotation remains. I recognize the sin of sloth in us all that prevents us from looking up references, and I am still eager for readers to feel directly the impact of the biblical ambiguity.

Bible quotations are from the New Revised Standard Version unless otherwise noted. I salute its move toward more inclusive language and regret the abundance of remaining masculine pronouns that refer to God. I have not attempted to alter that, but have quoted texts as they stand with one exception. I have replaced "Son of Man" with "the Human One," believing that to be a quite accurate translation of *bar enash* and *huios tou anthrōpou*. The ambiguity regarding war and peace and the historical fact that our texts come from a patriarchal society are not unrelated.

Introduction

Paralyzing Ambiguity

Thus says the LORD of hosts, . . . "Go and attack
Amalek, and utterly destroy all that they have;
do not spare them, but kill both man and
woman, child and infant, ox and sheep, camel
and donkey."

(1 Sam. 15:2–3)

It is not the will of my Father who is in
heaven that one of these little ones
should perish.

(Matt. 18:14, RSV)

Introduction: Paralyzing Ambiguity

The dream of a warless world is hoary with antiquity. It is at least as old as the words of a Hebrew prophet, written centuries before the time of Jesus:

> They shall beat their swords into plowshares,
> and their spears into pruning hooks;
> nation shall not lift up sword against nation,
> neither shall they learn war any more;
> but they shall all sit under their own vines
> and under their own fig trees,
> and no one shall make them afraid.
> (Micah 4:3–4)[1]

Phrases from this dream live on in this, perhaps the most warlike century in human history. We are asked to contribute to the Plowshares Defense Fund. The Vine and Fig Tree Community is located in Alabama. We sing around the campfire the African American spiritual "I Ain't Gonna Study War No More."

But the dream is not confined to radical visionaries, who can be so labeled and dismissed. World War I was widely hailed as "the war to end wars." And at least twice in our century hardheaded politicians and diplomats, shaken by the horrors of modern warfare, have dared to dream the dream. In the prologue of the Covenant of the League of Nations they wrote:

> The High Contracting Parties, in order to promote international cooperation and to achieve international peace and security by the acceptance of obligations not to resort to war . . . agree to this Covenant of the League of Nations.

The League failed; the world went to war again, a yet more horrible war. In its aftermath there was another attempt to abolish war:

> We the peoples of the United Nations determined to save suc-
> ceeding generations from the scourge of war, which twice in our
> lifetime has brought untold sorrow to mankind . . . to ensure . . .
> that armed force shall not be used, save in the common interest
> . . . have resolved to combine our efforts to accomplish these
> aims.

Armed force has been used, not in the common interest, every year since those brave words were written. The inexpressible sadness of our era is that as soon as the dream is revived it dies, overwhelmed by the harsh realities of a world where finally only military might settles international disputes and where even the prospect of total annihilation cannot generate a sustained effort for the abolition of war.

The Church's Timidity

One would suppose that the prophet's dream would be cherished among the prophet's heirs. The Christian church accepts the Bible, where the dream is found, as the authoritative word of God. Therefore one would expect the abolition of war to be high on the church's agenda. Not so. By and large Christians have not talked seriously or acted resolutely for it. For most of its history the energies of the church have been focused, not on how to abolish war, but on how to go to war justly (*jus ad bellum*) and how to fight a war in a just manner (*jus in bello*).

The historic peace churches are an exception. They have believed that there is no way for a state to go to war justly or for a Christian to fight justly once war has been declared. However, it is fair to say that their energies have been focused on conscientious objection to war more than on the abolition of war.

At the height of the cold war, when the reality of the nuclear threat began to sink in, there were stirrings for peace in the churches in the United States. Unprecedented statements against war were released by the Roman Catholic bishops[2] and the United Methodist bishops.[3] Almost every mainline Protestant church issued statements and launched some kind of peacemaking program, but the rank and file of church members have seemed paralyzed, unable to act decisively, unwilling to insist in any clear and public way that the nations of the world, including their own, move toward the abolition of war and the realization of the prophetic dream. Indeed, there has been no clear statement of that goal in the pronouncements of their leaders.

Meanwhile, there was among the powerful TV evangelists and other evangelicals great support for the arms buildup and an ardent embrace of the warlike policies of the Reagan and Bush administrations and even of the military adventures of Colonel Oliver North and his colleagues in "the Enterprise."[4]

Why are Christians thus divided and paralyzed? Why are they so easily caught up in the carefully manipulated fervor of Desert Storm and the like? Why are even those most enthusiastic for peace timid to speak of the abolition of war?

The Ambiguity of the Bible

There are doubtless many reasons: economic and political, psychological and cultural,[5] but a fundamental reason for paralysis and division among Christians is the ambiguity of the Bible.[6] This is evident to the most casual reader. The dream of the abolition of war is given us in the Bible, but the reason most Christians hesitate to accept that dream and act upon it comes also from the Bible, from all the wars that are recorded and celebrated by God's people, all the wars that are authorized and even commanded by God. God is the God of peace, who does not will the destruction of even one little child, but God is also the God of war, who orders war throughout the whole history of the Old Testament and even in the last book of the New.

The Bible is ambiguous with regard to many ethical problems,[7] but Paul D. Hanson, who has made special studies of the diversities and polarities in scripture,[8] says that the ambiguity regarding war and peace is regarded by many as the most troublesome and offensive of all. It can lead to silence on the subject, the justification of war, or the heresy of Marcionism.[9]

Attempted Solutions

Modern Christians have tried in various ways to resolve the scriptural ambiguity. One way is to abandon the Old Testament. Marcion tried this long ago, and was condemned as a heretic. But there has been a tendency, now and again, for "peace churches" to speak of themselves as "New Testament churches." Jean Lasserre, the staunch and erudite French pacifist, asks: "Why do I take up my position on the ground of the New Testament?" He answers that although Jesus bases his teaching on the Old Testament, he gives Old Testament texts an entirely new meaning. So, the Old Testament may illuminate the New, but it cannot contradict or challenge it. It cannot be normative directly. We must find our answers to moral questions in the New Testament alone.[10] Even an Old Testament scholar like T. R. Hobbs, after summarizing the Old Testament view of war, says that it cannot be an example for Christians; they must depend on the New Testament for that.[11] But the New Testament is utterly incomprehensible without the Old, which is its indispensable background. And, as I shall seek to demonstrate, to eliminate the Old Testament eliminates not only a huge number of wars but also the essential picture of what peace is all about, of God as giver of peace, of how peace is to be maintained and ordered—its connection with justice—and of the final peace that is promised and hoped for. The baby would be thrown out with the bath water.

Another attempted solution is the idea of the evolution of religious concepts. Human beings started out with a rather primitive, bloodthirsty conception of God. Slowly but surely their understanding improved until finally, with Jesus, they arrived at the idea of a loving heavenly Parent.[12] There are several problems with this. For one thing, the Bible does not claim to be a study in evolving human concepts; it claims to be revelation, a series of words from God of which human beings could never have conceived on their own. For another, the God of peace occurs from the very beginning, in the most primitive strata of scripture, and the God of war is still there on the final pages.

A third solution is the celebrated two-kingdom solution of Martin Luther. As citizens of Christ's kingdom, Christians do not fight or wage war. But they are also citizens of some earthly kingdom. In that capacity they do fight and wage war, just as the citizens of Israel and Judah did long ago. In a book that is excellent in many respects, Peter Craigie finally comes down, it seems to me, to a form of this solution. Christians are citizens of the kingdom of God, but they are also citizens of some state, and all states are founded on violence, nothing else. Christians cannot change either the kingdom of God or the violent state. Pacifists ignore the reality of the state. Advocates of just war ignore the reality of the kingdom of God. We must live in the tension, attempting the transformation of the state, even though that is impossible! We need both Isaiah's vision of a warless world and Koheleth's common sense that there is a time for war and a time for peace.[13]

One more solution is to say that the peacemaking injunctions of Jesus in the Sermon on the Mount were directed at individuals in their conflicts with other individuals. They are therefore applicable to individuals and perhaps possible for individuals, but they are not applicable to conflicts between states and are not possible for states to obey. Reinhold Niebuhr's *Moral Man and Immoral Society*[14] was a very sophisticated development of this thesis, which had devastating effects on the post–World War I peace movement in the United States and was widely used to justify U.S. participation in World War II. The Old Testament certainly contains abundant illustrations of national actions that fall below the ordinary level of individual morality. Interestingly enough, it is the Old Testament that insists clearly that peace is a national matter, a political matter, not to be confined to some inward peace in the individual heart or to good relationships between one individual and another.

If the ambiguity of the Bible does not yield to these or perhaps other solutions, what shall we do? How shall we start to assess it, to understand it, and ultimately to deal with it?

A Canonical Approach

First of all, it seems to me, we need to take the canon of scripture as it stands. Not only should we not delete the Old Testament, we should not use the tools of biblical criticism to delete any passage in either Testament that does not suit our argument. To say that it is "a later addition" to the authentic writing of the prophet, or "clearly reflects the mind of the early church rather than the mind of Jesus," does not mean it is not scripture.

What has functioned authoritatively in the church from early times, and still so functions today, is not the changing reconstructions of the critics, but the established contents of the canon. A discussion of war and peace in which all can join will need to be based there.[15]

This does not mean, on the other hand, that insights from literary-historical criticism, form criticism, redaction criticism, sociological criticism, rhetorical criticism, or narrative criticism will be ignored. Such matters neither produce nor eliminate the biblical ambiguity regarding war and peace, but they have their importance, as we shall see.

The Starting Point

A second basic question of method is: where shall we begin to examine and perhaps to resolve this massive ambiguity? In *Alice in Wonderland* the King of Hearts solemnly advised Alice to begin at the beginning and go to the end.[16] That would seem logical here, but there is a better way. Let us begin at the center, with Jesus. Are we to interpret the teachings of Jesus by the holy war doctrine of Joshua and Samuel, or are we to interpret the holy war doctrine by the teachings of Jesus? Surely Luther was right with his *"was Christum treibt."* For Christians, the true heart of God's word is that which promotes, "pushes" Christ. The internal principle for interpreting scripture can be no other than the mind of Christ.[17] Christ is Lord of scripture as surely as he is Lord of the Sabbath, Lord of the church, Lord of all.

Our first task, then, will be to see if we can understand the mind of Jesus with regard to peace and war. That will become our key to unraveling the ambiguity of the Law and the Prophets, and the ambiguity of the apostolic writings. It will not be as simple as it sounds, for the ambiguity that characterizes the Bible as a whole also characterizes its internal principle of interpretation, the biblical picture of Jesus himself. Ulrich Mauser says that the tension in Jesus' teaching on peace "must not be quickly and cheaply released, otherwise the subject itself becomes very seriously distorted."[18] So we turn in the first two chapters to wrestle with it.

Part One

The Ambiguity of Jesus

Do not think that I have come to bring peace to
the earth; I have not come to bring peace, but a
sword.

(Matt. 10:34)

Put your sword back into its place; for
all who take the sword will perish by
the sword.

(Matt. 26:52)

1

Jesus: "Not Peace, but a Sword"

New Testament scholarship has taught us just how difficult it is to break the biblical picture of Jesus down into its components. There was most assuredly a historical Jesus who lived at a particular spot on our map and at a particular time on our calendar. But to extricate that historical Jesus from the Christ of faith is no easy matter. We do have words that he said, but form criticism has shown us that to extricate those *ipsissima verba* from the forms they have taken in the preaching and teaching of the early church is a hazardous project. Moreover, redaction criticism has shown us that the gospel writers, who arranged the pieces of the tradition, were not mere copyists or scissors and paste artists. Each was a theologian in his own right, writing for the needs of a particular Christian community. To separate what the eyewitnesses remembered from what the theologians wanted to teach is a risky and difficult task. Sociological, rhetorical, and narrative criticism reveal additional layers between us and "the Jesus of history."

It is the total biblical picture of Jesus, made up of all those layers, which has historically been the seat of authority for the church. It is the canonical Jesus who is Lord of the canon. So, in accord with our basic decision for a canonical approach, we shall not spend our time in this chapter or the next on the critical sifting of the tradition. We shall take the biblical picture as it lies and explore its ambiguity regarding peace and war. In this chapter we shall look at those passages that are often quoted by the advocates of peace through strength and neglected by peacemakers.

Jesus Accepted the Fact of a Warring World

Jesus lived in a situation which the liberation theologians have taught us to call institutionalized violence. He and his people were oppressed by a foreign military power and could not forget it any moment of any day. We know from secular sources that insurrections against the Romans occurred every year of Jesus' life, and we see traces of this in the account of the Galileans whose blood Pilate mingled with their sacrifices (Luke 13:1) and the mention of Barabbas, who had started an insurrection in Jerusalem (23:19).

Jesus often pictured this warring world in his parables and sayings without any moral comment: neither praise nor blame. One of his parables concerns a king who goes to encounter another king in war, but first he sits down and estimates the odds. Finding his army outnumbered, he sends a delegation and asks terms of peace (Luke 14:31–32). In another parable a nobleman who has received kingly power says, "As for these enemies of mine who did not want me to be king over them—bring them here and slaughter them in my presence" (Luke 19:27). Again, "The king was enraged. He sent his troops, destroyed those murderers, and burned their city" (Matt. 22:7). The owner of the vineyard will destroy the tenants who beat his servants and killed his son (Mark 12:9 and par.). Jesus spoke of civil wars, of a kingdom divided against itself and laid waste (Matt. 12:25; Mark 3:24; Luke 11:17). He spoke of the strong man, fully armed, who attempts to defend his property by use of force; and of the stronger assailant who binds him, takes away his armor, and plunders his house (Luke 11:21–22; cf. Matt. 11:29; Mark 3:27). Fighting was endemic to all earthly kingdoms. "If my kingdom were from this world," says Jesus to Pilate, "my followers would be fighting" (John 18:36).

Jesus predicted that the world would continue to be this way. There will be "wars and rumors of wars . . . nation will rise against nation, and kingdom against kingdom" (Mark 13:7–8 and par.). He did not say, as he is often quoted as saying, that there would always be wars to the end of time, but he certainly predicted them for some time to come.

Jesus befriended and praised warriors. One of his disciples was a Zealot, a member of a party that advocated, and from time to time attempted, the overthrow of the Roman military occupation by force of arms (Mark 3:18; Matt. 10:4). He praised the faith of a Roman army officer without, as far as we know, attempting to persuade him to change his profession (Matt. 8:5–10; Luke 7:5–10; cf. John 4:46–53).

Jesus seems to have accepted the necessity of paying taxes, not only to support the temple worship (Matt. 17:24–27) but even when a good part of the taxes went to support the legions by which Rome kept its military grip on the world. While "Give to the emperor the things that are the emperor's" (Mark 12:13–17 and par.) does not clearly say, "Yes, go ahead and pay your taxes," it has often been interpreted to mean that. Caesar's image was on the coin, so the coin should go to Caesar. God's image is on the human person, so the person belongs to God.[1]

Jesus Was the Center of Conflict

Among the building blocks of the Gospels are not only miracle stories and pronouncement stories, but conflict dialogues. Jesus was in conflict, not primarily with the Roman overlords, but with the religious leaders of his own people. One of the features of Mark's Gospel is a skillful collection of conflict stories in 2:1–3:6. Early in his ministry, Jesus confronts the Pharisees over such issues as forgiving sins, eating with sinners, fasting, plucking grain on the Sabbath, healing on the Sabbath. In Matthew and Luke we find the famous series of woes upon "scribes and Pharisees, hypocrites" (Matt. 23:1–36; Luke 11:37–52). And the central section of the Fourth Gospel is an almost uninterrupted conflict between Jesus and "the Jews," meaning, again, the religious leaders of his people (John 5–12).

Jesus does not fit the conventional picture of a peacemaker in these conflicts. He pulls no punches. Occasionally he is moved to anger, as Mark candidly records, "He looked around at them with anger; he was grieved at their hardness of heart" (Mark 3:5). Once his anger erupted into action, when Jesus strode into the temple with a whip of cords, drove out the sheep and oxen, overturned the tables of the money changers, and poured out their coins (John 2:13–17; Matt. 21:12–13; Mark 11:15–17; Luke 19:45–46). It was this conflict that led to his death.

Jesus' Teaching Includes Militant Sayings

Jesus is quoted as saying to his disciples:

> Do not think that I have come to bring peace to the earth; I have not come to bring peace, but a sword.
>   For I have come to set a man against his father,
>   and a daughter against her mother,
>   and a daughter-in-law against her mother-in-law;
>   and one's foes will be members of one's own household.
>
> (Matt. 10:34–36)

While it may be argued that the sword here is not meant literally (the parallel passage in Luke 12:51–53 has the word "division"), the divisiveness and strife are entirely literal, hardly the work of peace-making as it is commonly understood. We know, in fact, that Christianity has often divided families, sometimes bitterly.

As a part of his praise for John the Baptist, Jesus said, "From the days of John the Baptist until now the kingdom of heaven has suffered violence, and the violent take it by force" (Matt. 11:12). A parallel saying in Luke reads, "The law and the prophets were in effect until John came; since then the good news of the kingdom of God is proclaimed, and everyone tries to enter it by force" (Luke 16:16). Surely this is one of the most mysterious of Jesus' sayings. Commentators disagree as to whether "the violent" are the oppressors and persecutors of the kingdom or its extremely zealous advocates. However that may be, Jesus is not speaking here of "the peaceable kingdom," but of a kingdom connected in some way with violence.

Luke reports that at the Last Supper Jesus announced what seems to be a change of policy regarding carrying defensive weapons:

"When I sent you out without a purse, bag, or sandals, did you lack anything?" They said, "No, not a thing." He said to them, "But now, the one who has a purse must take it, and likewise a bag. And the one who has no sword must sell his cloak and buy one. For I tell you, this scripture must be fulfilled in me, 'And he was counted among the lawless'; and indeed what is written about me is being fulfilled." They said, "Lord, look, here are two swords." He replied, "It is enough." (Luke 22:35–38)

It has been argued that Jesus did not intend the swords to be used, because that would have prevented the fulfillment of the prophecy which he cited. However, he could easily have had the disciples' self-defense in view, not their defense of him. It has also been argued that two swords were scarcely enough to defend him or themselves when the arresting party arrived later that night. They were not enough for a skirmish in the garden, let alone a war. Jesus' final "Enough!" could have meant, "Enough of this! You have misunderstood my saying"; but Jesus does not say clearly that they misunderstood. It is certainly possible to understand the saying as an approval of carrying arms in a dangerous situation.[2]

Summary

This is the picture of one side of the ambiguity of Jesus.[3] Taken all together, and in isolation from the other side, can these texts be interpreted to make Jesus a militarist? There are those who would like to do so.

In 1929–30, Robert Eisler published a two-volume work alleging that Jesus espoused and participated in armed revolution against the Roman oppressors of his people.[4] According to Eisler, Jesus, under the influence of the Rechabites, was at first critical of the Zealots and taught the nonretaliation that we find in the Sermon on the Mount. Later, perhaps influenced by the Zealots among his own followers, Jesus was convinced that God would intervene only if he took more decisive action of a military kind. He took the sword in order to perish by the sword (Matt. 26:52), believing that his execution would compel God to act for the deliverance of the Jews.

Such a reconstruction of history is obviously not supported by the canonical texts we have cited. Eisler based much of his argument on the Slavonic Josephus. When the scholarly consensus identified the Slavonic Josephus as a medieval fraud, Eisler's work was widely repudiated.

This did not deter S. G. F. Brandon from advancing a similar thesis in 1967.[5] Brandon alleges that Jesus was in sympathy with the Zealots all along and in the end joined in armed insurrection against the Roman power out of purely political motives, for which he was executed on the cross. This obviously requires a more radical emendation and interpretation of the biblical texts than Eisler attempted. Mark, says Brandon, writing for Roman Christians, suppressed all the material that showed that Jesus and the early Jewish Christians, along with the rest of the Jews, violently resisted the Roman rule. But traces of that earlier tradition persist, and on the basis of them we can recover the true picture of Jesus as a militant revolutionary. Brandon's thesis has been used to support the legitimacy of wars of liberation in the third world, but it has not gained wide support from biblical scholars.[6]

While the texts we have cited hardly make Jesus a militarist, it is fair to say that they can be used to picture a Jesus with whom the majority of Christians in the developed nations of today's world could feel quite comfortable. This commonsense Jesus recognizes and accepts war as a fact of life. He participates vigorously in conflicts with opposing viewpoints. He occasionally indulges in outbursts of anger and even combative behavior. He approves the use of weapons in self-defense. He is a good citizen of a state which he knows to be founded upon and sustained by violent military power.

But that is only one side of the ambiguity.

2

Jesus: "Put Away Your Sword"

The other side of the ambiguity of Jesus is well known. The word "peace" was often on his lips. To the woman who was a sinner, and to the woman with the issue of blood, he said, "Go in peace" (Luke 7:50; 8:48; Mark 5:34). Since peace means "health and wholeness," this may have been his customary word to people he healed. Certainly his customary greeting, which served to identify him after the resurrection, was "Peace be with you" (Luke 24:36; John 20:19, 21, 26). And there are the familiar Johannine sayings: "Peace I leave with you; my peace I give to you. I do not give to you as the world gives" (John 14:27). "I have said this to you, so that in me you may have peace" (16:33). These words are much loved by Christians and do not seem incompatible with the picture of the commonsense, respectable Jesus sketched at the end of chapter 1.

When we turn, however, to the record of Jesus' dealing with his enemies, or to the "hard sayings" of the Sermon on the Mount, or to his warning to his nation regarding the Roman occupation, the ambiguity becomes inescapable. It is this side of the ambiguity that has given the church an uneasy conscience regarding war and peace. Volumes have been devoted to the effort to soften it or explain it away.

Actions speak louder than words, so we shall start with Jesus' own actions in face of the hostility and persecution that confronted him personally.

Jesus' Personal Actions

One story indicates Jesus' attitude toward revenge. When he was rejected and turned away from a Samaritan village, his disciples said, "Lord, do you want us to command fire to come down from heaven and consume them?" Jesus turned and rebuked them, and they went on to another village (Luke 9:52–56).

What about fighting in self-defense? There are many strange stories. At the outset of Jesus' ministry, the crowd at Nazareth wanted to push him off a precipice. "But he passed through the midst of them and went on his way" (Luke 4:29–30). When the Pharisees took counsel with the Herodians to destroy him, he withdrew to the sea (Mark 3:6–7). When Herod threatened to kill him, he sent word back that he would simply continue his exorcizing, healing ministry (Luke 13:31–32). The Fourth Gospel is full of such stories. His enemies took up stones to throw at him, but Jesus hid himself, and went out of the temple (John 8:59; cf. 10:31). Several times officers were sent to arrest him, but they came back empty-handed (7:32, 44–47; 8:20; 10:39). After the raising of Lazarus, Jesus no longer went about openly (11:54).

But the confrontation could not be avoided forever. Jesus knew it was coming. The Gospels contain many of his predictions as to what would happen to him (Mark 2:20; 8:31–32; 9:30–32; 10:32–34, 45; 12:7–8; 14:8, 21, 27 and par.; also John 2:19–21; 3:14–15; 7:33–34; 8:21, 28; 10:11, 14–15, 17–18; 12:7, 23–24). Jesus struggled against his fate and prayed to escape from it (Mark 14:31–42; Matt. 26:36–46; Luke 22:40–46; cf. John 12:27–28). But in the end he accepted it nonviolently.

When the arresting party captured him in the Garden of Gethsemane, some of his followers attempted armed resistance. Peter drew a sword and cut off the ear of Malchus, a slave of the high priest. Whatever Jesus may have meant when he told his followers to buy swords (see the discussion of Luke 22:35–38 in chapter 1), when the sword was actually used, he rebuked the user, healed the wounded man,[1] and said, "Put your sword back into its place; for all who take the sword will perish by the sword" (Matt. 26:51–52; Luke 22:49–51; John 18:10–11).

During his trials that followed, Jesus was mostly silent, so much so that Pilate marveled (Matt. 27:14; Mark 15:5). There is no record that he offered any resistance to the scourging or to the nailing to the cross. When he was taunted and cursed, he did not reply in kind, but prayed for the forgiveness of his tormentors (Luke 23:34).[2]

There are those who argue that Jesus' extraordinary behavior was not necessarily an example as to how his followers should behave. Obviously, Jesus' case was unique. He and he alone was the Messiah, the Lamb of God who takes away the sin of the world. He was following a prewritten script. He had to fulfill the prophecies that had been written of him. This is attested by a number of Jesus' sayings: "Do you think that I cannot appeal to my Father, and he will at once send me more than twelve legions of angels? But how then would the scriptures be fulfilled, which say it must happen in this way?" (Matt. 26:53–54). "For [the Human One] goes as it is written of him" (Mark 14:21). "For it is written, 'I will strike the shepherd, and the sheep will be scattered' " (Mark 14:27). "See, we are going up to Jerusalem, and everything that is written of [the Human One] by the prophets will be accomplished" (Luke 18:31). "Oh, how foolish you are, and how slow of heart to believe all that the prophets have declared! Was it not necessary that the Messiah should suffer these things and then enter into his glory?" (Luke 24:25–26). In sum, Jesus' nonresistance was theologically motivated, to fulfill prophecy, to make atonement; it was not ethically motivated, to do the right thing. Therefore it does not necessarily apply to anyone else.

This argument could easily allay the uneasy conscience of the church—unless Jesus explicitly taught his followers that they should follow his example in conflict situations. The records state that he did.

Jesus' Instructions to His Followers

Jesus not only followed a course of nonviolence and nonresistance himself; he commanded his disciples to do likewise: "Do not resist an evildoer" (Matt. 5:39). "If anyone strikes you on the right cheek, turn the other also" (Matt. 5:39; Luke 6:29). "If anyone wants to sue you and take your coat, give your cloak as well" (Matt. 5:40; Luke 6:29). "If anyone forces you to go one mile, go also the second mile" (Matt. 5:41).

Jesus went beyond the condemnation of murder to condemn anger and contempt (Matt. 5:21–22). He went beyond limited revenge—"an eye for an eye and a tooth for a tooth" (v. 38)—to unlimited forgiveness, "Not seven times, but, I tell you, seventy-seven times" (Matt. 18:22; cf. Luke 17:4). Do not judge or condemn your enemies, he says (Matt. 7:1; Luke 6:37); rather, "love your enemies, do good to those who hate you, bless those who curse you, pray for those who abuse you" (Luke 6:27–28; Matt. 5:43–44). To sum up: "Blessed are the peacemakers, for they will be called children of God" (Matt. 5:9). Not those who "keep the peace," for the "peace" they keep may be simply the preservation of injustice and institutionalized violence. Rather, those who "make peace," who through their willingness to suffer pain and even death transform the situation to one in which real peace becomes possible. The commands to follow Jesus' example are also promises to share his glory as "children of God."

How the church has struggled with these sayings! They have been called counsels of perfection, applicable to monks and nuns, but not required of Christians living out in the real world. They have been called an interim ethic, appropriate only if the world is momentarily coming to an end, but inappropriate for the long haul. Perhaps, it is said, they do apply to individual Christians in their daily interpersonal dealings, but there is no way they could be applied to affairs between nations, to matters of war and peace. Yet Jesus did have some things to say to his nation, suffering constantly from institutionalized violence and oppression.

Jesus' Warning to His Nation

Jesus seems clearly to have seen that his people, constantly hatching armed insurrection, were on a collision course with Roman power.

The first three Gospels all attribute to him long discourses about the coming fall of Jerusalem, when not one stone would be left on another (Matt. 24; Mark 13; Luke 21). On the way to the cross he says,

> Daughters of Jerusalem, do not weep for me, but weep for your-
> selves and for your children. For the days are surely coming when
> they will say, "Blessed are the barren, and the wombs that never
> bore, and the breasts that never nursed." Then they will begin to
> say to the mountains, "Fall on us"; and to the hills, "Cover us."
> For if they do this when the wood is green, what will happen when
> it is dry? (Luke 23:28–31)

Could this terrible doom have been averted? It seems so.

> As he came near and saw the city, he wept over it, saying, "If you,
> even you, had only recognized on this day the things that make for
> peace! But now they are hidden from your eyes. Indeed, the days
> will come upon you, when your enemies will set up ramparts
> around you and surround you, and hem you in on every side.
> They will crush you to the ground, you and your children within
> you, and they will not leave within you one stone upon another;
> because you did not recognize the time of your visitation." (Luke
> 19:41–44; cf. 13:34–35; Matt. 23:37–39)

What were "the things that make for peace"? Where is Jesus' alternative program for his nation? Where but in the instructions he gave to his followers, and to the surrounding multitude, who also heard them (see Matt. 7:28; Luke 6:17–19)!

> You have heard that it was said, "You shall love your neighbor
> [your fellow Jew] and hate your enemy [the Gentile oppressor]."
> But I say to you, Love your enemies and pray for those who
> persecute you, so that you may be children of your Father in
> heaven; for he makes his sun rise on the evil and on the good, and
> sends rain on the righteous and on the unrighteous. For if you love
> those who love you, what reward do you have? Do not even the
> tax collectors do the same? And if you greet only your brothers and
> sisters [your fellow Jews], what more are you doing than others?
> Do not even the Gentiles do the same? Be perfect, therefore, as
> your heavenly Father is perfect. (Matt. 5:43–48)

The context would indicate that the perfection spoken of here is not perfect sinlessness, but treating friends and enemies with equal kindness, just as God does. Luke, in the parallel passage, has, "Be merciful, just as your Father is merciful" (Luke 6:36). That would be a thing that makes for peace.

It would most likely be a Roman soldier who would force one of Jesus' hearers to "go one mile," perhaps to carry his pack. It would be a thing that makes for peace to carry it two miles (Matt. 5:41).

The "evildoer," who slaps one of Jesus' hearers on the cheek, is apt to be a member of the occupation force. Not to seek or take revenge would be a thing that makes for peace.

Summary

The ambiguity in the biblical picture of Jesus is real, but the main thrust seems clear enough. For me, at least, it is impossible to conceive of Jesus as approving war as a method of settling international disputes. It is difficult to imagine him with his hand on the nuclear button, threatening the destruction of one hundred million people, including millions of little children, maintaining that "deterrence," based on that threat, is the only way to peace. It is easier to imagine him sitting on the edge of Moscow, and on the edge of Washington, and on the edge of Beijing and Johannesburg and Tel Aviv and Baghdad, and all other seats of military power, and weeping: "If you, even you, had only recognized on this day the things that make for peace!"

Now, how did Jesus, who was nursed on the Old Testament along with his mother's milk, come to such a position? Could it be that the Hebrew scriptures are not an unbroken record of war and bloodshed as is often supposed? Are they ambiguous, containing the seeds of Jesus' advocacy of peace as well as the war passages that are undoubtedly there? Jesus says he came not to abolish the Law and the Prophets, but to fulfill them (Matt. 5:17). Jesus says the scripture cannot be annulled (John 10:35). Did he have a way of reading the Old Testament that made it possible for him to be a peacemaker, that even insisted that he be a peacemaker? That will be our inquiry in Part Two.

Part Two

The Ambiguity of Israel's Faith and Practice

Prepare war,
   stir up the warriors.
Let all the soldiers draw near,
   let them come up.
Beat your plowshares into swords,
   and your pruning hooks into spears;
   let the weakling say, "I am a warrior."
                    (Joel 3:9–10)

              They shall beat their swords into
                 plowshares,
                and their spears into pruning hooks;
            nation shall not lift up sword against
                 nation,
                neither shall they learn war any
                 more.

                               (Micah 4:3)

3

Israel: Warlike People

The Hebrew Bible, on which Jesus was nurtured, is full of wars; the blood of battle oozes from its pages. And the people of Israel celebrated war with their finest literary efforts, glorying in victory, lamenting in defeat. We need to start with an honest appraisal of these two facts.

Wars, Wars, and More Wars

The annals of almost all peoples are records of wars. It is only in recent years that historians have begun to write social and economic histories; before that histories were primarily records of defeats and victories in battle. God's chosen people were no exception. The annals of ancient Israel are studded with accounts of war after war after war.

A Setting for Constant Warfare

How odd of God to choose Palestine as the place where the name and habitation of Yahweh were to be put! All we know of geopolitics would predict that Palestine would be a center of constant warfare. It occupies the narrowest part of the Fertile Crescent, a narrow land bridge with the Great Sea to the west and the desert to the east. Across that bridge marched the armies of successive powers of the Tigris-Euphrates Valley to confront the power of the Nile Valley, and the power of the Nile Valley to confront the powers of the

Tigris-Euphrates Valley. Later it was Persia and Macedonia and Rome. It is a focus of conflict at the present day.

Only rarely have the peoples that occupy the land bridge been united. Most of the time they have been at war among themselves. The litany of their ancient names rings in the minds of Sunday school children and all who have studied or read the Bible: Moab and Ammon and Edom and Amalek and the Philistines and the Arameans or Syrians. They were easy pawns in the hands of the great powers who knew how to set them against each other, how to divide and conquer. But often their wars were not externally fomented. They knew how to do it all by themselves. This, too, is true at the present day.

The people of God were part of the picture, warring with neighboring tribes and kingdoms, even as doom peered over the horizon from Egypt or Assyria; also warring among themselves in tribal rivalries and in the north-south division of Israel and Judah.

A Survey of Israel's Wars

It may be worth our time to make quick survey of the principal wars in which Israel was involved. To mention every skirmish or palace coup would stretch the account beyond all reasonable bounds.

In the Pentateuch

Israel's national history began in a warlike event. The Hebrew slaves, fleeing Egypt, were pursued by Pharaoh's army. They were delivered when the army was drowned in the Red Sea (Exodus 14–15).

En route to Sinai, they were attacked by Amalek and fought in self-defense (Ex. 17:8–16).

In an attempt to take Canaan from the south, in disobedience to Moses, they were defeated by the Amalekites and the Canaanites (Numbers 14).

As they prepared to enter Canaan, they moved up the east bank of Jordan and seized the territories of Sihon, king of the Amorites

(Num. 21:21–31; Deut. 2:26–37), and Og, king of Bashan (Num. 21:33–35; Deut. 3:1–7). In the same campaign, Numbers mentions wars with the king of Arad (Num. 21:1–3) and the five kings of Midian (31:1–12).

In Joshua

The book of Joshua records the "conquest of Canaan" through a series of wars, often bloody and genocidal. First there was a strike through the center at Jericho and Ai (Joshua 6–8). Next a confederation of kings in the southern half of Canaan was defeated (ch. 10). Then a similar confederation in the north was defeated (ch. 11). Joshua 12 lists thirty-one kings defeated by Joshua.[1]

In Judges

The period of the Judges was a period of intermittent warfare. The book of Judges pictures a time when Israel was a loose confederation of tribes, scattered about in Canaan, oppressed by the Canaanite city-states and by other tribal groups who swept in from the desert or from the seacoast. Israel had no standing army, but from time to time there was a rallying of tribes (not often all of them) under a charismatic leader (a "judge") to throw off the oppressor's yoke. In this pattern there were wars with Aram Naharaim (Judg. 3:7–11), Moab (vs. 12–30), Hazor (a Canaanite city) (chs. 4; 5), Midian (6:1–7:21), Ammon (10:6–11:33), and the Philistines (3:31; chs. 13–16). Not all the wars recorded were wars of liberation or defense. In addition to the aggressive warfare of the (partial) conquest (1:1–26), there was the attack by the tribe of Dan on the unsuspecting city of Laish (ch. 18). There was also fratricidal warfare among the tribes: Abimelech against Shechem and Thebez (ch. 9); Gilead against Ephraim (ch. 12); the other tribes against Benjamin (chs. 19–21).

The Era of Samuel

The era of Samuel, the last of the judges, was marked by periodic warfare with the Philistines. Israel was disastrously defeated and the ark of the covenant was captured (1 Samuel 4). Later, the tables were turned as a repentant Israel, aided by the Lord's thunder, drove the Philistines out of Israelite territory (ch. 7).

The Philistine pressure eventually led Israel to make a major change in its military policy: they demanded a king. Kings in the ancient Near East were first and foremost military leaders. "We are determined to have a king over us," they said, "so that we also may be like other nations, and that our king may govern us and go out before us and fight our battles" (1 Sam. 8:19–20). It seems clear that two very different accounts of the inauguration of the kingdom are intertwined in 1 Samuel. However they may be unraveled, the fact remains that there was indeed a transition from the tribal league with its occasional rallies of Israelite peasantry to fight for their freedom to a monarchy with a standing army, career military commanders, up-to-date armaments, the capacity to take and hold new territory.

The Era of Saul

Saul, the first king, started out like a judge. He rallied the peasantry in charismatic fashion to go to the rescue of Jabesh-gilead against Nahash, king of the Ammonites (1 Samuel 11). After the victory, however, some who had rallied were not sent home; they were retained as a standing army (13:2). This army continued to be augmented from time to time by the traditional rally of the peasantry (14:20–23). Saul, we are told, led Israel in wars against Moab, the Ammonites, Edom, Zobah, the Philistines, and the Amalekites (14:47–48). The struggle with the Philistines was continuous. It was the setting for the familiar story of David and Goliath (ch. 17). In the end, Saul died in battle against the Philistines (ch. 31).

The Era of David and Solomon

David was Israel's most successful warrior. He was credited with many victories in Saul's ongoing struggle with the Philistines (1 Sam. 18:12–16, 27, 30). Eventually Saul's jealousy forced him to lead the life of an outlaw, with his own private army (22:2). He even deserted to the Philistines to save his skin. When the Philistines launched the attack in which Saul died, David was at war with the Amalekites, to avenge their sack of Ziklag, the city which the Philistines had given him, and to rescue his wives and others who had been taken captive (chs. 29–30).

David became king only after long warfare between Judah, which supported him, and the northern tribes, which supported the house of Saul (2 Samuel 2–4). With his private army he took Jerusalem and made it his capital (5:6–10). Once established as king, he was able to augment his private army with thousands of Israelite soldiers, under the command of seasoned and able generals. During his reign he decisively defeated the Philistines (5:17–25; 8:1) and the Arameans (8:5–6; 10:6–19), putting garrisons among them and exacting tribute. He defeated the neighboring tribes: Edom (8:12), Moab (v. 2), the Ammonites (10:1–14; 11:1; 12:26–31), and Amalek (8:12).

David's wars were not all wars of conquest. There was the sad civil war in which his own son Absalom usurped the throne and was finally defeated and killed (2 Sam. 13–18); and yet another civil war when Sheba the son of Bichri rebelled and divided the kingdom, the northern tribes against Judah, once again (ch. 20).

There is no record of war during the reign of Solomon, but Solomon completed "the conquest of Canaan" by enslaving the descendants of the Canaanites (1 Kings 9:20). He modernized the army with great numbers of horses and chariots (vs. 19, 22).

The Era of the Divided Kingdom

After Solomon's death, the kingdom divided again, north and south, with Solomon's son Rehoboam king over Judah in the south and Jeroboam, an official of Solomon's bureaucracy who had rebelled and fled to Egypt, as king over Israel in the north. Rehoboam prepared for a major war to try to reclaim the north, but was dissuaded by the prophet Shemaiah (1 Kings 12:21–24). Nevertheless there were continual border battles between the two kingdoms in Rehoboam's time (14:30) and in the reign of his son Abijam (15:6) and his grandson Asa. Asa established a dangerous precedent by calling on the Arameans to help him against the king of Israel (vs. 16–21). In Israel there was bloody coup after bloody coup. During this period of simmering civil war there were outside wars as well. Judah suffered the first incursion of a major power when Shishak, king of Egypt, invaded and exacted tribute (14:25–26). Israel renewed the wars with the Philistines (16:15–16).

The Arameans (Syrians) now emerged as a great threat, and Ahab, king of Israel, fought many battles against them (1 Kings 20:1–30). After a period of truce, Ahab persuaded Jehoshaphat, king of Judah, to join forces with him to retake Ramoth-gilead from the Arameans. In the ensuing battle, Ahab was killed (22:1–4, 29–37). War with Aram continued intermittently through the reigns of many Israelite kings (2 Kings 6–7; 8:28; 10:32–33; 12:17–18; 13:3, 22–25). There is also the record of a campaign against Moab, undertaken jointly by Israel, Judah, and Edom (3:4–27). Also an unsuccessful campaign against Edom was undertaken by Joram, king of Israel (8:20–24), and a successful one by Amaziah of Judah (14:7).

The Aramean threat had ended the strife between Israel and Judah, but it was renewed by Amaziah of Judah, who was defeated by Jehoash of Israel (2 Kings 14:8–14).

Jeroboam II, son of Jehoash of Israel, was a mighty warrior. He recaptured for Israel all its lost territory and ended the Aramean threat for the time being by capturing Damascus (2 Kings 14:25, 28).

The Assyrian Campaigns

After another series of palace coups, Menahem came to the throne in Israel. He launched a raid on Tiphsah (2 Kings 15:16). During his reign, Assyria, the great power in the Tigris Valley, invaded Israel and was bought off by heavy tribute (vs. 19–20). Two kings later, in the reign of Pekah, the Assyrians were back and carried many people captive (v. 29). Pekah formed an anti-Assyrian alliance with Aram and besieged Judah to compel Ahaz of Judah to join. The response of Ahaz was to call for Assyrian help. The Assyrians promptly came and destroyed Aram (15:37; 16:5–9; cf. Isaiah 7). The end of the Northern Kingdom came rapidly. Pekah was assassinated by Hoshea. The Assyrians came again and made

Hoshea a vassal. Hoshea sought help from Egypt. The Assyrians came again and after a three-year siege took Samaria, the Israelite capital, and carried the people away (2 Kings 17).

Judah, under its king Hezekiah, remained alone, exposed to the Assyrian threat. He undertook war against the Philistines (2 Kings 18:8), but he was soon under attack by Sennacherib, king of Assyria, who captured all his fortified cities, exacted tribute, and threatened to sack Jerusalem and destroy the temple (ch. 18). Encouraged by Isaiah the prophet, Hezekiah laid the situation before the LORD in prayer. Disaster (possibly a plague) befell the Assyrian army and Sennacherib withdrew (ch 19; cf. Isaiah 37).[2]

The record in 2 Kings is silent concerning wars under Manasseh and Amon, who seem to have paid tribute to Assyria. The next king, Josiah, the great reformer, attacked Pharaoh Neco of Egypt as the Egyptian army was on its way to a decisive battle on the Euphrates.[3] Josiah was killed and brought back dead to Jerusalem (2 Kings 23:29–30).

The Babylonian Campaigns

Babylon was now the power in the Tigris-Euphrates Valley and the kings of Judah soon became Babylonian vassals. We read of raids on Judah by bands of Chaldeans, Arameans, Moabites, and Ammonites (2 Kings 24:2). The Babylonian army besieged Jerusalem when tribute was not paid, taking the young king Jehoiachin, the city's treasures, and the cream of the population away to Babylon (vs. 10–17). The last king, Zedekiah, again rebelled; another siege followed; and Jerusalem was taken and leveled, the temple destroyed, the walls broken down (2 Kings 25:1–12; cf. Jeremiah 52).

This list could be expanded by adding wars mentioned in Chronicles and others alluded to by the prophets. Of course we could go into the wars of the Maccabees and others in the intertestamental period. But enough is enough. It is evident from this long and tedious record that warfare was a way of life for the ancient people of God. There seem to have been no conscientious objectors among them. The fighting of some wars and the failure to fight others may have been questioned as instances of disobedience to God, but the institution of warfare as such was not questioned.[4]

War was brutal and cruel in the ancient Near East. The record states without compunction that Israel engaged in the mutilation of prisoners (Judg. 1:6–7); the execution of prisoners (1 Sam. 15:32–33); the mutilation of dead bodies (2 Sam. 4:12); the ripping up of pregnant women (2 Kings 15:16); the slaughter of all males in a country (1 Kings 11:15–16). There was no attempt to protect civilian population: Israel engaged in the ban, or *herem,* in which every inhabitant of a conquered city was killed: men, women, the old, little children (Josh. 8:25–26; 1 Sam. 15:3). We would call it genocide.

Truly the blood of battle oozes from the pages of the Old Testament.

The War Poetry of Israel

The people of God not only engaged in war after war after war, they celebrated those wars in song. A major portion of Israel's literary output is war poetry. In volume and in literary quality, the Old Testament is one of the world's great collections of the poetry of war.

Ancient Poems

The oldest poems of the Hebrew people are war poems. The Song of Deborah is a prime example. Its literary excellence can easily be appreciated by comparing the poetry of Judges 5 with the prose account of Judges 4.

Later poems, like David's lament for Saul and Jonathan (2 Sam. 1:19–27), have been greatly admired.

The Prophets

War poetry reached its zenith in the prophets. It is in the poetry of the prophets that we catch the sights, sounds, smells of battle itself. Almost every prophetic book contains poetic descriptions of war. We shall cite here only two outstanding examples.

Nahum

Nahum's bitter book is devoted to a description of the fall of Nineveh, Assyria's capital, in the most graphic terms. He describes the attacking army's red shields and crimson uniforms, the flashing chariot wheels, the prancing chargers (Nahum 2:3). He mocks the panic of the defenders (2:10–11; 3:11–13). He exults over Israel's ancient enemy in words like these:

> Ah! City of bloodshed,
>   utterly deceitful, full of booty—
>   no end to plunder!
> The crack of whip and rumble of wheel,
>   galloping horse and bounding chariot!
> Horsemen charging,
>   flashing sword and glittering spear,
> piles of dead,
>   heaps of corpses,
> dead bodies without end—
>   they stumble over the bodies!
>   (Nahum 3:1–3)

Jeremiah

Perhaps the greatest of the war poets was Jeremiah. He offers a series of snapshots, as it were—unforgettable word pictures that stamp an indelible image on the reader's mind.

The Sights and Sounds of Battle. The first great descriptions of warfare occur in Jeremiah 4–6. The passage opens with a strident alarm sounded on the trumpet (4:5), and the din of battle deafens us throughout: the sound of the trumpet, the alarm of war, disaster overtaking disaster (vs. 19–20). As the trembling people sweep into the fortified cities, we get glimpses of the enemy and his armaments: a cloud of dust on the horizon, horses swifter than eagles, chariots like the whirlwind (v. 16). The noise of his approach is deafening; it strikes terror to the heart of whole cities; towns are deserted as the people go into thickets and climb to rocky crags for refuge (v. 29). Plunder and pillage: the enemy eats his fill of the harvest and destroys the rest; flocks are eaten, driven off, and destroyed (5:17). Then to the walled cities he goes, hewing down trees, casting up siege ramps, destroying palaces by night (6:5–6).

Once again, in the oracles against the nations (chs. 46–51) we find vivid descriptions of battle. The battle of Carchemish (46:3–12) is a masterpiece. Graphic details abound in the oracles against the Philistines (ch. 47), Moab (48:40–46), and Babylon (50:11–16; 51:27–33).

The Dreadful Aftermath. War is not all battle: the sound of the trumpet, the neighing of steeds, the clash of armor. There is that moment of awful stillness when the battle has swept on. And it is not the warriors alone who bear the brunt. The suffering of noncombatants is not a recent invention. Jeremiah himself was a noncombatant, and it is natural that many of his most vivid pictures of the horrors of war concern, not the battlefield, but the people within the walls and the survivors who look on the utter desolation that war has left.

War means suffering for children and youth, for the wife with the husband, nor are the aged spared (Jer. 6:11). Men see their wives and their fields taken by others (6:12; 8:10). War means death. Almost continually we see Jeremiah standing amid a multitude of corpses:

> If I go out into the field,
>   look—those killed by the sword!
> And if I enter the city,
>   look—those sick with famine!
>   (Jer. 14:18)

> "Death has come up into our windows,
>   it has entered our palaces,
> to cut off the children from the streets
>   and the young men from the squares."
> Speak! Thus says the Lord:
> "Human corpses shall fall
>   like dung upon the open field,
> like sheaves behind the reaper,
>   and no one shall gather them."
>   (Jer. 9:21–22)

The end of it all is desolation. Cities are left waste and without inhabitant—how often that phrase is on Jeremiah's lips! Jackals howl amid the ruins (9:11; 10:22). As the lonely nomad passes the desolate and blackened tell, he hisses with astonishment (18:16; 50:13; 51:37).

The defeated nation is like a fallen tent, collapsing suddenly when the stakes are removed (Jer. 4:20; 10:20); like a thoroughly gleaned vineyard (6:9); like winnowed chaff (15:7).

All in all, war is most comparable to a cosmic upheaval. It has the qualities of an eclipse and an earthquake:

> I looked on the earth, and lo, it was waste and void;
> and to the heavens, and they had no light.
> I looked on the mountains, and lo, they were quaking,
> and all the hills moved to and fro.
> I looked, and lo, there was no one at all,
> and all the birds of the air had fled.
> I looked, and lo, the fruitful land was a desert,
> and all its cities were laid in ruins
> before the LORD, before his fierce anger.
>
> (Jer. 4:23–26)

The similarity between that poem and modern descriptions of the aftermath of a nuclear shoot-out[5] is eerie!

This is but a sample of the war poetry of the prophets. There is war poetry in the Psalms as well. We shall see more of both in chapters 4 and 7. By then we may be ready to agree with those who hold that, from a literary standpoint, the war poetry of the Bible can hold its own with Homer's *Iliad* or Milton's war in heaven in *Paradise Lost*.

There are important distinctions to be made within the body of war poetry. The Song of Deborah comes "from below"; it is the voice of an oppressed peasantry protesting the overweening power of the Canaanite city-states. Nahum speaks for the Guatemalas and Nicaraguas of his day, the small states constantly oppressed and periodically attacked by the great powers. Jeremiah sings of war as an implement of God's inexorable justice, punishing Judah, its neighbors, and the great powers for their sins.

Our main point, however, is neither literary appreciation nor rhetorical distinctions. It is the honest admission of enormous ambiguity. The people from whom Jesus came were continually at war and able to describe it with great genius. They never seemed to question it. What is more, they saw their God as deeply involved in it.

4

Yahweh: Warrior God

We began chapter 3 by saying that the annals of almost all peoples are records of wars. We must move on to say that in the annals of almost all peoples, the wars have a religious dimension, the gods are involved. Again, the people of God are no exception. We read in Numbers 21:14 of a lost document: "The Book of the Wars of Yahweh." That title could fit large parts of the Old Testament! Israel's God is deeply involved in many of the wars recorded. Yahweh is involved as Israel's ally, and Yahweh is involved as Israel's enemy: Yahweh is a warrior.

Yahweh: Israel's Ally

Yahweh's participation in Israel's battles is pictured in a bewildering variety of stories and poems. One approach is to develop a sort of continuum of the various levels of Yahweh's involvement, ranging from what we might call monergistic wars in which Yahweh fights alone, through synergistic wars in which Yahweh and Israel cooperate in fighting, to secular wars in which Israel fights alone.

Yahweh Fights Alone

Sometimes the Hebrew scriptures show Yahweh as doing all the fighting, while Israel does not fight at all. We will look first at several accounts of monergistic warfare in the primary history (Genesis through 2 Kings), then at scattered assertions of monergism, and finally at the piety of the Psalms.

Monergistic Warfare in the Primary History

1. In Israel's battle with Egypt at the Red Sea (Exodus 14–15), Israel does not fight; Yahweh wins the victory. Miriam's song (Ex. 15:21) says it all:

> Sing to the LORD, for he has triumphed gloriously;
> horse and rider he has thrown into the sea.

In the expanded Song of the Sea (Ex. 15:1–18), Yahweh's right hand shattered the enemy, Yahweh's majesty overthrew the adversaries, Yahweh's fury consumed them, the blast of Yahweh's nostrils piled up the waters.

The prose account in Exodus 14, admittedly later, only makes explicit what is implicit in the poem. Though Israel went up out of the land of Egypt "prepared for battle" (Ex. 13:18), they soon found themselves hopelessly trapped between Pharaoh's army and the sea. Moses said to them, "Do not be afraid, stand firm, and see the deliverance that the LORD will accomplish for you today; for the Egyptians whom you see today you shall never see again. The LORD will fight for you, and you have only to keep still" (Ex. 14:13–14). One aspect of Yahweh's fighting, which we shall encounter again and again, was the confusion and panic that spread through the army of Israel's enemy. "At the morning watch the LORD in the pillar of fire and cloud looked down upon the Egyptian army, and threw the Egyptian army into panic" (v. 24). Another aspect was a nature miracle, in which Israel passed through the sea dry-shod, while the pursuing Egyptians were drowned. By these means Yahweh alone won the battle, unaided by Israel.

In two of the Elisha stories in 2 Kings, there is similar monergism. In the first, the king if Aram is at war with Israel and Elisha foils his plans. He sends out a great army to capture Elisha, but the cosmic army of Yahweh, the horses and chariots of fire, protect the prophet. Afterward, Yahweh strikes the Syrian army with blindness. They are captured, spared, and the Syrian raids cease (2 Kings

6:8–23). In the second, Samaria is besieged by Ben-hadad of Aram. The famine is severe. But the LORD sends confusion on the enemy. They hear the sound of a great army and flee in panic. Israel is delivered without fighting (6:24–7:20).[1]

Next to the deliverance of Israel from Egypt, the most striking instance of monergistic warfare is the deliverance of Jerusalem from Sennacherib's army in the reign of Hezekiah (2 Kings 18–19; cf. Isaiah 36–37). Tiny Judah is under attack by a great world power: Assyria. The other small kingdoms of the Fertile Crescent have already fallen. Hezekiah, terrified by the threats of Sennacherib, turns to Isaiah the prophet for help. Isaiah replies with a word of assurance, "Fear not!" Yahweh himself will "put a spirit" in Sennacherib. Does this mean that a member of the divine council will be dispatched to handle the matter? (Compare 1 Kings 22:19–23.) Sennacherib will hear a "rumor." Is this another instance of the "confusion" by which Yahweh routs the enemies of Israel? In any event, Hezekiah spreads the written threats of the Assyrians before the LORD in the temple with fervent prayer, Isaiah utters a defiant oracle of victory, a great disaster befalls the Assyrian army, Sennacherib returns to Nineveh, and Jerusalem is saved.

> And the might of the Gentile, unsmote by the sword,
> Hath melted like snow in the glance of the Lord![2]

There is a notorious historical problem surrounding the defeat of Sennacherib.[3] Our point here is simply that this tradition, historical or not, was an article of Israel's faith. Israel believed that Yahweh on occasion fought for them unaided and alone (cf. Hos. 1:7).

In using the term "monergism" to describe these stories, we do not imply that Israel does nothing. Israel must believe. It takes great faith to "keep still" in a situation of grave danger. Moreover, the role of the prophet is significant. The prophet Moses was very active in the confrontations with Pharaoh which led up to the victory at the Red Sea and in the miracle of the parting of the waters. Elisha likewise played an active part in the victories over Aram, and Isaiah played a critical role in the defeat of Sennacherib. By monergism we simply mean that Israel did not wage war.

Assertions of Monergism

Monergism as an article of faith occurs many places in the Old Testament. We find it in the basic creed of Israelite faith:

> The LORD brought us out of Egypt with a mighty hand and an outstretched arm, with a terrifying display of power, and with signs and wonders; and he brought us into this place and gave us this land, a land flowing with milk and honey. (Deut. 26:8–9)

Compare Deuteronomy 6:21–23; Exodus 19:4; Leviticus 26:13; Exodus 20:2.

We find it in the liturgy for the renewal of the covenant in Joshua 24:2–13, especially in verse 12: "I sent the hornet ahead of you, which drove out before you the two kings of the Amorites; it was not by your sword or by your bow."

We find it all through the prophets. See, for example, Amos 2:9–10; Isaiah 51:10. We find it in the prayer of Ezra (Neh. 9:6–25, esp. vs. 11, 22–24). But most of all we find it in the Psalms.

The Piety of the Psalter

In the late Jewish piety attested by the Psalms, monergism has become the dominant understanding of how Yahweh is involved in the wars of the nation.

1. The monergistic victories of Yahweh cited above are celebrated in song. The victory at the Red Sea:

> He rebuked the Red Sea, and it became dry;
> > he led them through the deep as through a desert.
> So he saved them from the hand of the foe,
> > and delivered them from the hand of the enemy.
> The waters covered their adversaries;
> > not one of them was left.
>
> (Ps. 106:9–11)

See also Psalms 66:6; 77:16–20; 78:13, 53; 114:3; 136:13–15.

The monergistic defense of Elisha against the armies of Aram (2 Kings 8:23) may be reflected in these lines:

> The angel of the LORD encamps
> around those who fear him, and delivers them.
>
> (Ps. 34:7)

The monergistic victory of Yahweh over Sennacherib seems to be reflected in Psalms 76 and 48. Whether it refers to the Sennacherib incident or not, Psalm 46 is a strongly monergistic text. God defends the city (v. 5) God brings wars to an end, stripping the enemy of all his weapons (v. 9). "Be still, and know that I am God!" (v. 10) is not primarily a call for silence in a worship service. It is an echo of Moses' words at the Red Sea: "The LORD will fight for you, and you have only to keep still" (Ex. 14:14). Israel will win the battle without human fighting because "the LORD of hosts is with us; the God of Jacob is our refuge" (Ps. 46:7, 11). That is, the Commander of the heavenly army is with us; the God of Jacob, who enabled Jacob, unarmed, to face Esau with four hundred men (Genesis 33), is our refuge.

2. More striking is the way that victories which the primary history records as synergistic are sung about as monergistic. In Psalms 135:10–12 and 136:17–22 there is no mention of any human cooperation in the victories over Sihon, king of the Amorites, or Og, king of Bashan.

Again, Joshua gets no credit for the conquest of Canaan. It is Yahweh alone who has conquered Canaan and given it to Israel:

> You with your own hand drove out the nations,
> but them you planted;
> you afflicted the peoples,
> but them you set free;
> for not by their own sword did they win the land,
> nor did their own arm give them victory;
> but your right hand, and your arm,
> and the light of your countenance,
> for you delighted in them.
>
> (Ps. 44:2–3)

See also Psalms 47:3–4; 80:8–9; 105:44; 111:6, and the explicit reference to the kingdoms of Canaan in Psalm 135:11.

The wars of the Judges are mentioned only once, in Psalm 83:9–11, and here again they are reinterpreted as wars fought by Yahweh alone.

3. There is a repeated emphasis in the Psalms that Israel does nothing to win the victories:

> A king is not saved by his great army;
>   a warrior is not delivered by his great strength.
> The war horse is a vain hope for victory,
>   and by its great might it cannot save.
>   (Ps. 33:16–17)

> For not in my bow do I trust,
>   nor can my sword save me.
>   (Ps. 44:6)

> O grant us help against the foe,
>   for human help is worthless.
> With God we shall do valiantly;
>   it is he who will tread down our foes.
>   (Ps. 60:11–12 = 108:12–13)

See also Psalms 124; 127:1.

More general statements of God's monergistic warfare for the nation are found in Psalms 2; 9:5–6, 15–16; 10:16; 28:8; 59:6; 79:8–10; 81:14; 98:1–3. One of the most striking is the LORD's command to an Israelite ruler to sit still while Yahweh makes the ruler's enemies a stool for his feet (Ps. 110:1).

4. Psalms not only sing of Yahweh's monergistic warfare in behalf of the nation; they sing even more frequently of Yahweh's monergistic warfare in behalf of individuals against their personal enemies. Alert readers of the Psalms are aware that "enemies" are mentioned in the vast majority of the psalms, including the beloved Twenty-third Psalm, where the word can easily be missed.

The psalmists *express confidence* that the LORD will deal with their enemies:

> The LORD is my light and my salvation;
>   whom shall I fear?

> The LORD is the stronghold of my life;
>> of whom shall I be afraid?
> When evildoers assail me
>> to devour my flesh—
> my adversaries and foes—
>> they shall stumble and fall.
> Though an army encamp against me,
>> my heart shall not fear;
> though war rise up against me,
>> yet will I be confident . . .
> Wait for the LORD;
>> be strong, and let your heart take courage;
>> wait for the LORD!
>>
>> (Ps. 27:1–3, 14)

Note the same monergistic sit still, wait.

The psalmists *cry out for deliverance:*

> How long, O LORD? Will you forget me forever?
> How long will you hide your face from me?
> How long must I bear pain in my soul,
>> and have sorrow in my heart all day long?
> How long shall my enemy be exalted over me?
>>
>> (Ps. 13:1–2)

The psalmists even *pray for vengeance,* for terrible punishments to overtake their enemies. The imprecatory psalms, such as Psalms 58, 69, and 109, call upon God to execute punishments that far exceed the "eye for eye, tooth for tooth" of the Mosaic law (Lev. 24:20).[4] But, as Walter Brueggemann has made clear, the psalmists do not propose to wreak this terrible vengeance themselves. By bringing their anger to speech and submitting it to the LORD, they obtain the relief that otherwise only vengeful action would bring.[5] Even these terrible psalms are monergistic: God alone is to do the punishing, without human assistance.

Once one becomes alert to affirmations of confidence, cries for help, and prayers for vengeance as expressions of monergism, it almost seems that the entire Psalter is devoted to Yahweh's monergistic warfare on the psalmists' behalf. See Psalms 3, 4, 5, 6, 7, 9, 10, 11, 12, 13, 14 = 53, 17, 22, 23, 25, 27, 28, 31, 34, 35, 36, 37, 40, 52, 54, 55, 56, 57, 58, 59, 62, 64, 69, 70, 71, 86, 91, 92, 94, 109, 118, 129, 137, 140, 143.[6]

But the Psalter is ambiguous, like the rest of scripture. There are psalms that reflect other understandings of Yahweh's involvement in Israel's warfare. We shall see that as we proceed with our continuum.

Yahweh and Israel Cooperate in Fighting

When we return to the primary history, we find many accounts of wars in which there was cooperation between Yahweh and the armies of Israel. We may call this synergism. There are many levels of synergistic warfare, ranging from those where the heavy emphasis is on Yahweh's action to those where the heavy emphasis is on fighting by Israel.

Yahweh Wins; Israel Pursues

Closest to the idea of monergism are stories where the victory itself is won by the power of Yahweh and the role of Israel is to pursue and plunder the already defeated foe.

1. The sack of Jericho is such a story. Before Israel has crossed the Jordan, Yahweh has already put fear and confusion into the minds and hearts of the inhabitants of Jericho (Joshua 2). Suddenly Israel is across the river and has Jericho under siege. Joshua has a vision which assures him that the divine army will fight along with the armies of Israel (5:13–15). Yahweh orders a ceremonial march around the city for seven days. On the seventh day, the people give a great shout, and the walls fall flat. Without a blow the formidable defenses of Jericho are destroyed and victory is assured. Only then does Israel fight, slaughtering all the inhabitants except Rahab and her family, "devoting" the city to Yahweh (ch. 6).

2. The ancient Song of Deborah (Judg. 5) is an even better example. The participation (and nonparticipation) of the various tribes is a prominent theme (vs. 9–18),[7] but the primary fighting was

between Yahweh and the Canaanite kings. Yahweh marches from the south, from Edom and Sinai (vs. 4–5). Yahweh fights, with the divine army, of which the stars are a part,[8] against the kings and their general, Sisera. The heavy rain produces a flash flood that sweeps the enemy away (vs. 19–21). The echoes of the Song of the Sea are evident. Although the triumph of Yahweh is identified with the triumph of his peasantry in Israel (v. 11b, c), all that is actually described at this point is the march of the peasantry down to the gates (vs. 11d, 13). The only human action that is specifically described is that of Jael, a Kenite woman, who kills Sisera (vs. 24–27). The prose account of the same battle (Judges 4) is later. It does not mention the flood, but rather the panic into which Sisera and his army fell when they viewed the approach of Barak with ten thousand warriors, coming down from Mount Tabor. Sisera's army was defeated before a blow was struck. Indeed it was Yahweh alone who defeated it, throwing the army into a panic similar to the panics described in the stories we have already reviewed. Israel's role was then to pursue the army and annihilate it (v. 16).

3. The story of Gideon's defeat of the Midianites (Judges 6–8) is similar. Gideon's army is reduced to a handful, to show that the victory will be Yahweh's. "The troops with you are too many for me to give the Midianites into their hand. Israel would only take the credit away from me, saying, 'My own hand has delivered me'" (7:2). Instructed to spy on the Midianities, Gideon discovers that Yahweh has already made them afraid of him (vs. 9–15). In the middle of the night, Gideon's warriors break jars, revealing torches, and sound trumpets. Without a blow being struck, the Midianites fall into confusion, begin to kill each other, and flee. Only after the victory is Israel called out to fight, to hold the fords of the Jordan, to pursue and slaughter the enemy.

4. Another such story is found in 1 Samuel 7. The Philistines are thrown into confusion by the LORD's thunder, routed without a blow's being struck. Then Israel pursues the Philistines and strikes them down.[9]

5. It is possible that David's defeat of the Philistines in 2 Samuel 5:22–25 belongs here. Is the sound of marching in the tops of the

balsam trees the sound of God's army, the divine host? Does the LORD "strike down the army of the Philistines" by the "divine confusion"? David's striking them down from Geba to Gezer would seem to be the pursuit of a fleeing foe.

One psalm seems to share the stance of these stories. It is the Song of David (Psalm 18 = 2 Samuel 22). The victory over all David's enemies is clearly Yahweh's victory:

> The LORD is my rock, my fortress, and my deliverer,
>   my God, my rock in whom I take refuge,
>   my shield, and the horn of my salvation, my stronghold.
>   (Ps. 18:2)

The coming of Yahweh to David's aid is described in mythic, cosmic language that reminds one of the Song of Deborah (vs. 7–15). At one point the language seems monergistic:

> He delivered me from my strong enemy,
>   and from those who hated me;
>   for they were too mighty for me.
>   (Ps. 18:17)

But then, with Yahweh's help, David begins to fight. He crushes a troop, leaps over a wall (v. 29), bends the bow (v. 34), pursues his enemies (v. 37), strikes them down (v. 38), beats them like dust and casts them out like mire in the streets (v. 42).

Israel Wins with Yahweh's Aid

Next on our continuum we may place *stories where the battle is clearly fought by Israel, but is won only because of Yahweh's aid.*

1. Israel's victory over Amalek in the wilderness, where Israel prevailed only as long as Moses held up the staff of God in his hand (Ex. 17:8–13), is an example.

2. Joshua's victory over the kings of the south at Gibeon, where the LORD aided by throwing the enemy into panic, showering them with hailstones, and prolonging the light of day (Josh. 10:1–15), also belongs here.

3. The victory over the Philistines, which was started by Jon-

athan's daring attack, attended only by his armor bearer, is such a story. Yahweh came to his aid through the divine panic and an earthquake. Israel then rallied and the defeat was a great one (1 Sam. 14:1–23).

4. David's victory over Goliath (1 Samuel 17) is hard to classify. The record does not ascribe any particular deed of Yahweh's as aiding David; but David insists that it is only through such aid that he wins the victory (vs. 37, 46).[10] Indeed, David's rhetoric belongs in the tradition of monergism: "The LORD does not save by sword and spear; for the battle is the LORD's and he will give you into our hand" (1 Sam. 17:47; cf. Josh. 24:12).

5. The victory over Mesha, the king of Moab, when the LORD provided water for Israel and its allies, and the Moabites, thinking the water was blood, rushed in to seize the spoil, only to be ambushed (2 Kings 3:4–27), is also to be included.

Many of the royal psalms describe just this kind of synergism. The king fights and Yahweh assists in the fighting:

> Now I know that the LORD will help his anointed;
>   he will answer him from his holy heaven
>   with mighty victories by his right hand.
> Some take pride in chariots, and some in horses,
>   but our pride is in the name of the LORD our God.
> They will collapse and fall,
>   but we shall rise and stand upright.
> Give victory to the king, O LORD;
>   answer us when we call.
>
> (Ps. 20:6–9)

See also Psalms 21; 72; 89:23; 110; 118, 144.

Yahweh Directs the Strategy

Next we may place stories where Yahweh directs the strategy of Israel's armies through the priestly oracle: the ephod or the Urim and Thummim. These include Judah's victory over Adoni-bezek (Judg. 1:1–7); the other tribes' battles against Benjamin (Judges 20); David's victory and escape at Keilah (1 Sam. 23:1–13); David's

victory over the Amalekites who had raided Ziklag (1 Samuel 30);
and David's victory over the Philistines at Baal-perazim (2 Sam.
5:17–21).

Yahweh Responds to Vows

In a few stories, Yahweh grants victory in response to a vow: the
victory over the king of Arad (Num. 21:1–3) and Jephthah's victory
over the Ammonites (Judges 11).

Yahweh Raises Up Leaders

Somewhere on the continuum belong wars where the function
ascribed to Yahweh was to "raise up" the leader of the battle, or where
the *ruach-Yahweh* (spirit of the LORD) inspired such a leader. Examples are Othniel (Judg. 3:9), Ehud (v. 15), Gideon (6:34), Jephthah
(11:29), Samson (chs. 13–16 passim), and Saul (1 Sam. 11:6).

Yahweh Commands; Israel Obeys

Next we come to stories where Yahweh merely issues the orders
to fight and Israel obeys. These include the defeat of Sihon, king of
the Amorites, and Og, king of Bashan (Deut. 2:26–3:7); the sack of
Ai (Josh. 8:1–29); the destruction of the southern cities by Joshua
"as the LORD God of Israel commanded" (Josh. 10:16–43; see v.
40); the defeat of the northern league (Josh. 11:1–15);[11] Saul's war
against Amalek (1 Samuel 15); Ahab's wars against Ben-hadad (1
Kings 20:13–30a).

One Psalm may reflect this kind of synergism:

> Let the high praises of God be in their throats
> and two-edged swords in their hands,
> to execute vengeance on the nations
> and punishment on the peoples,
> to bind their kings with fetters
> and their nobles with chains of iron,
> to execute on them the judgment decreed.
> This is glory for all his faithful ones.
> Praise the LORD!
>
> (Ps. 149:6–9)

The *Herem*

In connection with wars which Yahweh orders, we must pause to consider the ban, or *herem*, the custom of destroying cities utterly, leaving no one alive: man, woman, or child. This was a cultic acknowledgment that the real victor was Yahweh and therefore the human warriors were not entitled to take any spoils. The conquered cities were "whole burnt offerings" to Yahweh. This custom was followed by other nations in the Fertile Crescent for similar religious reasons.

Did Israel actually practice this custom which seems so barbaric to us? Some scholars have argued that they did not. There is serious question as to the historicity of "the conquest of Canaan" in Joshua. Clearly, the accounts in Joshua of a clean sweep of the Canaanites are exaggerated. Judges 1:1–3:6 gives a different picture, stating flatly that the inhabitants of the land were not driven out or destroyed; they remained to become adversaries and a snare to Israel. We continue for centuries to meet the descendants of "utterly destroyed" peoples.

There are varying views as to "what really happened": (1) The Hebrews infiltrated from time to time, settling in the hills, and leaving the plains to the Canaanites. There were doubtless skirmishes or even battles, but not the bloody conquest that Joshua describes. This is the view of Albrecht Alt, Martin Noth, and Gerhard von Rad.[12] (2) There was indeed a violent conquest, though not exactly as Joshua describes it. This is the view of W.F. Albright and John Bright.[13] (3) The "conquest" was really an uprising of the oppressed underclass in the Canaanite territory. This is the view of George Mendenhall and Norman Gottwald.[14]

This does not solve the problem. The *herem* does not rest on Joshua alone. Numbers says it was practiced east of Jordan (21:3, 34–35; ch. 31). Deuteronomy legislates it (7:1–2; 13:12–18; 20:10–18).[15] Judges records a savage *herem* against Benjamin, carried out by the other tribes of Israel (20:37). 1 Samuel states that David practiced it (27:9). There is plenty of archaeological evidence that cities in the area were repeatedly sacked and burned. Even if it could be proven that Israel never actually practiced the *herem*, the problem would still remain that Israel boasts of it in its sacred books. The more serious problem is that Israel taught that its God, Yahweh, commanded the *herem* and punished those who did not obediently carry it out. The defeat of Israel at Ai resulted because the *herem* of Jericho was not perfectly carried out (Joshua 7). Saul was rejected from being king because he did not perfectly carry out the *herem* of the Amalekites (1 Samuel 15). Ahab was rebuked for sparing the life of Ben-hadad, who should have been "devoted" (1 Kings 20:30b–43).

The book of Deuteronomy seeks to give a rationale for the *herem*. If the Canaanites had not been annihilated, they would have corrupted the pure religion of Israel with their idolatries (Deut. 2:3–6; 20:18). But Israelites were expert at idolatry before they entered Canaan (remember the golden calf in Ex. 32). And they were continually plagued with it (the *herem* didn't work).

How could the merciful God found elsewhere in the Old Testament, as well as in the New, command the *herem?* There is no explanation or justification. We are simply here at the extreme edge of the enormous ambiguity of scripture.

Israel Fights Alone

We began our continuum with monergistic wars in which Yahweh does everything and Israel does nothing. We end it with wars in which Israel does everything and Yahweh does nothing. These are secular wars, wars to which no religious meaning is ascribed. Most of the civil wars within Israel fall here: the wars of Abimelech (Judges 9); the war between Ephraim and Gilead (Judges 12); the wars between David and the house of Saul (2 Samuel 2–4); Absalom's revolt (2 Samuel 13–18); Sheba's revolt (2 Samuel 20); the border wars between Israel and Judah (1 Kings 14:30; 15:6–7, 16–22, 32; 2 Kings 14:8–14). Certain aggressive expeditions are also treated in this way: the tribe of Dan against Laish (Judges 18); David's raids on Geshur (1 Sam. 27:8–12); the capture of Jerusalem from the Jebusites (2 Sam. 5:6–10); Josiah's attack on Pharaoh Neco (2 Kings 23:29–30).

Interestingly enough, the wars that were most important from a political and military standpoint had no overt religious dimension and consequently received scant attention from the biblical writers. The territorial wars of David which greatly enlarged Israel's borders and made it a kingdom like other kingdoms in the Fertile Crescent receive little more than a bare mention in 2 Sam. 8:1–13. Some elaboration occurs in 2 Sam. 10 (war with the Arameans) and 12:26–31 (war with the Ammonites)—all secular wars.[16] Likewise the wars of Jeroboam II which regained the lost territory tory of the Northern Kingdom are barely mentioned (2 Kings 14:25–28).

The "Holy War" Discussion

Recently there has been a considerable body of Old Testament studies regarding "holy war." If we are to face squarely the ambiguity of the Bible, we must deal seriously with this scholarship and with its analysis of Yahweh's involvement in warfare as Israel's ally.

Von Rad's Thesis

It was Gerhard von Rad who placed the matter of holy war at the center of Old Testament discussion with his slender volume *Holy War in Ancient Israel*.[17] Von Rad maintained that holy war was a religious institution in ancient Israel, as integral to the worship of Yahweh as the sacrificial system or the law. From the accounts of warfare that we have listed above he gathered together the following traits and characteristics of this religious institution:

1. There was no standing army in holy war. A spirit-filled leader sounded the trumpet (Judg. 3:27; 6:34; 1 Sam. 13:3) or sent out dismembered flesh (Judg. 19:29–30; 1 Sam. 11:7) to rally troops for battle. When the battle was over the troops were dismissed with the cry: "To your tents, O Israel!" (2 Sam. 20:1; 1 Kings 12:16).

2. There was no draft. The army was composed of willing volunteers (Judg. 5:2, 9; cf. Deut. 20:5–9).

3. The army was ritually holy. The people "sanctified" themselves (Josh. 3:5). The soldiers were ascetics, refraining from sexual intercourse (1 Sam. 21:4–6; 2 Sam. 11:11). Vows were undertaken (Num. 21:2; Judg. 11:29–32; 1 Sam. 14:24). Ritual cleanliness was to be practiced in the camp (Deut. 23:9–14). Sacrifices were offered before battle (1 Sam. 7:8–10; 13:9, 12). If there was defeat, there was ceremonial mourning (Judg. 20:23, 26; 1 Sam. 11:4; 30:4). Even the weapons were holy (2 Sam. 1:21).

4. The army was Yahweh's army. The assembled troops were called "the people of Yahweh" (Judg. 5:11, 13; 20:2). The wars were called Yahweh's wars (Num. 21:14; 1 Sam. 18:17; 25:28). The troops marched into battle "before Yahweh" (Num. 32:20, 21, 27, 29, 32; Josh. 4:13), as though Yahweh were on the reviewing stand. Yahweh, in turn, went before the troops, leading the way, the traditional role of a king in the Near East (Deut. 20:4; Josh. 3:11; Judg. 4:14; 2 Sam. 5:24). Yahweh fought for Israel (Ex. 14:14; Deut. 1:30; Josh. 10:14, 42; 11:6; 23:10; Judg. 20:35; 1 Sam. 14:23, 39). Yahweh directed Israel's strategy and tactics through the priestly ephod and the Urim and Thummim (Judg. 20:23, 27–28; 1 Sam. 23:2, 4, 6, 9–12; 30:7–8; 2 Sam. 5:19, 23–25). The enemies of Israel were Yahweh's enemies (Judg. 5:31; 1 Sam. 30:26).

5. The victory was Yahweh's victory. Again and again it was said: "Yahweh has given [the various enemies] into our hands" (Josh. 2:24; 6:2, 16; 8:1, 18; 10:8, 19; Judg. 3:28; 4:7, 14; 7:9, 15; 18:10; 20:26; 1 Sam. 14:12; 17:46; 23:4; 24:5; 26:8; 1 Kings 20:28). Thus, the numbers of troops do not matter (Judg. 7:2; 1 Sam. 14:6), and to number the army is wrong (2 Sam. 24:1–10). To the victor belong the spoils, and thus the spoils of battle were to be "devoted" or sacrificed to Yahweh. This is the logic of the *herem,* or ban (Num. 21:2; Deut. 2:34; 3:6; 7:1–2; 20:16; Josh. 6:21; 8:26; 10:28–40; 11:11; 1 Sam. 15).

6. Israel's faith was essential. Israel is told repeatedly: "Do not be afraid" (Ex. 14:13; Deut. 20:3; Josh. 8:1; 10:8, 25; 11:6; Judg. 7:3; 1 Sam. 23:16). Conversely, Yahweh's most essential activity was

to strike fear into the heart of Israel's enemies (Ex. 15:14–16; 23:27–28; Deut. 2:25; 11:25; Josh. 2:9, 24; 5:1; 10:2; 24:12; 1 Sam. 4:7–8). Yahweh's great weapon was the divine terror (Ex. 23:27; Deut. 7:23; Josh. 10:10; Judg. 4:15; 7:22; 1 Sam. 5:11; 7:10; 14:15).

Von Rad admits that the idealized holy war described above never happened. That is, the records never relate all of the above characteristics in describing a particular war; nor is there consistency regarding particular characteristics, such as the *herem*, or ban. Yet the basic design of holy war colors every account.[18]

In thus clearly defining the sacral institution of holy war, von Rad admits to two basic assumptions which seem to me to be imposed on the data rather than derived from the data. One is that holy war was always defensive. This rules out any genuine instances of holy war during the conquest of Canaan. Indeed, the basic idea of a conquest is called in question. The other assumption is that holy war was always a cooperative venture between Israel and Yahweh; Yahweh never fought alone for Israel. The word "synergism," which we have used above, is von Rad's. This rules out the story of the Red Sea or any similar stories.

One result of these two assumptions is that the actual historical situation of holy war is the time of the Judges, the period of the Tribal League. With the shift to the monarchy, it was rather quickly replaced by typical Near Eastern warfare, fought by kings through a professional army, enhanced by drafted troops. There was an attempt to revive holy war in the time of Josiah, which explains the heavy emphasis on it in the book of Deuteronomy. With the death of Josiah, holy war came to an end, but the holy war ideal continued to occupy and stimulate Israel for centuries.

In order to explain away any records of what we have called monergistic warfare, von Rad develops his theory that such records have been colored by "the post-Solomonic Enlightenment." In the time following Solomon, Israel was exposed to foreign influences, particularly Near Eastern "wisdom." A school of writers arose who turned the ancient stories of holy war into novellas. We owe the Red Sea story in its present form to them, as well as the narratives of the conquest of Canaan, particularly the story of the fall of Jericho.

Their hand is evident in the stories of Gideon, and of David and Goliath.

Isaiah, the prophet in whom the ideas of holy war were strongest, took these novellas at face value and advocated leaving the defense of Jerusalem totally in God's hands (Isa. 7:4; 30:15–16; 31:1–5).[19]

In accord with his basic assumption that such monergistic warfare never occurred, von Rad discounts the account in Isaiah 36–37 = 2 Kings 18:17–19:37. The true history, he maintains, is the account in 2 Kings 18:14–16, verses omitted in Isaiah. Isaiah had firmly believed and stoutly maintained that if Judah would have faith, sit still, entrust its defense to Yahweh alone, they would be saved. But Judah did not do so. Instead, Hezekiah bought off the invader with the temple treasures. Judah was devastated. Only the city of Jerusalem was spared, "like a shelter in a cucumber field" (Isa. 1:8). Israel's greatest prophet died a failure, unheeded to the end, bitter (Isaiah 22) but compassionate (Isaiah 1).[20]

Critiques of von Rad

Various aspects of von Rad's thesis have been attacked. Rudolph Smend maintained that the Tribal League was a cultic league, not a military or political one.[21] The very name von Rad coined, "holy war," is not scriptural. It would be better to speak of "wars of Yahweh" or "Yahweh wars."[22] The wars, as recorded, were so diverse that it is questionable whether the kind of pattern or design that von Rad discerns ever existed even in the minds of biblical writers, much less in the actual events.[23] In particular, von Rad's insistence that holy war was always defensive cannot be supported.[24]

An important critique of von Rad's thesis is advanced by Millard Lind in his book *Yahweh Is a Warrior*. Lind accepts holy war as a cultic institution that deeply influenced Israel's life and history, but he does not agree that synergism is its typical form.[25]

Lind starts with the view that Exodus 15, the Song of the Sea, to which von Rad assigns a very late date,[26] is very ancient.[27] Here there is no synergism. The battle for Israel's deliverance from Egypt, the foundational event of the nation's existence, was won by Yahweh alone.

Lind maintains that in the Red Sea event we discover the true paradigm of holy war. The accounts of synergistic warfare represent a falling away from the ideal. In many of them the true shape of holy war can still be discerned.[28] This stands on its head von Rad's contention that the synergistic accounts portray the true holy war and the accounts where Yahweh alone fights are pious corruptions.

Yahweh: Israel's Enemy

In our continuum we have been analyzing the various ways in which Yahweh is said to have fought for and with the chosen people. But Yahweh also fought against them! This is not a unique understanding that belongs only to Israel,[29] but Israel emphasizes it more largely and systematically than any other people.

Yahweh's Passive Enmity Against Israel

Yahweh may fight against Israel passively, simply by not accompanying them into battle. In the familiar story of the twelve spies sent out to survey the Promised Land, the people of Israel believed the ten fearful spies and refused to go up and take the land, and Yahweh condemned them to forty years of wilderness wandering. The next day, against the orders of Moses, the people decided to go up anyway. Yahweh did not go with them and they were badly defeated (Numbers 13–14).

When Israel did not observe the *herem* against Jericho, but Achan took some of the devoted things and hid them in his tent, Yahweh did not go with them against Ai, the next city, and they were defeated (Joshua 7).

Because of the sins of Eli and his sons, Yahweh did not go with Israel to battle against the Philistines. Even taking the ark of the covenant into the field did not guarantee the LORD's presence. So Israel was defeated and the ark captured (1 Samuel 4).

Saul, rejected as king of Israel, could get no answer from Yahweh by dreams, by Urim, or by prophets (1 Sam. 28:6). Despite warnings from Samuel through a medium, he went into battle against the

Philistines, unaccompanied by Yahweh. Israel was defeated and
Saul and his sons were killed (ch. 31).

Despite the warnings of Micaiah, Ahab listened to his own court
prophets and went to war against Ramoth-gilead. Yahweh was not
with him and he was killed in battle and Israel was scattered in
defeat (1 Kings 22).

Yahweh's Active Warfare Against Israel

Not only did Yahweh fight against Israel passively by not going
with them, Yahweh fought against Israel actively, using their enemies as instruments. The incursions of the great empires were
brought about by Yahweh in order to punish the people for their
sins. This was constantly predicted by the prophets, and we shall
consider those predictions at length in chapter 7. After the predictions came true and Israel fell to Assyria and Judah fell to Babylon,
the historians and poets spoke eloquently of the antagonistic warfare of Yahweh.

In 2 Kings 17 the removal of Israel, the Northern Kingdom, by
the armies of Assyria is said to be Yahweh's punishment upon them
for their idolatry. When they would not listen to the warnings of the
prophets, but worshiped all the host of heaven, served Baal, and
made their sons and daughters pass through fire, "the LORD was
very angry with Israel and removed them out of his sight; none was
left but the tribe of Judah" (v. 18).

In 2 Chronicles 36 the exile of Judah, the Southern Kingdom, is
attributed to the antagonistic warfare of Yahweh. When they kept
mocking his messengers, despising his words, and scoffing at his
prophets, "the wrath of the LORD against his people became so great
that there was no remedy" (v. 16). It was the LORD who brought
against them the king of Chaldeans, to slaughter the people, take
away the treasures, burn the temple, break down the walls of
Jerusalem (vs. 17–19).

Once again, this theme is reflected in the piety of the Psalter.
There are plaintive laments of Yahweh's passive enmity:

> Yet you have rejected us and abased us,
>   and have not gone out with our armies.
> You made us turn back from the foe,
>   and our enemies have gotten spoil.
>
>   (Ps. 44:9–10)

See also Psalms 60:10 = 108:11; 74; 77.

In other psalms, Yahweh actively fights against the people. In an eloquent passage in Psalm 78:56–64, the psalmist declares:

> He gave his people to the sword,
>   and vented his wrath on his heritage.
>
>   (Ps. 78:62)

In Psalm 106:40–46 we read:

> He gave them into the hand of the nations,
>   so that those who hated them ruled over them.
>
>   (Ps. 106:41)

See also Psalms 80:12; 89:38–45.

Some of the clearest statements regarding Yahweh's antagonistic warfare against Israel are found in the collection of poems known as the book of Lamentations. Chapter 2:2–5 is an excerpt that represents the tone of the whole. It ends thus:

> The Lord has become like an enemy;
>   he has destroyed Israel;
> he has destroyed all its palaces,
>   laid in ruins its strongholds,
> and multiplied in daughter Judah
>   mourning and lamentation.
>
>   (Lam. 2:5)

Individuals, as well as the nation, suffer from Yahweh's antagonistic warfare. They suffer from God's absence and neglect (Psalms 42–43) and from God's active attack:

> For your arrows have sunk into me,
>   and your hand has come down on me.
>
>   (Ps. 38:2)

> Remove your stroke from me;
>   I am worn down by the blows of your hand.
> (Ps. 39:10)

> Your wrath has swept over me;
>   your dread assaults destroy me.
> (Ps. 88:16)

> You have lifted me up
>   and thrown me aside.
> (Ps. 102:10)

> He bent his bow and set me
>   as a mark for his arrow.
> He shot into my vitals
>   the arrows of his quiver.
> (Lam. 3:12–13)

A Cease-Fire in Yahweh's War

Now comes an unexpected turn of events. God declares a cease-fire in his warfare against the people:

> Speak tenderly to Jerusalem,
>   and cry to her
> that her warfare is ended,
>   that her iniquity is pardoned,
> that she has received from the LORD's hand
>   double for all her sins.
> (Isa. 40:2, RSV)

God raises up another strange and warlike nation, a great world power, to be God's instrument. The purpose this time is not to punish Israel, but to redeem them, to set them free, to restore them to their land.

Cyrus, king of Persia, is the LORD's anointed (Messiah!), raised up for this purpose. The LORD will grasp his right hand, subdue nations before him, open doors, level mountains. He will build the LORD's city and set the LORD's people free (Isa. 45:1–4, 13; see also 41:2, 25; 43:14).

So it happened. In a series of military campaigns, Cyrus the Persian conquered Babylon and released the Jewish exiles to return and rebuild Jerusalem. They never lifted a hand or a sword. It was like their release from Egypt long before. The prophet sees the connection and speaks of the LORD

> who says to the deep, "Be dry—
>   I will dry up your rivers";
> who says of Cyrus, "He is my shepherd,
>   and he shall carry out all my purpose";
> and who says of Jerusalem, "It shall be rebuilt,"
>   and of the temple, "Your foundation shall be laid."
>
>   (Isa. 44:27–28)

The imagery of the exodus runs all through this magnificent poem. We have come full circle. We have returned to the monergistic warfare with which Israel's story began.

Even if we follow Lind and decide that monergism is the true understanding of Yahweh's involvement in Israel's warfare, we still face serious problems. When Yahweh fights as Israel's ally, there are still human victims who suffer and die. The dead Egyptians still wash up on the shore. Sennacherib's army is decimated, and "the widows of Ashur are loud in their wail."[30] Cyrus moves to free the Jewish exiles by a path marked by the death and destruction of thousands. And when Yahweh fights against the chosen people, the siege of Jerusalem can be so horrible that women eat their own offspring, the children they have borne (Lam. 2:20). The debate over monergism and synergism may have some bearing over whether Israel should fight, but there is no disguising the belief that Yahweh fights, that Yahweh is a warrior.

Yahweh Is a Warrior

Israel never sought to disguise the belief that Yahweh is a warrior. Israel celebrated it. The Song of the Sea exults:

> The LORD is a warrior;
>   the LORD is his name.
>   (Ex. 15:3)

The liturgy of Psalm 24 declares:

> Lift up your heads, O gates!
>   and be lifted up, O ancient doors!
>   that the King of glory may come in.
> Who is the King of glory?
>   The LORD, strong and mighty,
>   the LORD, mighty in battle.
>
> (Ps. 24:7–8)

See also Isaiah 42:13; Zephaniah 3:17.

Yahweh's Army

This brings us to the affirmation that the Divine Warrior has a divine army. Patrick D. Miller, Jr., in *The Divine Warrior in Early Israel*[31] compares divine warfare in Israel with divine warfare in the literature of Syria-Palestine. As there was a divine assembly in the Canaanite religions, so there was a divine assembly in the religion of Israel. Psalm 82:1 says, "God has taken his place in the divine council; in the midst of the gods he holds judgment." The members of the council, here called "gods," are elsewhere called "sons of God" (Job 1:6), "servants" (Job 4:18), "ministers" (Pss. 103:21; 104:4), "spirits" (1 Kings 22:21), and so on. In the Canaanite religions, the divine assembly was clearly polytheistic, made up of many rival gods and their retinues. In Israel, the members of the assembly are subordinate to God, under the name of El or Yahweh.

While the divine assembly had judicial functions, its primary function was a military one. Thus the "host" or "army" of Yahweh is another name for the divine council (1 Kings 22:19; Ps. 103:20–21). The cosmic army of Yahweh is on the march in the most ancient poems of the Old Testament:

> The LORD came from Sinai,
>   and dawned from Seir upon us;
>   he shone forth from Mount Paran.
> With him were myriads of holy ones;
>   at his right, a host of his own.
>
> (Deut. 33:2)

See also Judg. 5:4–5 and Ps. 68:7–8, 17.[32]

The cosmic army also figures in poems of the royal period (1 Sam. 22:7–16 = Ps. 18:6–15; Hab. 3:3–15). In these poems we see Yahweh marching to battle at the head of an army, not the troops of Israel, but the hosts of heaven. It is true that the familiar name for God, "LORD of hosts" = "Yahweh of armies," later came to be associated with the armies of Israel, but it initially pictured God as commander of a cosmic army.

This point is pressed home in unforgettable fashion in the story where the great army of the Arameans comes by night to surround the prophet Elisha in Dothan. Elisha's servant rises early, sees the army, and panics. "Do not be afraid," says the prophet, "for there are more with us than there are with them." He prays that the servant's eyes may be opened. Yahweh opens the servant's eyes and he sees the mountain full of horses and chariots of fire around Elisha. The cosmic hosts of the LORD are there to defend the prophet (2 Kings 6:15–17).

The most striking difference from the Canaanite parallels is that the Canaanite deities lead their armies against each other or against cosmic forces. While some conflict with cosmic forces is predicated of Yahweh,[33] the principal emphasis is that Yahweh leads Yahweh's hosts to do battle against the earthly enemies of Israel.

Yahweh's Weapons

The weapons of the Divine Warrior are described in Habakkuk 3:

> You brandished your naked bow,
>   sated were the arrows at your command. . . .
> The moon stood still in its exalted place,
>   at the light of your arrows speeding by,
>   at the gleam of your flashing spear.
> In fury you trod the earth,
>   in anger you trampled nations.
>   (Hab. 3:9, 11–12)

A similar description is found in the Song of Moses (Deut. 32:39–43).

The Armor of Yahweh

Even the armor of the Divine Warrior is described in a familiar and moving passage:

> The LORD saw it, and it displeased him
>   that there was no justice.
> He saw that there was no one,
>   and was appalled that there was no one to intervene;
> so his own arm brought him victory,
>   and his righteousness upheld him.
> He put on righteousness like a breastplate,
>   and a helmet of salvation on his head;
> he put on garments of vengeance for clothing,
>   and wrapped himself in fury as in a mantle.
> According to their deeds, so will he repay;
>   wrath to his adversaries, requital to his enemies.
>   (Isa. 59:15–18)

The Ambiguity of the Divine Warrior

The portrait of God the Warrior in a certain way sums up all the diverse materials of this long chapter. Scholars like G. Ernest Wright do not find this portrait offensive. In *The Old Testament and Theology,*[34] Wright maintains that the Old Testament understands God in three primary ways: as creator, as Lord, and as warrior. The Old Testament understanding of God is historical and political, not metaphysical. Human history and politics are continuously marked by conflict; and if God is involved in that history and politics as creator and Lord, God is also involved as protagonist, as combatant, as warrior. In exercising the divine sovereignty, in working out the divine purposes in history, God had to engage in real conflict in a real world. For example, God had to remove the Canaanites to make a place for the covenant people Israel.

Wright admits that there are problems here. We must say that God uses war for God's purposes without in any way sanctifying the human participants. We must say that Israel's wars of conquest become no mandate for wars by God's people today. Language about the Warrior Lord means that there is a force in the universe set against the forces of evil. "Now if one thinks this type of language is too strong, let him only remember that God the Warrior is simply the reverse side of God the Lover or of God the Redeemer. . . . [Love] is power in action in a sinful world."[35]

I cannot deal with the portrait of God as warrior so easily. I can see positive value in the fact that the biblical God is not the Unmoved Mover of Greek philosophy, that God is an involved God, working God's purpose out in a real world filled with real people. But that does not eliminate the negativity. War in any form is cruel, barbarous, deadly. Are we to say that with God the end justifies the means, when we know it does not work that way among human beings? What is ascribed to God here does mystify and offend us. In the *herem* God orders conduct that is clearly condemned by the proponents of the just war theory, let alone by those who believe that Jesus taught nonviolence. The main problem is not that the people of God were warriors, but that the Old Testament affirms that God is a warrior. Here is where the ambiguity of scripture reaches a point of agony, for the same Old Testament affirms that the same God is also the author and giver of peace.

5

Yahweh: Giver of *Shalom*

The Warrior God is also the God of peace who gives peace to the people of God. In this chapter we shall speak of Yahweh as the giver of *shalom*. We use the Hebrew word, not to appear erudite, but because *shalom* has a range of meanings that go far beyond the meanings we usually associate with the English word "peace." We begin with an exploration of those meanings.[1]

The Meaning of *Shalom*

The Absence of War

In several passages *shalom* is an antonym for war and means "the absence of war," as it does so often in customary English usage. Thus we find it in the familiar list of antonyms in Ecclesiastes (3:8):

> a time to love, and a time to hate;
> a time for war, and a time for *shalom*.

The same contrast is found in Psalm 120:6–7:

> Too long have I had my dwelling
>   among those who hate *shalom*.
> I am for *shalom*;
>   but when I speak,
>   they are for war.

And the same contrast is found in biblical narratives. David condemned Joab for killing Abner and Amasa, "retaliating in time of peace for blood that had been shed in war," literally "he shed bloods of war in *shalom*" (1 Kings 2:5). David may not build the temple, for he is a man of war; Solomon shall build it, for he is a man of *shalom* (1 Chron. 22:8–9). Ben-hadad, king of Aram, issued orders that said: "If they have come out for *shalom*, take them alive; and if they have come out for war, take them alive" (1 Kings 20:18).

Shalom simply means the absence of war in the statements that "there was *shalom* between King Jabin of Hazor and the clan of Heber the Kenite" (Judg. 4:17), or that "there was *shalom* also between Israel and the Amorites" (1 Sam. 7:14), or that Solomon "had *shalom* on all sides" (1 Kings 4:24). Such peace was often the result of a formal peace treaty or "covenant of *shalom*" as between Isaac and Abimelech (Gen. 26:26–31) or Joshua and the Gibeonites (Josh. 9:15) or the other tribes and Benjamin (Judg. 21:13) or David and Jonathan (1 Sam. 20:42) or Solomon and Hiram (1 Kings 5:12).

There are often anxious questions as to whether someone is coming with peaceful or with warlike intent. The men of Bethlehem ask, when Samuel suddenly visits them, "Do you come peaceably?" literally, "*Shalom* do you come?" To which Samuel replies, "Peaceably," literally, "*Shalom*" (1 Sam. 16:4–5). Bathsheba asks Adonijah, "Is your coming *shalom*?" To which he replies "*Shalom*" (1 Kings 2:13). As Jehu moves toward the palace of King Joram, he is asked repeatedly, "Is it *shalom*?" (2 Kings 9:17–19, 22, 31). In that case it was not peace, but a bloody coup.

The Fullness of Well-being

But *shalom* is not merely an emptiness, an absence of war or internal strife.[2] It is a fullness, a promise of general well-being. It is in this positive fullness, which goes far beyond the mere negation of war, that *shalom* possesses a richness not usually found in our English word "peace." A simple way to explore the cluster of meaning that surrounds *shalom* is to examine the various translations for it offered in the New Revised Standard Version of the Bible:

"To be all right." When the wealthy woman of Shunem came to see the prophet Elisha on a day which was neither new moon nor Sabbath, he sensed something might be wrong. So he sent his servant Gehazi to ask: "Do you have *shalom?* Does your husband have *shalom?* Does the child have *shalom?*" The NRSV translates, "Are you all right? Is your husband all right? Is the child all right?" To which she replies, *"Shalom.* It is all right" (2 Kings 4:26). To have *shalom* is to be all right. It is to have health when disease is possible, safety when danger is possible, enough when deprivation is possible, life when death is possible. Of course the Shunammite was not telling the truth, because the child was dead. The prophet discerned it was not *shalom* because she was in bitter distress. The same translation is found in 2 Kings 4:23; 5:21–22; 9:11.

"To be well." Frequently the noun *shalom* is translated by various verbal expressions centering on well-being or being well. Jacob sent Joseph "to see the *shalom* of his brothers and the *shalom* of the flock." The translation is: "Go now, see if it is well with your brothers and with the flock" (Gen. 37:14). In a similar situation, when Jesse sent David to the battlefield to see his brothers "for *shalom,*" the translation is, "See how your brothers fare" (1 Sam. 17:18). In like fashion, Mordecai would walk around in front of the court of the harem "to know the *shalom* of Esther," which is translated "to learn how Esther was" (Esth. 2:11). In an extraordinary juxtaposition of war and peace, David asked Uriah "for the *shalom* of Joab and for the *shalom* of the people, and for the *shalom* of the war." The translation is, "David asked how Joab and the people fared, and how the war was going" (2 Sam. 11:7). Later, Joab asked after the *shalom* of a rival commander, Amasa. The translation is, "Is it well with you, my brother?" A treacherous question, for he seized him by his beard as if to kiss him and stabbed him in his belly (2 Sam. 20:9–10).

In the notion of well-being, there are undertones of health. When Joseph's brothers came a second time to Egypt for grain, Joseph inquired about their *shalom* and said, "Does your father

have *shalom,* the old man of whom you spoke? Is he still alive?"
They replied, "Your servant, our father has *shalom;* he is still alive."
The translation is, "He inquired about their welfare, and said, 'Is
your father well . . . ?' They said, 'Your servant, our father is well' "
(Gen. 43:27–28). Jacob made a similar inquiry about Laban (29:6).
At other times, the undertone is one of safety. David anxiously
inquired of the runners who brought word of the battle, "Does the
young man Absalom have *shalom?*" The translation is, "Is it well
with the young man Absalom?" (2 Sam. 18:28–29, 32).

   "*Shalom to you*" often functions as a greeting when people meet
(Judg. 19:20; 1 Sam. 25:5–6; 1 Chron. 12:18). The implication is,
"All is well; you have nothing to fear." Thus when Joseph says
"*Shalom* to you" to his brothers, the NRSV translates "Rest assured"
(Gen. 43:23). Similarly, "Go in *shalom*" or "Go to or for *shalom*" is
a traditional parting formula (Gen. 44:17; Ex. 4:18; Judg. 18:6; 1
Sam. 1:17; 25:35; 29:7; 2 Sam. 15:9, 27; 2 Kings 5:19). There is a
real question whether these formulas were ever routine, like "how
are you?" or "goodbye" in modern English. There seems to have
been in all these cases an assurance of safety, a wish for health, a
genuine concern for the other person's well-being.

   In the biblical stories there are predictions, true or false, that
individuals or the whole people will have *shalom.* David says to
Jonathan, "If Saul says, 'Good!' it will be well with your servant" (1
Sam. 20:7). Jeremiah says, "Ah, Lord GOD, how utterly you have
deceived this people and Jerusalem, saying, 'It shall be well with
you,' even while the sword is at the throat!" (Jer. 4:10). And he says
concerning the false prophets, "They keep saying to those who
despise the word of the LORD, 'It shall be well with you'; and to all
who stubbornly follow their own stubborn hearts, they say, 'No
calamity shall come upon you' " (23:17). In each case it is *shalom*
that is being translated.

   "*Welfare, weal.*" Sometimes the noun *shalom* is translated more
literally by an English noun "welfare." We have already seen Joseph
inquiring about the "welfare" (*shalom*) of his brothers in Gen.
43:27. Similarly Moses and Jethro ask after each other's welfare in
Ex. 18:7. And the psalmist sings:

> Let those who desire my vindication
>   shout for joy and be glad,
>   and say evermore,
> "Great is the LORD
>   who delights in the welfare of his servant."
>   (Ps. 35:27)

Welfare is not confined to the well-being of individuals; cities and nations and generations are in view. In an important passage, Jeremiah urges the exiles in Babylon to seek the "welfare" (*shalom*) of the city to which they have been exiled, "for in its welfare you will find your welfare" (Jer. 29:7). See Deuteronomy 23:6; Esther 10:3; Proverbs 3:2; Isaiah 38:17; Jeremiah 15:5; 29:11; 38:4 for other places where *shalom* is translated "welfare." In the familiar and difficult word of the LORD in Isaiah 45:7, "I make weal and create woe," the word "weal" translates *shalom*.

"To be safe, safety." We have already seen that safety is often an important undertone in the more general idea of well-being. To return from battle in *shalom* is to return "safe." After the slaughter of the five kings, "all the people returned safe to Joshua in the camp" (Josh. 10:21). Mephibosheth professes to have been concerned above all else that the king (David) should return home in safety (2 Sam. 19:14), or safely (v. 30). In 1 Kings 22:27–28 = 2 Chronicles 18:26–27, before going into battle, Ahab orders the prophet Micaiah put in prison on bread and water "until I come in peace." Micaiah replies, "If you return in peace, the LORD has not spoken by me." Here the translation "peace" has been chosen, but the idea of a safe return from battle is clear. Ahab died in the battle, but Jehoshaphat, king of Judah, returned in safety (*shalom*) to his house in Jerusalem (2 Chron. 19:1). Jeremiah predicts that Nebuchadnezzar will ravage Egypt and that he will depart from there safely (43:12), and the Prophet of the Exile says of Cyrus that he pursues the nations and passes on safely (Isa. 41:3).

Shalom also describes safety from individual enemies. Jonathan goes to great effort to determine whether David will be safe (in *shalom*) from Saul (1 Sam. 20:13, 21).

In the great poetic debate in Job, Eliphaz includes safety from wild animals as part of *shalom.* "If you accept the Almighty's discipline," he says,

> You shall be in league with the stones of the field,
>   and the wild animals shall be at peace with you.
> You shall know that your tent is safe (*shalom*).
>   (Job 5:23–24)

Not so, replies Job. Look rather at the wicked:

> Their houses are safe (*shalom*) from fear,
>   and no rod of God is upon them.
>   (Job 21:9)

Compare Deut. 29:19, where the wicked think in their hearts, "We are safe (*shalom* shall be to me) even though we go our own stubborn ways."

"*Health.*" As we have already seen, in the inquiries whether things are "all right" or whether it is "well" with this person or that, a concern for health is evident. Clearly, *shalom* could often be translated as "health," but that translation occurs only sparingly in the NRSV.

> There is no soundness in my flesh
>   because of your indignation;
> there is no health (*shalom*) in my bones
>   because of my sin.
>   (Ps. 38:3)

Most important, we find this in the description of the Suffering Servant in Isa. 53:

> But he was wounded for our transgressions,
>   crushed for our iniquities;
> upon him was the punishment that made us whole,
>   [the punishment of our *shalomim*]
>   and by his bruises we are healed.
>   (Isa. 53:5)

The "healths" of each of us are dependent on his punishment, our healing on his bruises.

"*Prosperity.*" *Shalom* involves not only safety in the face of danger, health in the face of sickness or death, but material prosperity in the face of possible famine and deprivation. This translation is demanded in the following example of poetic parallelism:

> I will extend prosperity (*shalom*) to her like a river,
>> and the wealth of nations like an overflowing stream.
>>> (Isa. 66:12)

The *shalom* which the wicked enjoy often takes the form of material prosperity.

> Terrifying sounds are in their ears;
>> in prosperity (*shalom*) the destroyer will come upon them.
>>> (Job 15:21)

> For I was envious of the arrogant;
>> I saw the prosperity (*shalom*) of the wicked.
>>> (Ps. 73:3)

Prosperity is associated with abundant crops and therefore roots in the land.

> But the meek shall inherit the land,
>> and delight themselves in abundant prosperity (*shalom*).
>>> (Ps. 37:11; see also 72:3)

Prosperity depends on obedience to the Torah:

> O that you had paid attention to my commandments!
>> Then your prosperity (*shalom*) would have been
>>> like a river,
>> and your success like the waves of the sea.
>>> (Isa. 48:18)

There are other gracious predictions that promise prosperity (*shalom*) to the people of God: Isaiah 54:13; Jeremiah 33:6, 9; Haggai 2:9.

"*Friendship.*" *Shalom* is the basis of trust and friendship. Thus David says to the Benjaminites, "If you have come to me in friendship (*shalom*), to help me, then my heart will be knit to you"

(1 Chron. 12:17). The expression "man of my *shalom*" is translated "bosom friend" (Ps. 41:9), "close friend" (Jer. 20:10), "trusted friend" (Jer. 38:22), "confederate" (Obad. 1:7). On occasion the context demands that the simple word *shalom* be translated "friend" (Ps. 55:20) or "ally" (Ps. 69:22). Sadly, most of these passages have to do with betrayal by friends, which constitutes a terrible breach of *shalom.*

"*Integrity.*" In being "all right" (*shalom*) there is surely an underlying concept of wholeness, of "having it all together." We are not surprised, then, to find the translation "integrity" used in a remarkable oracle addressed to the priests by the prophet Malachi:

> Know, then, that I have sent this command to you, that my covenant with Levi may hold, says the LORD of hosts. My covenant with him was a covenant of life and well-being (*shalom*), which I gave him; this called for reverence, and he revered me and stood in awe of my name. True instruction was in his mouth, and no wrong was found on his lips. He walked with me in integrity (*shalom*) and uprightness, and he turned many from iniquity. (Mal. 2:4–6)

Other Translations. It is obvious that to inquire after someone's *shalom* was a conventional way to greet that person. So the NRSV sometimes translates "to ask after the *shalom* of" as simply "to greet" (Judg. 18:15; 1 Sam. 10:4; 17:22; 25:5; 30:21; 2 Sam. 8:10; 1 Chron. 18:10). In one case it goes so far as to translate "to come [to inquire] for the *shalom* of" as "to visit" (2 Kings 10:13). Elsewhere speaking *shalom* becomes "a favorable answer" (Gen. 41:16) or "friendly words" (Jer. 9:8), and returning in *shalom* from battle goes beyond safety to become "victory" (Judg. 8:9). There are also adverbial translations like "peaceably" (Gen. 37:4) and "wholly" (Jer. 13:19).

"*Peace.*" The majority of the occurrences of *shalom* are translated "peace," as one would expect. Examination of the immediate context has helped us understand other translations, but will not be of particular help here. It will be more helpful to examine *shalom* = peace in the broader context of the Hebrew scriptures as a whole. At this point the help of Old Testament scholars, who have a comprehensive grasp of that broader context, will prove invaluable.

Walter Brueggemann, in his collection of addresses entitled *Living Toward a Vision,* begins by attacking our individualistic "habits of the heart," typified by the familiar chorus, *"I've* got the peace that passes understanding down in *my* heart." No, says Brueggemann, *shalom* is not for isolated, insulated individuals. *"Shalom* comes only to the inclusive, embracing community that excludes none."[3] He goes on to point out three dimensions of *shalom.* In its cosmic dimensions *shalom* is "orderly fruitfulness." In its political dimensions, it is "equitable justice." In its personal dimensions, it is "generous caring."[4] To the have-nots, the slaves in Egypt, or the poor of the land when the kings ruled, or the exiles in Babylon, *shalom* means "freedom, liberation." There must be radical change before things will be all right and going well for them, before they can enjoy welfare, safety, prosperity, friendship, health, and personal integrity. To the haves, on the other hand, *shalom* means "order, stability." There must be proper management of the existing welfare, safety, prosperity and so on, so they can continue to enjoy and celebrate what they have. To the have-nots, *shalom* is salvation; to the haves, *shalom* is blessing. And *shalom* = peace must embrace both.[5]

Paul D. Hanson, in an amazingly compact essay on "War and Peace in the Hebrew Bible," starts with the struggle between order and chaos. *Shalom* is the order established by God in the act of creation. How are we to live in that order? Israel takes the exodus, its founding event, as the clue. There Yahweh is revealed as righteous, compassionate, and majestic. So Israel must live in what Hanson calls "a triangle" of righteousness, compassion, and worship. This is to live in a *shalom* that corresponds to the divinely established order. When the community lives in the triangle, God's *shalom* emanates into all creation. When they repudiate the covenant of *shalom,* the whole world falls into chaos. "If one were to choose a single word to describe the reality for which God created the world, and in which he seeks to sustain the community of those

who respond to his initiating grace . . . , that word would be
'*shalom.*'"[6]

We are far from exhausting the meaning of *shalom,* but already
we can discern at least the following:

1. *Shalom* is very clearly a broader and more positive word
   than our English "peace."

2. *Shalom* is a focal, central concept in the Hebrew scriptures.

3. *Shalom* is earthy, material. *Shalom* is something you can
   see. It is almost never an invisible, inward, psychological,
   or "spiritual" state—"peace of mind, peace of heart."[7]

4. Israel, though a warlike people, did not devalue *shalom*
   as a boring interlude between wars, as many other warlike peoples have done. *Shalom* is valued, desired, longed
   for.

Yahweh as Giver of *Shalom*

The Gift of *Shalom*

In passage after passage it is emphasized that Yahweh is the
creator, the source, the giver of this marvelous thing called *shalom.*
Thus we read in Job:

> Dominion and fear are with God;
> he makes *shalom* in his high heaven.
> (Job 25:2)

Individuals receive *shalom* from Yahweh:

> I will both lie down and sleep in *shalom;*
> for you alone, O LORD, make me lie down in safety.
> (Ps. 4:8)

> Those of steadfast mind you keep [in] *shalom—*
> [in] *shalom* because they trust in you.
> (Isa. 26:3)

The nation receives *shalom* in the same way:

> He grants *shalom* within your borders;
>   he fills you with the finest of wheat.
>   (Ps. 147:14)

Prayers for Shalom

Since Yahweh is the giver of peace, prayer is made to Yahweh for the gift of *shalom:*

> Pray for the *shalom* of Jerusalem:
>   "May they prosper who love you.
> *Shalom* be within your walls,
>   and security within your towers."
> For the sake of my relatives and friends
>   I will say, "*Shalom* be within you."
>   (Ps. 122:6–8)

The prayer for *shalom* in its shortest form is "*Shalom* be upon Israel!" (Pss. 125:5; 128:6).

The Blessing of Shalom

Closely related to the prayer for peace is the blessing of peace. Hear the priestly blessing of Israel, so frequently incorporated into Christian worship:

> The LORD bless you and keep you;
>   the LORD make his face to shine upon you,
>   and be gracious to you;
>   the LORD lift up his countenance upon you,
>   and give you *shalom*.
>   (Num. 6:24–26)[8]

The threefold repetition of "the LORD" = Yahweh leaves no doubt who the giver of *shalom* is. A briefer, but similar benediction is found in Psalm 29:

> May the LORD give strength to his people!
> May the LORD bless his people with *shalom*!
>   (Ps. 29:11)

In Psalm 85 it is Yahweh himself who speaks the blessing of peace:

> Let me hear what God the Lord will speak,
>   for he will speak *shalom* to his people,
>   to his faithful, to those who turn to him in their
>   hearts.
>
> (Ps. 85:8)

The Promise of Shalom

Promises abound that the prayers for peace will be answered, the blessings of peace bestowed.

> Steadfast love and faithfulness will meet;
>   righteousness and *shalom* will kiss each other.
> Faithfulness will spring up from the ground,
>   and righteousness will look down from the sky.
> The Lord will give what is good,
>   and our land will yield its increase.
>
> (Ps. 85:10–12)

> O Lord, you will ordain *shalom* for us,
>   for indeed, all that we have done, you have done
>   for us.
>
> (Isa. 26:12)

> Then justice will dwell in the wilderness,
>   and righteousness abide in the fruitful field.
> The effect of righteousness will be *shalom*,
>   and the result of righteousness, quietness and trust
>   forever.
> My people will abide in a habitation of *shalom*,
>   in secure dwellings, and in quiet resting places.
>
> (Isa. 32:16–18)

> Shalom, shalom, to the far and the near,
>   says the Lord;
>   and I will heal them.
>
> (Isa. 57:19)

> I will appoint *Shalom* as your overseer
>   and Righteousness as your taskmaster.
> Violence shall no more be heard in your land,
>   devastation or destruction within your borders;
> you shall call your walls Salvation,
>   and your gates Praise.
>
> (Isa. 60:17–18)

For surely I know the plans I have for you, says the LORD, plans for your *shalom* and not for harm, to give you a future with hope. (Jer. 29:11)

The Covenant of Shalom

Yahweh does not give *shalom* by whim. Yahweh is pledged, covenanted to bestow *shalom* on the people of Yahweh.

> For the mountains may depart
>   and the hills be removed,
> but my steadfast love shall not depart from you,
>   and my covenant of *shalom* shall not be removed,
> says the LORD, who has compassion on you.
>
> (Isa. 54:10)

I will make a covenant of *shalom* with them; it shall be an everlasting covenant with them; and I will bless them and multiply them, and will set my sanctuary among them forevermore.

> (Ezek. 37:26)

See also Numbers 25:12; Ezekiel 34:25; Malachi 2:5.

Yahweh Is Shalom

Clearly, *shalom* is not something that human beings can create or give to themselves. They can receive it and obediently maintain it, but *shalom* is created and given by Yahweh. Yahweh makes *shalom*, Yahweh alone makes us lie down in safety, Yahweh keeps us in *shalom*, Yahweh grants *shalom*, Yahweh gives *shalom*, Yahweh blesses with *shalom*, Yahweh speaks *shalom*, Yahweh ordains *shalom*, Yahweh appoints *shalom*, Yahweh plans *shalom*, Yahweh covenants *shalom*.

Perhaps the best summary of the material adduced thus far is

found in a primitive story about Gideon (Judg. 6:1–24). The angel of
the LORD (who is somehow the LORD himself; vs. 14, 16) appears to
Gideon and he is frightened for his life, crying: " 'Help me, Lord
GOD! For I have seen the angel of the LORD face to face.' But the
LORD said to him, '*Shalom* be to you; do not fear, you shall not die.'
Then Gideon built an altar there to the LORD, and called it, "Yahweh
is *shalom*" (vs. 22–24). Here in the midst of a warlike story is the
astounding affirmation: "Yahweh is *shalom.*" The creator, bestower,
covenantor of *shalom* is himself *Shalom!* This is the counterbalance
to the equally primitive statement, "Yahweh is a warrior" (Ex. 15:3).
The basic ambiguity of the biblical picture of God could hardly be
expressed more vividly.

How Yahweh Gives *Shalom*

If *shalom* is the focal, central concept in Hebrew scripture that
we have said it is, and if Yahweh is the giver of *shalom*, then we
would expect that giving to take place in the most focal, central
actions of God. Let us see if that is not the case.

Creation

Whatever theological orthodoxy may have to say about *creatio ex
nihilo* (creation out of nothing), the Hebrew scriptures see it as
bringing order out of chaos.

1. In certain passages, chaos is symbolized as a sea dragon with
whom the Creator is engaged in a life-or-death struggle. This is a
bold borrowing from surrounding Canaanite mythology. See Psalms
74:13–17; 89:9–11; Isaiah 51:9–10.

2. The sea itself is a symbol of chaos. When the Creator sets
bounds to the sea, chaos is limited and order is established. See Job
28:8–11; Psalm 24:1–2; Proverbs 8:29; Jeremiah 5:22.

3. In the priestly account of creation in Genesis 1, the primeval
chaos is ordered by the orderly, spoken commands of God: "In the
beginning when God created the heavens and the earth, the earth
was a formless void and darkness covered the face of the deep, while
a wind from God swept over the face of the waters. Then God said,

'Let there be light.'. . . . 'Let there be a dome in the midst of the waters, and let it separate the waters from the waters.'. . . . 'Let the waters under the sky be gathered together into one place, and let the dry land appear.'. . . 'Let the earth put forth vegetation.'. . . 'Let there be lights in the dome of the sky.'. . . 'Let the waters bring forth swarms of living creatures.'. . . 'Let the earth bring forth living creatures of every kind.'. . . 'Let us make humankind' " (Gen. 1:1–3, 6, 9, 11, 14, 20, 24, 26).

According to Hanson, the true antonym of *shalom* is chaos; war is an antonym because it is the quintessence of chaos. *Shalom* "describes the realm where chaos is not allowed to enter, and where life can be fostered free from fear of all which diminishes and destroys."[9] Thus, in creation, God is already at work giving peace.

Liberation

To the have-nots, we remember, *shalom* means liberation, deliverance, salvation. The slaves in Egypt were have-nots, and the exodus, their deliverance from bondage, was a *shalom*-action. The Hebrew poets have not missed the connection between God's victory over chaos in creation and the dividing of the sea in exodus.

> Was it not you who cut Rahab in pieces,
>   who pierced the dragon?
> Was it not you who dried up the sea,
>   the waters of the great deep;
> who made the depths of the sea a way
>   for the redeemed to cross over?
>   (Isa. 51:9–10)

Again and again the liberation from Egypt is described as Yahweh's act, Yahweh's gift:

You have seen what I did to the Egyptians, and how I bore you on eagles' wings and brought you to myself. (Ex. 19:4)

I am the LORD your God, who brought you out of the land of Egypt, out of the house of slavery; you shall have no other gods before me. (Ex. 20:2–3)

I am the LORD your God who brought you out of the land of Egypt,
to be their slaves no more; I have broken the bars of your yoke and
made you walk erect. (Lev. 26:13)

See also Num. 15:41; Deut. 8:14; 13:5, 10; 20:1.

The language of *shalom* is not used in connection with the
liberation of the slaves from Egypt, but it is clearly used in connection with the liberation of the exiles from Babylon.

> Comfort, comfort my people,
>   says your God.
> Speak tenderly to Jerusalem,
>   and cry to her
> that her warfare is ended,
>   that her iniquity is pardoned,
> that she has received from the LORD's hand
>   double for all her sins.
>   (Isa. 40:1–2, RSV)

The exile is here described as "warfare" (*saba'*). The end of the exile
is therefore peace, *shalom*. This is true if the "warfare" is simply
understood as a term of military service, and therefore a hard and
difficult time (NRSV). It is even more true if the allusion is to
Yahweh's antagonistic warfare against Yahweh's own people, which
is now coming to its end: Yahweh is announcing peace at last.

> How beautiful upon the mountains
>   are the feet of the messenger who announces *shalom*,
> who brings good news,
>   who announces salvation,
>   who says to Zion, "Your God reigns."
> Listen! Your sentinels lift up their voices,
>   together they sing for joy;
> for in plain sight they see
>   the return of the LORD to Zion.
>   (Isa. 52:7–8)

Here "the return of the LORD to Zion," which the context makes
clear is the return of the exiles from Babylon, is simply called
shalom.

> For you shall go out in joy,
>   and be led back in *shalom;*
> the mountains and the hills before you
>   shall burst into song,
>   and all the trees of the field
>   shall clap their hands.
>
>   (Isa. 55:12)

The LORD gives *shalom* by liberating the oppressed.

Fruitful Land

Liberation from bondage has no great meaning unless there is some place to go, and it is a temporary blessing unless there is posterity to enjoy it in that place.

Walter Brueggemann asserts that "land is a central, if not *the central theme* of biblical faith." The symbolic meaning of land, he says, is "wholeness of joy and well-being characterized by social coherence and personal ease in prosperity, security, and freedom."[10] This is virtually identical with the cluster of meanings we have seen gathered around the idea of *shalom.* The connection between land and *shalom* is a very close one.

God the Covenant Maker promised land and family to marginal, landless, childless people (Genesis 12, 15, 17). God the Provider brought them through the howling wilderness (Exodus; Numbers). God the Warrior conquered their foes and gave them the land (Joshua). God the Peace Giver makes them dwell in families in the land in *shalom.*

The land which Yahweh gives is not empty, barren land like the wilderness. It is fruitful land. Israel never tires of describing it as a land flowing with milk and honey (Ex. 3:8, 17; 13:5; 33:3; Lev. 20:24; Num. 14:8; Deut. 6:3; 11:9; 26:9, 15; 27:3). For fuller descriptions of the land's fruitfulness, see Deut. 8:7–10; 11:10–12; Ps. 65:9–13.

Yahweh is a fertility deity, as both Walter Harrelson and Walter Brueggemann agree.[11] The idealized pictures and the future promises of the *shalom* that Yahweh gives are frequently agricultural in nature: threshing overtaking vintage and vintage overtaking sowing

(Lev. 26:5); Israel flourishing like a garden (Hos. 14:7); mountains dripping sweet wine (Amos 9:13); showers of blessing (Ezek. 34:26); splendid vegetation (v. 29). "For there shall be a sowing of *shalom;* the vine shall yield its fruit, the ground shall give its produce, and the skies shall give their dew; and I will cause the remnant of this people to possess all these things" (Zech. 8:12).

Torah

Yahweh gives peace in creation, by setting limits on the sea and all other forms of chaos. But that is not enough. Yahweh gives peace in liberation, by setting free marginalized, oppressed, powerless people. But that is not enough. Yahweh gives peace by providing liberated people a place. a fruitful land. But that is not enough, for within that land people will marginalize and oppress each other and there will be no peace. So Yahweh gives peace in Torah, instruction, direction, laws, statutes, commandments, for right living in the fruitful land.

> Great *shalom* have those who love your Torah;
> nothing can make them stumble.
> > (Ps. 119:165)

> My child, do not forget my Torah,
> but let your heart keep my commandments;
> for length of days and years of life
> and abundant *shalom* they will give you.
> > (Prov. 3:1–2)

> O that you had paid attention to my commandments!
> Then your *shalom* would have been like a river,
> and your success like the waves of the sea.
> > (Isa. 48:18)

> All your children shall be taught by the LORD,
> and great shall be the *shalom* of your children.
> > (Isa. 54:13)

A great portion of the Torah has to do with the right distribution and the right use of the land. Walter Brueggemann writes that

"Torah consists in guidelines for land management. . . . It is . . . interested in care for the land, so that it is never forgotten from whence came the land and to whom it is entrusted and by whom. . . . The link between Torah and land is essential."[12] The following are some of the salient provisions of the Torah regarding the distribution and use of the land:

1. *You are to remember that the land is a gift.* It was promised to your ancestors as a gift:

> Remember Abraham, Isaac, and Israel, your servants, how you swore to them by your own self, saying to them, "I will multiply your descendants like the stars of heaven, and all this land that I have promised I will give to your descendants, and they shall inherit it forever." (Ex. 32:13)

See also Genesis 12:7; 13:15, 17; 15:7, 18; 17:8; 24:7; 26:3; 28:4, 13; 35:12; 48:4; 50:24; Exodus 6:4; 32:13; 33:1; Numbers 14:23; Deuteronomy 6:18, 23; 8:1; 9:5; 10:11; 19:8; 26:15; 34:4.

The land was delivered into your hands by the monergistic warfare of Yahweh:

> And because he loved your ancestors, he chose their descendants after them. He brought you out of Egypt with his own presence, by his great power, driving out before you nations greater and mightier than yourselves, to bring you in, giving you their land for a possession, as it is still today. (Deut. 4:37–38)

See also Exodus 3:8; 6:8; 12:25; Leviticus 14:34; 20:22, 24; 23:10; 25:2, 38; Numbers 27:12; 32:7, 9; Deuteronomy 1:21; 4:1; 5:31; 6:18–19; 9:3–4; 11:31; 12:1, 10, 29; 15:4, 7; 16:20; 17:14; 18:9; 19:1, 3, 14; 25:19; 26:1, 2, 8–9; 27:2; 28:8; 32:49, 52.

Never forget this.

> When the LORD your God has brought you into the land that he swore to your ancestors, to Abraham, to Isaac, and to Jacob, to give you—a land with fine, large cities that you did not build, houses filled with all sorts of goods that you did not fill, hewn cisterns that you did not hew, vineyards and olive groves that you did not plant—and when you have eaten your fill, take care that

you do not forget the LORD, who brought you out of the land of
Egypt, out of the house of slavery. (Deut. 6:10–12)

2. *You are to treat the land with great respect.* For example, just
as you are to enjoy your sabbaths, so the land is to enjoy its sabbaths.

Speak to the people of Israel and say to them: When you enter the
land that I am giving you, the land shall observe a sabbath for the
LORD. Six years you shall sow your field, and six years you shall
prune your vineyard, and gather in their yield; but in the seventh
year there shall be a sabbath of complete rest for the land, a
sabbath for the LORD: you shall not sow your field or prune your
vineyard. (Lev. 25:2–4; cf. Ex. 23:10–11)

It is good agricultural policy for fields to lie fallow from time to time,
but more than that is at stake here. As Brueggemann puts it, "Land
has its own rights over against us and even its own existence. It is in
covenant with us but not totally at our disposal."[13] Its ultimate
owner is God.

3. *Land is not to be permanently alienated from the families to
whom Yahweh gave it:*

The land shall not be sold in perpetuity, for the land is mine; with
me you are but aliens and tenants. Throughout the land that you
hold, you shall provide for the redemption of the land. (Lev.
25:23–24)

This is why the distribution of the land, the free, gifted distribution
to the tribes, is so painstakingly recorded (Joshua 13–19; 21). This is
why the lines of family descent are so faithfully preserved (1
Chronicles 1–9). This is why the preservation of the tribes is so
important. Even in the lawless times of the Judges, the threat that
Benjamin might die out was a calamity. "They lifted up their voices
and wept bitterly. They said, 'O LORD, the God of Israel, why has it
come to pass that today there should be one tribe lacking in
Israel?' " (Judg. 21:2–3). Extraordinary measures were taken to
secure wives for the Benjaminites (vs. 4–24). This is why the brother
of a deceased man must marry his widow, to raise up descendants
for him (Deut. 25:5–10).

People become marginalized and oppressed when they lose their inherited family land. This can happen if the land is sold, or if people go into debt or even sell themselves into slavery. Very quickly the society can be polarized into haves and have-nots and *shalom* can be lost. The Torah proposed several interesting pieces of legislation to avoid this.

There shall be a sabbath of debts: every seventh year, all debts within the community are to be forgiven (Deut. 15:1–11). There shall be a sabbath of slavery: every seventh year slaves are to be set free (Ex. 21:1–11; Deut. 15:12–18). There shall be a year of jubilee (Lev. 25:8–17). Every fiftieth year (after seven sevens) all land shall be returned to the families that originally owned it. This means that the land itself is not what is really sold: only the number of crops until the next year of jubilee. Whether these laws were ever universally enforced, or whether indeed the year of jubilee was ever practiced at all are matters of debate among scholars. However, the intent of the legislation was clear enough. There was to be no permanent underclass in Israel. There was to be a time limit on the rich growing richer and the poor growing poorer. Poetically stated, every family was to sit under its own vine and under its own fig tree, with none to make them afraid (Micah 4:4; cf. 2 Kings 18:31). This would be *shalom*: everyone with a stake in the commonwealth and access to the means of production.

4. *Those who are landless still have rights in the land.* The Torah makes special provisions for the poor in general and for the alien or sojourner, the widow, and the orphan in particular:

> When you reap your harvest in your field and forget a sheaf in the field, you shall not go back to get it; it shall be left for the alien, the orphan, and the widow, so that the LORD your God may bless you in all your undertakings. When you beat your olive trees, do not strip what is left; it shall be for the alien, the orphan, and the widow. When you gather the grapes of your vineyard, do not glean what is left; it shall be for the alien, the orphan, and the widow. Remember that you were a slave in the land of Egypt; therefore I am commanding you to do this. (Deut. 24:19–22; cf. Lev. 19:9–10)

What grows during the fallow year (Ex. 23:11), what is not reaped in the corners of the field (Lev. 19:9), and what the landed owner is forbidden to glean (see above) is not charity; it is the patrimony of the poor.

The Torah is Yahweh's final provision for the peace of the chosen people. Above and beyond the land laws it breathes a concern for the powerless poor. You are not to be hard-hearted or tightfisted toward your needy neighbor (Deut. 15:7). Aliens, widows, and orphans are not to be oppressed in any way (Ex. 22:21–23; 23:9; Deut. 24:17; 27:19). Aliens, widows, and orphans shall share in the tithe of your produce (Deut. 26:12–13). No interest shall be charged to the poor (Ex. 22:25; Lev. 25:36; Deut. 23:19). Garments taken in pledge must be restored before the sun goes down (Ex. 22:26–27; Deut. 24:12–13). Millstones may not be taken in pledge, for that would be taking a life in pledge (Deut. 24:6). The justice due the poor shall not be perverted in lawsuits (Ex. 23.6). The Sabbath rest is specially for slaves and aliens (Ex. 23:12; Deut. 5:12–15). Wages shall be paid the day they are earned (Lev. 19:13; Deut. 24:14–15). Indeed, if a fellow Israelite becomes poor and cannot maintain himself, you shall maintain him (Lev. 25:35).

Ruth as a Picture of *Shalom*

A society so ordered will have *shalom*: rest, security, health, wholeness, well-being, prosperity. As we have seen, the historical record shows a very imperfect internal peace for Israel, broken by revenge, and royal oppression, and continual coups. We are fortunate to have the book of Ruth, a book that records no wars and depicts the life of the village of Bethlehem, where the Torah is honored. Set in the period of the Judges, it was written after the times it describes.[14] It may be an idealized picture, but it portrays in concrete, down-to-earth terms the *shalom* which Yahweh, the giver of *shalom*, intends for the people of God.

Two widows, landless, marginalized, powerless people, come to Bethlehem. Naomi is a former resident, who went as a refugee to Moab and lost there her husband and two sons. Ruth is an alien,

Naomi's daughter-in-law. Ruth goes to glean in the field of Boaz, claiming the patrimony of the poor, which is her right as an alien and a widow. Labor-management relations are good there. Boaz says to the reapers, "The LORD be with you." They reply, "The LORD bless you." Boaz, who turns out to be close kin to Naomi's deceased husband, is kind to Ruth and she gleans there for the whole harvest. On Naomi's advice, Ruth offers herself to Boaz as wife. Boaz challenges the one kinsman who is closer than he to redeem Naomi's husband's land, to keep it in the family. When the kinsman learns that with the field he will acquire the duty to marry Ruth and keep the family line going, he surrenders his rights to Boaz. Boaz marries Ruth. Then the village shows its nature as a *shalom* community. The people rejoice with Boaz, the middle-aged bachelor who has found the happiness of marriage and the prospect of children. Ruth bears a son and the women rejoice with Naomi, "Blessed be the LORD, who has not left you this day without next-of-kin; and may his name be renowned in Israel! He shall be to you a restorer of life and a nourisher of your old age; for your daughter-in-law who loves you, who is more to you than seven sons, has borne him" (Ruth 4:14–15). So the family line was preserved, a line from which came David the king and Jesus the Christ. In this story of sorrow and joy we see the face of *shalom*.[15]

6

The Prophets: Champions of *Shalom*

The *shalom* that God gives through creation, liberation, land, and Torah is always under threat. What happens to the precarious *shalom* of the little village of Bethlehem when the Torah is disregarded, when every individual is a law to himself or herself, doing whatever is right in his or her own eyes (Judg. 21:25)? What happens when there is no organized defense and Moab or Midian or Ammon sweeps in from the desert to confiscate the crops of the fruitful land? What happens when the Philistines settle the seacoast and subject Israel to seemingly permanent domination with their weapons of iron?

Israel's solution was to demand a king who would meld the loose confederation of tribes into a strong central state, who would defend them from their enemies (1 Sam. 8:19–20), who would study and enforce the Torah (Deut. 17:14–20). The king would be responsible for managing and perpetuating the *shalom* which God had given them.

The danger was that the king would imitate the kings of neighboring kingdoms and become the enemy of *shalom*. He would draft their sons as soldiers and armament manufacturers. He would draft their daughters as perfumers, cooks, and bakers. He would take their land, tax their produce, make them slaves (1 Sam. 8:10–14).

So Yahweh, the giver of *shalom,* did one more thing. Yahweh raised up the prophets to counterbalance the kings. It is true that the prophets at times cooperated with the kings. Nathan the prophet delivered the oracle regarding Yahweh's convenant with

David (2 Sam. 7:1–17) and was a leader in the movement to secure the throne to Solomon as David's successor (1 Kings 1). Elisha was a supporter of several of the kings of Israel (2 Kings 3, 5–7, 13). Isaiah counseled Hezekiah (Isa. 37). Jeremiah praised Josiah (Jer. 22:15–16). Nevertheless, the prophets remained the primary representatives of the continuing kingship or *imperium* of Yahweh. It was the kingship of Yahweh that had constituted Israel, and Israel would survive only as that *imperium* continued, overarching and overruling the power of human kings.[1] So when the prophets said, "Thus says the LORD," they were representing the ancient, original, final, and legitimate authority in Israel. One of the concerns of that authority was to defend *shalom* against the efforts of the kings and the nobles and the wealthy to undermine it.

The Defense of *Shalom*

Upholding Torah

Two dramatic stories show the earlier prophets in their role as defenders of *shalom*. In the first, King David, after the manner of eastern monarchs, has taken to bed Bathsheba, the wife of Uriah the Hittite. When she finds she is pregnant, David sends for Uriah to come home from the wars and to "cover up" what has been done. When Uriah does not cooperate, he is sent back to the front, bearing his own death warrant, a letter from David to Joab instructing him to make sure Uriah is killed in battle. Although a soldier in David's army, Uriah was an alien. But the Torah says that aliens are not to be oppressed or defrauded, and the king, like everyone else, is subject to the Torah. *Shalom* has been breached, so Yahweh sends Nathan the prophet to confront David the king. By a skillful parable Nathan enables David to see what he has done and predicts that this breach of *shalom* will haunt David's house for generations to come (2 Samuel 11–12).

In the second story, King Ahab covets the vineyard of Naboth. He offers to trade land for it, or to pay cash, but Naboth refuses, because he understands that *shalom* depends on each family's keeping its own inheritance. Ahab is terribly upset. His wife Jezebel, daughter of the king of Sidon, does not understand this way of doing things. Kings take what they want. She "frames" Naboth and has him stoned to death and tells Ahab to go and take possession of the vineyard he wanted so badly, but there in the vineyard stands Elijah the prophet, the champion of *shalom*. He predicts the doom of Ahab's house, a doom Ahab does not live to see because he repents abjectly (1 Kings 21).

Preaching Against Injustices

The great prophets of the eighth century B.C.E. inveigh against the injustices[2] that erode Israel's *shalom*. Hosea weeps that there is "no faithfulness or loyalty, no knowledge of God in the land" (Hos. 4:1).

Amos condemns those who trample the head of the poor into the dust of the earth, selling them into slavery for small debts, lying beside the altars on garments taken in pledge and not returned before night (Amos 2:6–8). The rich grow richer, with their winter houses and summer houses, their houses of hewn stone and even of ivory (3:15; 4:11), their luxurious life-style (6:1–6). The poor grow poorer, unable to get justice in the courts (5:12), cheated by false weights and measures (8:4–6).

Micah pronounces woe upon those who covet fields, and seize them; and houses, and take them away; who oppress householder and house and rob families of their inheritance (Micah 2:2). He describes them as cannibals, tearing the skin off the people, eating their flesh, breaking their bones, chopping them up like meat in a kettle (3:2–3).

Isaiah says,

> The LORD enters into judgment
>   with the elders and princes of his people:
> It is you who have devoured the vineyard;
>   the spoil of the poor is in your houses.
> What do you mean by crushing my people,
>   by grinding the face of the poor?
>   says the Lord GOD of hosts.
>
> (Isa. 3:14–15)

He pronounces woe upon those who join house to house, who add field to field, until there is no more room (5:8); and upon those who make iniquitous decrees, who write oppressive statutes, to turn aside the needy from justice and to rob the poor of Yahweh's people of their right, who make widows their spoil and orphans their prey (10:1–2). *Shalom* can be established only by a return to Torah:

> Cease to do evil,
>> learn to do good;
> seek justice,
>> rescue the oppressed,
> defend the orphan,
>> plead for the widow.
>> (Isa. 1:16–17)

A century later Jeremiah identifies the enemies of *shalom:*

> For scoundrels are found among my people;
>> they take over the goods of others.
> Like fowlers they set a trap;
>> they catch human beings.
> Like a cage full of birds,
>> their houses are full of treachery;
> therefore they have become great and rich,
>> they have grown fat and sleek.
> They know no limits in deeds of wickedness;
>> they do not judge with justice
> the cause of the orphan, to make it prosper,
>> and they do not defend the rights of the needy.
>> (Jer. 5:26–28)

He also calls for a return to Torah as the basis for dwelling peacefully in the land:

> For if you truly amend your ways and your doings, if you truly act justly one with another, if you do not oppress the alien, the orphan, and the widow, or shed innocent blood in this place, and if you do not go after other gods to your own hurt, then I will dwell with you in this place, in the land that I gave of old to your ancestors forever and ever. (Jer. 7:5–7)

In the Persian period, Zechariah reviews how Israel lost *shalom* by not heeding the words of the prophets who preceded him:

> The word of the LORD came to Zechariah, saying: Thus says the LORD of hosts: Render true judgments, show kindness and mercy to one another; do not oppress the widow, the orphan, the alien, or the poor; and do not devise evil in your hearts against one another. But they refused to listen, and turned a stubborn shoulder, and stopped their ears in order not to hear. They made their hearts adamant in order not to hear the Torah and the words that the LORD of hosts sent by his spirit through the former prophets. Therefore great wrath came from the LORD of hosts. Just as, when I called, they would not hear, so, when they called, I would not hear, says the LORD of hosts, and I scattered them with a whirlwind among all the nations that they had not known. Thus the land was left desolate, so that no one went to and fro, and a pleasant land was made desolate. (Zech. 7:8–14)

Criticizing False Prophets

One of the problems that the prophets faced was the multitude of false prophets who supported the kings in whatever they wanted to do.[3] We meet them in the story of the prophet Micaiah: Ahab had four hundred prophets who encouraged his military adventures (1 Kings 22:6–12). Micah speaks of prophets who lead the people astray, crying *"Shalom"* when they have something to eat and declaring war against those who put nothing into their mouths (Micah 3:5; cf. v. 11). Isaiah speaks of the prophets who teach lies (Isa. 9:15). Zephaniah calls the prophets "reckless, faithless persons" (Zeph. 3:4).

It is Jeremiah who deals most extensively with this phenomenon. Jeremiah 23:9–40 is a long denunciation of the false prophets. Chapter 28 is the detailed account of Jeremiah's controversy with the false prophet Hananiah. The tragedy of false prophecy is summarized succinctly:

> An appalling and horrible thing
> has happened in the land:

the prophets prophesy falsely,
and the priests rule as the prophets direct;
my people love to have it so,
but what will you do when the end comes?
(Jer. 5:30–31)

The nub of the controversy is that false prophets prophesy a false *shalom*.

Then I said: "Ah, Lord GOD! Here are the prophets saying to them, 'You shall not see the sword, nor shall you have famine, but I will give you true *shalom* in this place.' " And the LORD said to me: The prophets are prophesying lies in my name; I did not send them, nor did I command them or speak to them. They are prophesying to you a lying vision, worthless divination, and the deceit of their own minds. (Jer. 14:13–14; cf. 5:12–13; 27:14–15; 29:8–9)

The most familiar saying about false *shalom* is found twice in Jeremiah:

For from the least to the greatest of them,
everyone is greedy for unjust gain;
and from prophet to priest,
everyone deals falsely.
They have treated the wound of my people carelessly,
saying, "*Shalom, shalom,*"
when there is no *shalom*.
(Jer. 6:13–14; see 8:10–11)

See also Ezekiel 13:10, 16, where the prophet says that to say *shalom* when there is no *shalom* is like attempting to strengthen a wall by merely whitewashing it!

The false prophets were quick to promise *shalom* or announce its arrival, a cheap *shalom,* based on the favoritism of Yahweh. This was to give the *imperium,* the final authority in Israel, to the kings, and to make Yahweh their lackey. The message of the true prophets was frequently "no *shalom*" because there was no justice. The God who gives *shalom* can and will take it away if justice is lacking.

Thus says the LORD: Do not enter the house of mourning, or go to lament, or bemoan them; for I have taken away my *shalom* from this people, says the LORD, my steadfast love and mercy. (Jer. 16:5)

> Upon all the bare heights in the desert
>> spoilers have come;
> for the sword of the LORD devours
>> from one end of the land to the other;
> no one shall be safe,
>> [Lit.: no *shalom* to all flesh].
>>> (Jer. 12:12; cf. 30:5)

"There is no *shalom*," says the LORD, "for the wicked."
(Isa. 48:22; see 57:21)

To say that Yahweh will punish those who breach *shalom*, to say that the Giver of *shalom* is also the Withdrawer of *shalom*, to speak of "the sword of the LORD," is to reiterate the ancient faith of Israel that Yahweh is a warrior. But the prophets give that faith an unexpected twist. Because Israel has rejected the *shalom* Yahweh gives, because they have neglected the justice and loyalty and humility that are fundamental to *shalom*, Yahweh will war against his own people! It is the prophets who emphasize Yahweh's *antagonistic* warfare against Israel and who describe it with unparalleled vividness. We shall devote a major portion of chapter 7 to those predictions.

The Critique of War

Against Atrocities

In the primary history, as we saw in chapter 3, the wars of Israel are simply recorded in all their brutality and disregard of the humanity of enemies; but in the prophets a critique emerges. Amos makes it clear that Yahweh is against the atrocities of warfare. He lists the destruction of crops (Amos 1:3), the exile of people from their lands (v. 6), the breaking of treaties (v. 9), the lack of pity (v. 11), the maintenance of perpetual feuds (v. 11), ripping up women with child (v. 13), dishonoring the dead (2:1). For such atrocities,

committed in wars among the small states of the land bridge,
Yahweh is bringing upon them the punishment of Assyria.

Against Trust in Weapons

The prophets go further. To trust in military might to defend and
save Israel is *not* to trust in God. It is idolatry, imposing in one's own
weaponry trust of which God alone is worthy. Hosea condemns
Israel for trusting in their own power and the multitude of their
warriors (Hos. 10:13–14). Isaiah indicts Israel for multiplying armaments and multiplying idols in the same breath:

> Their land is filled with horses,
>   and there is no end to their chariots.
> Their land is filled with idols;
>   they bow down to the work of their hands,
>   to what their own fingers have made.
>   (Isa. 2:7–8)

Micah relates the disarming of Israel to the destruction of idols.
When Yahweh destroys their horses and chariots, he will also
destroy images and pillars and they will no longer bow down to the
work of their hands (Micah 5:10–13).

And Isaiah once again:

> For thus said the Lord GOD, the Holy One of Israel:
> In returning and rest you shall be saved;
>   in quietness and in trust shall be your strength.
> But you refused and said,
> "No! We will flee upon horses"—
>   therefore you shall flee!
> and, "We will ride upon swift steeds"—
>   therefore your pursuers shall be swift!
>   (Isa. 30:15–16)

Against Alliances

As to reliance on allies, the prophetic critique is merciless. Hosea
sings:

> When Ephraim saw his sickness,
>   and Judah his wound,
> then Ephraim went to Assyria,
>   and sent to the great king.
> But he is not able to cure you
>   or heal your wound.
>   (Hos. 5:13; see also 6:11; 8:9; 12:1)

When Hezekiah tried to defend Judah against Assyria through an alliance with Egypt, Isaiah spoke for Yahweh:

> Alas for those who go down to Egypt for help
>   and who rely on horses,
> who trust in chariots because they are many
>   and in horsemen because they are very strong,
> but do not look to the Holy One of Israel
>   or consult the LORD! . . .
> The Egyptians are human, and not God,
>   their horses are flesh, and not spirit.
> When the LORD stretches out his hand,
>   the helper will stumble, and the one helped will fall,
>   and they will all perish together.
>   (Isa. 31:1, 3; cf. 30:1–3)

And so it proved. When Sennacherib threatened Jerusalem, the Egyptians marched out and then, like "the noble Duke of York and his ten thousand men," they marched right back again. It was the hand of Yahweh, not the Egyptian armies, that saved Jerusalem (Isaiah 36–37).

Those who will not learn from history are doomed to repeat its mistakes. A century later, in Jeremiah's time, there was strong trust in Egypt to save Judah from the armies of Babylon, and Jeremiah had to repeat Isaiah's warning:

> How lightly you gad about,
>   changing your ways!
> You shall be put to shame by Egypt
>   as you were put to shame by Assyria.
>   (Jer. 2:36; cf. 2:18; 37:7–8)

The Greater of Two Evils

It is in Jeremiah that the prophetic critique of war reaches an astounding extreme. He see Nebuchadnezzar of Babylon as the instrument of Yahweh's antagonistic warfare, Yahweh's punishment for Judah's sins. Therefore he counsels the kings not to fight, and not to trust Yahweh to deliver them, but to surrender. Jeremiah dramatized this advice by wearing a wooden yoke, such as oxen wear. He wore it when envoys of the petty kingdoms of the land bridge were in Jerusalem, consulting with King Zedekiah about how to throw off the yoke of Nebuchadnezzar. To them he said, "If any nation will not serve this king, Nebuchadnezzar of Babylon, and put its neck under the yoke of the king of Babylon, then I will punish that nation with the sword, with famine, and with pestilence, says the LORD, until I have completed its destruction by his hand. . . . But any nation that will bring its neck under the yoke of the king of Babylon and serve him, I will leave on its own land, says the LORD, to till it and live there" (Jer. 27:8, 11). Even after he had been imprisoned, Jeremiah persisted in this advice, saying to Zedekiah, "Thus says the LORD, the God of hosts, the God of Israel, If you will only surrender to the officials of the king of Babylon, then your life shall be spared, and this city shall not be burned with fire, and you and your house shall live. But if you do not surrender to the officials of the king of Babylon, then this city shall be handed over to the Chaldeans, and they shall burn it with fire, and you yourself shall not escape from their hand" (38:17–18). During the siege itself, Jeremiah said to the people, "Thus says the LORD: See, I am setting before you the way of life and the way of death. Those who stay in this city shall die by the sword, by famine, and by pestilence; but those who go out and surrender to the Chaldeans who are besieging you shall live and shall have their lives as a prize of war" (21:8–9). War is not always the lesser of two evils. In this case it would be the greater of two evils.

Reverse Fighting

It would seem that the prophetic critique of war could go no further, but it does. In the great prophecy of the exile (Isaiah 40–55) we meet one who conquers, not by dishing out punishment, but by enduring it. Vernard Eller has coined a phrase for this: "reverse fighting."[4] The "reverse fighter" is the servant of the LORD. Nebuchadnezzar, the instrument of Yahweh's antagonistic warfare, the punisher of Judah's sins, had been called the servant of the LORD (Jer. 25:9; 27:6; 43:10). This servant, however, is no warrior. A bruised reed he will not break, and a dimly burning wick he will not quench (Isa. 42:3). He gives his back to those who strike him and his cheeks to those who pull out his beard, not hiding his face from insult and spitting (50:6). He knows contempt and rejection, suffering and infirmity, wounds and bruises, oppression and injustice. In all this he does no violence, makes no complaint (53:3–9). Yet he wins the victory! The "reverse fighter" is honored in the sight of the LORD; God becomes his strength (49:5). Kings stand up in his presence; princes prostrate themselves (v. 7). He prospers, is exalted and lifted up, startles many nations; kings shut their mouths because of him (52:13–15). Yahweh allots him a portion with the great; he divides the spoil with the strong (53:12). This is the "warfare" to which Israel, as Yahweh's servant (41:8–9; 43:10; 44:1–2, 21; 45:4; 48:20; 49:3) is ultimately called.

The Extension of *Shalom*

Yahweh, the giver of *shalom,* gives *shalom* to Israel. That seems to have been the basic understanding of the Hebrew people.[5] They justified war as necessary to establish secure borders within which *shalom* could be nurtured and practiced, but the prophets dare to suggest an extension of *shalom* beyond the borders.

To the Nations

The nations, the Gentiles, the *goyim,* are going to seek Yahweh and Yahweh's Torah and *shalom.*

Many nations shall come and say:

> "Come, let us go up to the mountain of the Lord,
>   to the house of the God of Jacob;
>   that he may teach us his ways
>   and that we may walk in his paths."
> For out of Zion shall go forth Torah,
>   and the word of the Lord from Jerusalem.
>
> (Micah 4:2; cf. Isa. 2:3)

There are many prophetic passages that make this point: Isaiah 45:22–23; 55:5; 56:6–8; Zech. 2:11; 8:20–23.

It is worth noting here that some of the psalmists heard the prophets on this point. There are notable invitations to the nations to join Israel in the praise of Yahweh:

> May God be gracious to us and bless us
>   and make his face to shine upon us,
>   that your way may be known upon earth,
>   your saving power among all nations.
> Let the peoples praise you, O God;
>   let all the peoples praise you.
> Let the nations be glad and sing for joy,
>   for you judge the peoples with equity
>   and guide the nations upon earth.
>
> (Ps. 67:1–4)

See also Psalms 47, 66, 96, 97, 100, 117, 138, 148.

To the Enemy

More striking than the prophecies of a general extension of *shalom* are the predictions that *shalom* will be extended to Israel's worst and bitterest enemies. War seems to require that we dehumanize our enemies. They must be outsiders, aliens, some lesser breed without the law. If they are human beings just like ourselves, who could ever press the red button? So Israel kept the war spirit going by characterizing its enemies as godless heathen.

The prophets taught otherwise. In the book of Amos we find

these words, "Did I not bring Israel up from the land of Egypt, and the Philistines from Caphtor and the Arameans from Kir?" (Amos 9:7). Your traditional enemies each had their exodus, too! I guide their history as well, whether they know it or not.

And in Isaiah, we find this extraordinary passage:

> On that day there will be an altar to the LORD in the center of the land of Egypt, and a pillar to the LORD at its border. . . .
>
> On that day there will be a highway from Egypt to Assyria, and the Assyrian will come into Egypt, and the Egyptian into Assyria, and the Egyptians will worship with the Assyrians.
>
> On that day Israel will be the third with Egypt and Assyria, a blessing in the midst of the earth, whom the LORD of hosts has blessed, saying, "Blessed be Egypt my people, and Assyria the work of my hands, and Israel my heritage." (Isa. 19:19, 23–25)

Egypt my people? We thought Israel was Yahweh's people, and Egypt was the devil's people. Assyria the work of my hands? We thought Israel was the work of Yahweh's hands and Assyria was the work of the devil. One might as well say, "Blessed be communist China, Yahweh's people, and ruthless Iraq, the work of Yahweh's hands, and my own country, Yahweh's heritage."

Then there is Jonah. In the primary history, he is mentioned as a 100 percent Israelite patriot, a prophet who predicted and encouraged the military campaigns by which Jeroboam II recovered much of the lost territory of the Northern Kingdom (2 Kings 14:25). The book of Jonah is the story of how Yahweh sent Jonah to preach in Nineveh, the capital of Assyria. Of all Israel's enemies, the Assyrians were the most ruthless and cruel. The bitter book of Nahum calls for vengeance on Nineveh and exults in its downfall. Jonah obviously felt the same way. He tried to take his evangelistic campaign to Spain instead, but, as even children know from the familiar story of the whale, he wound up in Nineveh after all. Looking over the size of the place, he called for Yahweh's most massive destructive power and hunkered down in his bomb shelter to see the results. But Nineveh repented and nothing happened. Only a worm destroyed his bomb shelter—a flimsy affair anyway, consisting mainly of the leaves of a castor bean plant. Jonah was mad enough to die. Yahweh advises Jonah to think it over. He is concerned deeply for a bush he didn't even plant. And should Yahweh not be concerned about Nineveh, that great city, in which there are more than a hundred and twenty thousand innocent children too young to know their right hand from their left, and also many animals (Jonah 4:11)? So Nineveh gets included in the survival principles and the caring principles that had marked the *shalom* of Bethlehem, and the war is over. The enemy has become a neighbor.

The prophets share in the biblical ambiguity regarding war and peace. They place a high value on *shalom* and rush to the defense of the Torah principles on which it rests. Yahweh is the Giver of *shalom*. Yet they know that Yahweh can also be the Withdrawer of *shalom*. There are times when the true prophetic word is not "*shalom, shalom,*" but "no *shalom.*" They are severe critics of war, its atrocities, its trust in weapons, its reliance on alliances. Yet earlier prophets aided and abetted kings in their wars and later prophets predicted that Yahweh would use war to punish rebellious Israel and to assert moral authority over all nations, the great powers as well as the people of God. It is to those predictions that we turn in the next chapter.

7

Predictions of War

Before the prophets, Israel's theology was based on past saving events. Deuteronomy 26:1–11 shows how the recitation of Israel's founding events became an annual liturgical celebration and the basis for Israel's theological self-understanding. In Judah, the covenant with David furnished an additional basis for theology. God's decisive actions for God's people had taken place already. The past was the guarantee of the future. Change was to be avoided.

The prophets came to believe that the proper basis for Israel's theology, the life-or-death factor in Israel's existence, was a future event, something God had not yet done, but promised to do. God is a God of change, a God of surprises. The prophets stood in the divine council, heard of God's intended work, and urged Israel to repent and to have faith, not on the basis of the past, but on the basis of the future.[1]

The plans of Yahweh, which the prophets heard in the divine council, were ambiguous. They were plans for war, and also plans for peace. We look in this chapter at the predictions of war. The records of Israel's wars, which we surveyed in chapter 3, are extensive; the prophetic and apocalyptic predictions of war are equally extensive. Taken together, the records and the predictions fill the pages of the Old Testament with the din of battle.

Wars Against Israel

On almost every page of the prophets there are predictions that Yahweh will fight antagonistically *against* Israel if they do not repent of their sins. We have mentioned this already in chapters 4 and 6. The time has come to examine these predictions at length. Because the people have breached the *shalom* that God gives, there will be no *shalom,* but war instead. The great powers, in their incursions into the Fertile Crescent, will be instruments in Yahweh's hand to punish Yahweh's sinful and rebellious people.

In Amos, Yahweh speaks of his warfare against Israel: "I will press you down in your place, just as a cart presses down when it is full of sheaves" (Amos 2:13). "I will punish you" (3:2, 14). "I will tear down" your houses (3:15; 6:11). "I will deliver up the city and all that is in it" (6:8). "I will rise against the house of Jeroboam with the sword" (7:9). "I will kill with the sword; not one of them shall flee away, not one of them shall escape" (9:1). The imagery of warfare is everywhere: soldiers fleeing naked (2:16), strongholds plundered (3:11), walls breached (4:3), decimation of troops (5:5), wailing (5:16–17; 8:3, 10), exile (5:27; 6:7; 7:17), desolate sanctuaries (7:9). The LORD's instrument in this warfare will be "an adversary" (3:11), "a nation" (6:14). The fulfillment of these predictions was not long in coming. As we have seen, the Assyrians came in successive campaigns and finally destroyed the Northern Kingdom less than thirty years after Amos spoke at Bethel.

Speaking a few years later, Isaiah was not as reticent in naming the adversary. He predicted that Assyria would be God's instrument for the punishment of Judah as well:

> Ah, Assyria, the rod of my anger—
>   the club in their hands is my fury!
> Against a godless nation I send him,
>   and against the people of my wrath I command him,
> to take spoil and seize plunder,
>   and to tread them down like the mire of the streets.
>
> (Isa. 10:5–6)

Yahweh, says Isaiah, will whistle for a people at the ends of the earth, and they will come swiftly. None of them will be weary or stumble. Their armament will be in perfect order. They will seize their prey like lions. The whole land will be in darkness and distress (Isa. 5:26–30). This prediction, too, was rapidly fulfilled. Assyria greatly plundered Judah before the LORD turned and fought monergistically in defense of Jerusalem.

A century later, Yahweh antagonistically fought against Judah again. This time the chosen instrument was the Chaldeans or Babylonians. In Habakkuk, Yahweh declares:

> For I am rousing the Chaldeans,
>   that fierce and impetuous nation,
> who march through the breadth of the earth
>   to seize dwellings not their own.
>
> (Hab. 1:6)

He goes on to paint a fearsome picture of the coming foe: riding horses swifter than leopards, wolves, or eagles; gathering captives like the sand; scoffing at kings; laughing at fortresses; worshiping their own might (vs. 7–11).

Jeremiah makes similar predictions:

> I am going to bring upon you
>   a nation from far away, O house of Israel,
>   says the LORD.
> It is an enduring nation,
>   it is an ancient nation,
> a nation whose language you do not know,
>   nor can you understand what they say.
> Their quiver is like an open tomb;
>   all of them are mighty warriors.
> They shall eat up your harvest and your food;
>   they shall eat up your sons and your daughters;
> they shall eat up your flocks and your herds;
>   they shall eat up your vines and your fig trees;
> they shall destroy with the sword
>   your fortified cities in which you trust.
>
> (Jer. 5:15–17)

The fulfillment of this and similar predictions was the approach of the armies of Nebuchadnezzar, king of Babylon. Zedekiah, king of Judah, was hopeful that "the LORD will perform a wonderful deed for us, as he has often done, and will make him withdraw from us." Jeremiah replied, "Thus says the LORD, the God of Israel: I am going to turn back the weapons of war that are in your hands and with which you are fighting against the king of Babylon and against the Chaldeans who are besieging you outside the walls; and I will bring them together into the center of this city. I myself will fight against you with outstretched hand and mighty arm, in anger, in fury, and in great wrath" (Jer. 21:1–5). Jeremiah was so certain that Nebuchadnezzar was Yahweh's instrument that he advised surrender to the Babylonians. When his advice was rejected, he lived to see the destruction of the Southern Kingdom.

Ezekiel, carried to Babylon in the first group of exiles, predicts from there the final end of Jerusalem:

> Disaster after disaster! See, it comes.
>   An end has come, the end has come.
> It has awakened against you: see, it comes! . . .
> Soon now I will pour out my wrath upon you;
>   I will spend my anger against you.
> I will judge you according to your ways,
>   and punish you for all your abominations. . . .
> I will bring the worst of the nations
>   to take possession of their houses.
> I will put an end to the arrogance of the strong,
>   and their holy places shall be profaned.
>   (Ezek. 7:5–6, 8, 24)

Similar passages could be gathered from other prophets to demonstrate predictions of Yahweh's warfare *against* Yahweh's own people.

It is important to note that there is a conditional element in these predictions. Up to the last moment Israel can repent and God's plans can be changed. Amos is typical on this point. In the midst of his direst predictions he says:

> Seek good and not evil,
>   that you may live;
> and so the LORD, the God of hosts, will be with you,
>   just as you have said.
> Hate evil and love good,
>   and establish justice in the gate;
> it may be that the LORD, the God of hosts,
>   will be gracious to the remnant of Joseph.
>
>   (Amos 5:14–15)

Isaiah pleads again and again for just practices and quiet faith to avert the awesome punishment that is on the way (Isa. 1:19–20; 30:15). Up to the very end Jeremiah declares that Judah has other options (Jer. 4:1–4; 7:5–7; 18:1–11; 21:12; 22:1–4; 27:11; 36:1–3; 38:17).

Wars Against the Nations

The prophets do not confine their prophecies to Israel and Judah. They are prophets to the nations, and most of what they predict for the nations is war.

Amos begins his prophecy with predictions of devastating warfare against Damascus, Gaza, Tyre, Ammon, and Moab. Strongholds will be burned, bars will be broken, inhabitants and rulers will be cut off amid shouting and the sound of the trumpet (Amos 1:3–2:3). These are Israel's neighboring petty states in the Fertile Crescent. As we have seen, they are to be punished for atrocities in their warfare against each other. The instrument of punishment is not named, but we know it will be Assyria.

Isaiah says that Yahweh will use Assyria to punish Judah, but that does not mean that Assyria has Yahweh's approval or that Assyria will escape its own punishment.

> When the LORD has finished all his work on Mount Zion and on Jerusalem, he will punish the arrogant boasting of the king of Assyria and his haughty pride. . . .
> Shall the ax vaunt itself over the one who wields it,

> or the saw magnify itself against the one who
>   handles it? . . .
> For in a very little while my indignation will come to an end, and my
> anger will be directed to their destruction. (Isa. 10:12, 15, 25)

In Isaiah there are extensive oracles predicting war against Babylon (Isaiah 13–14, 21), Assyria (14, 30, 31), Philistia (14), Moab (15–16), Damascus (17), Ethiopia (18), Egypt (19), Edom (21, 34), Arabia (21), Tyre and Sidon (23).

It is not clear whether the bitter book of Nahum, which we cited in chapter 3 for the excellence of its poetry, is a description of the fall of Nineveh or a prediction.

Habakkuk is puzzled that God would use wicked Babylon to punish the sins of Judah, but he confidently predicts that in the end those whom Babylon has plundered will plunder Babylon (Hab. 2:8). The third chapter is an imitation of Israel's most ancient war poetry, in which the Divine Warrior comes forth in anger to trample the nations that have oppressed Israel.

Zephaniah predicts war for Gaza, Ashkelon, Ekron, Moab, Ammon, Ethiopia, Assyria (Zephaniah 2).

A whole section of Jeremiah is devoted to oracles predicting war against Egypt, Philistia, Moab, Ammon, Edom, Damascus, and Elam (Jeremiah 46–49), followed by a long oracle against Babylon (50; 51).

There is a similar section in Ezekiel 25–32. There Egypt gets the major attention.

The postexilic prophets continue this tradition. The book of Obadiah predicts the military overthrow of Edom, because at the time of Jerusalem's fall they pillaged, handed over survivors to the Babylonians, and gloated at Judah's defeat. Zechariah 9:1–6 predicts war against Israel's enemies: Damascus, Tyre, Sidon, and the cities of Philistia.

It is noteworthy that both the little peoples and the superpowers are included in these predictions.[2] Though in some cases punishment is predicted for Assyria and Babylon because of their involvement with Israel, at other times Israel is not in the picture at all.

Yahweh sits in judgment on Assyria and Babylon, on Tyre and Egypt, quite apart from his concerns for his chosen people.[3] Yahweh is the judge of all the earth and will do what is just (Gen. 18:25). Let superpowers in all ages hear and tremble!

Apocalyptic War

Scattered among the prophetic writings are predictions of a war involving all the nations of the world, a final war where God's judgment is executed on the whole earth. These predictions are not conditional. There is nothing Israel or any other nation can do to prevent, delay, or hasten these wars. They are part of an unalterable future scenario which is totally in God's hands. We are here at "the dawn of apocalyptic."

Apocalyptic writings spring up among people for whom the realities of this world have become unbearable. Human beings seem impotent to influence the flow of events or to determine the future. Human history will no longer support human hopes. Prophetic visions of possibilities within history are replaced by visions of another world breaking into this world, or even of the end of this world and of history altogether. This *eschaton,* or end event, cannot be hastened or delayed or changed by repentance or any other human action. God will bring it about in God's own time. But the vision of it is the only way in which faith can be renewed and life reordered.[4]

Isaiah 13 is entitled "The Oracle concerning Babylon." Before Babylon definitely comes into view (v. 14?), the war is Yahweh versus the world. Yahweh summons "my consecrated ones, my warriors, my proudly exulting ones" (v. 3). They come "from a distant land, from the end of the heavens" (v. 5). Is this the cosmic army, the host of heaven? An earthly army is also mustered from kingdoms and nations (v. 4). The troops are the weapons of Yahweh's indignation, "to destroy the whole earth" (v. 5). This is the famed "day of the LORD" (vs. 6, 9). The earth will be made desolate (v. 9). Neither stars, sun, nor moon will give light (v. 10). The heavens will tremble "and the earth will be shaken out of its place" (v. 13). Yahweh "will punish the world for its evil" (v. 11).

Isaiah 24 is a long poem about final war. "The LORD is about to lay waste the earth and make it desolate" (v. 1). "A curse devours the earth" (v. 6). The earth will resemble a beaten olive tree, a gleaned vineyard (v. 13). There will be no escape: those who flee "at the sound of the terror shall fall into the pit; and whoever climbs out of the pit shall be caught in the snare" (v. 18; cf. Amos 5:19). The whole earth will be broken, torn asunder, violently shaken (v. 19). Yahweh will punish the host of heaven as well as the kings of the earth (v. 21). "The moon will be abashed and the sun ashamed; for the LORD of hosts will reign . . . and manifest his glory" (v. 23).

The oracle against Edom in Isaiah 34 is prefaced by another picture of a final war. The LORD is enraged against all the nations and against all the host of heaven. The mountains shall flow with blood; the skies shall roll up like a scroll (vs. 1–4).

In Micah, also, there is a vision of a future war involving many nations. They are all assembled against Zion, but the LORD has gathered them as sheaves are gathered on a threshing floor (Micah 4:11–12).

> Arise and thresh,
>   O daughter of Zion,
> for I will make your horn iron
>   and your hoofs bronze;
> you shall beat in pieces many peoples,
> and shall devote their gain to the LORD,
> their wealth to the LORD of the whole earth.
>   (Micah 4:13)

The prophet Joel is mainly concerned with a plague of locusts, but in his third chapter he pictures the final war:

> Proclaim this among the nations:
> Prepare war,
>   stir up the warriors.
> Let all the soldiers draw near,
>   let them come up.
> Beat your plowshares into swords,
>   and your pruning hooks into spears;

> let the weakling say, "I am a warrior."
>
> (Joel 3:9–10)

The nations thus armed will gather in the valley of Jehoshaphat. There God will judge them. Sun and moon will be darkened. The heavens and the earth will shake. The LORD will be a refuge for the people of Israel (vs. 11–16).

There are similar apocalyptic visions of final war in Zephaniah 1:2–3, 14–18; Haggai 2:21–22; Zechariah 12:2–5; 14:1–5.

The most extensive prediction of a final war is in Ezek. 38–39.[5] Many years after Israel has returned from exile, a great army from many nations will be assembled under the leadership of a prince named Gog. It will fall on unprotected, peaceful Israel like a cloud covering the earth. Then Yahweh will fight to deliver Israel:

> On that day there shall be a great shaking in the land of Israel; the fish of the sea, and the birds of the air, and the animals of the field, and all creeping things that creep on the ground, and all human beings that are on the face of the earth, shall quake at my presence, and the mountains shall be thrown down, and the cliffs shall fall, and every wall shall tumble to the ground. I will summon the sword against Gog in all my mountains, says the Lord GOD; the swords of all will be against their comrades. With pestilence and bloodshed I will enter into judgment with him; and I will pour down torrential rains and hailstones, fire and sulfur, upon him and his troops and the many peoples that are with him. So I will display my greatness and my holiness and make myself known in the eyes of many nations. Then they shall know that I am the LORD. (Ezek. 38:19–23)

Note the allusions to features of the ancient warfare of Yahweh in behalf of Israel: the divine confusion, turning armies against themselves (Judg. 4:15; 7:22; Josh. 6:10; 1 Sam. 7:10; 2 Kings 7:6–7), torrential rains (Judg. 5:21), hail (Josh. 10:11), earthquake (1 Sam. 14:15).

Gog will be totally defeated. The weapons of his armies will be burned for fuel by Israel, enough fuel to last seven years. The birds of the air and the wild animals will feast on the slain. It will take

Israel seven months to bury all the bones. Peace will be restored and Yahweh will never hide his face from Israel again (Ezekiel 39).

As we have just seen, the predictions of apocalyptic war represent a reuse of the older war materials of the Old Testament. The Divine Warrior is prominent and for the most part the wars are monergistic, but there is a transformation. These wars are not just the defense of Israel from historic foes or the punishment of Israel by those foes. They are the final judgment on the whole earth, indeed on the whole cosmos, and frequently they usher in a final peace.

The one full-blown apocalypse in the Hebrew Bible is the book of Daniel. It is filled with predictions of wars by great world powers, such as Babylon, Persia, and Greece.[6] These predictions come in fanciful dreams: a statue whose golden head, silver chest and arms, bronze middle and thighs, iron legs, and feet of mixed iron and clay signify successive world empires (Daniel 2); or four great beasts coming up out of the sea, again signifying successive empires (ch. 7); or a ram and a goat with successive horns sprouting out and being broken, with the same significance (ch. 8).

Each dream ends with a final conflict. The statue is broken to bits by a stone, not cut by human hands; the eschatological kingdom of God brings to an end the succession of earthly kingdoms (Daniel 2). The Ancient of Days puts the boasting horn of the final beast on trial and executes him (ch. 7). The boasting horn of the male goat is broken, not by human hands (ch. 8).

After the final conflict comes a period of stability and order, we might say of *shalom*. The kingdom of God, signified by the stone, "shall never be destroyed, nor shall this kingdom be left to another people. It shall crush all these kingdoms and bring them to an end, and it shall stand forever" (Dan. 2:44). The Ancient of Days, after the execution of the arrogant earthly king, gives a kingdom to one like a human being who comes on the clouds of heaven.

> To him was given dominion
>   and glory and kingship,
> that all peoples, nations, and languages

should serve him.
His dominion is an everlasting dominion
   that shall not pass away,
and his kingship is one
   that shall never be destroyed.
                              (Dan. 7:14)

After the goat's-horn king has been destroyed, not by human hands,
"the sanctuary shall be restored to its rightful state" (Dan. 8:14).

These statements seem to correspond to the predictions in the
earlier stages of apocalyptic that after the final battle there would be
safety and stability for God's people. Perhaps it can be said that
though the predictions of war far outnumber the predictions of
peace, they are penultimate; they are not the last word.

8

Promises of Peace

The prophets, we said, saw God's future actions as truly decisive for the life or death of Israel. The predictions of war were designed to lead God's people to repentance. And the promises of peace were designed to lead them to faith, steadfastness, faithfulness.

Promises are closer to the heart of God's reality than threats. God's name, Yahweh, was revealed in the context of a promise of deliverance, not a threat of destruction (Exodus 3). Unlike the gods of surrounding nations, Yahweh does not appear mainly to create a sacred place, a cultic center, where human culture is protected by becoming close to unchanging divine reality. Yahweh appears to make promises: to Noah (Genesis 8–9); to Abraham (12, 13, 15, 17, 18, 22); to Isaac (26); to Jacob (28, 35).[1]

When we recall what was promised in the Genesis stories—the holding back of chaos, land, posterity—the possibility emerges that *shalom,* which embraces all that and more, may be the quintessential promise, the epitome of all Yahweh's promises.

There are many promises of *shalom* in the Hebrew Bible, too many for us to examine them all. We have already looked at a number of them in chapters 5 and 6, because it was only in terms of promised *shalom* that we could define what it is or explain how God gives it or examine how the prophets championed it. In this chapter we shall focus on a further sample of these promises.

Promises of Fertility and Stability

In defining *shalom*, we said that those who have land yearn for *shalom* in terms of continued fertility and stability. There are many promises that answer this longing and greatly enrich our understanding of what peace is.

In the Torah

At the close of the Holiness Code, a powerful sermon (Lev. 26:3–45) contains a promise of fertility and stability and calls it *shalom*:[2]

> If you follow my statutes and keep my commandments and observe them faithfully, I will give you your rains in their season, and the land shall yield its produce, and the trees of the field shall yield their fruit. Your threshing shall overtake the vintage, and the vintage shall overtake the sowing; you shall eat your bread to the full, and live securely in your land. And I will grant *shalom* in the land, and you shall lie down, and no one shall make you afraid; I will remove dangerous animals from the land, and no sword shall go through your land. (Lev. 26:3–6)

The agricultural aspects of *shalom* are emphasized, but there are also promises of freedom from fear, freedom from dangerous animals, and freedom from war. The biblical ambiguity is close at hand, for in 26:7–8 it is promised that Israel will put its enemies to flight in war. The longer part of the sermon (vs. 14–45) is a prediction of what will happen if they do not obey the Torah: terror, disease, defeat in war, failure of crops, attack by wild animals, devastation, landlessness.

In Deuteronomy, the promise of peace takes the form of a series of blessings:[3]

> If you will only obey the LORD your God, by diligently observing all his commandments that I am commanding you today, the LORD your God will set you high above all the nations of the earth; all these blessings shall come upon you and overtake you, if you obey the LORD your God:

Blessed shall you be in the city, and blessed shall you be in the field.

Blessed shall be the fruit of your womb, the fruit of your ground, and the fruit of your livestock, both the increase of your cattle and the issue of your flock.

Blessed shall be your basket and your kneading bowl.

Blessed shall you be when you come in, and blessed shall you be when you go out. (Deut. 28:1–6)

Once again the language is mainly agricultural. The biblical ambiguity is evident: the next verse promises defeat of the enemy in war. The long list of curses for disobedience (vs. 15–68) reverses all the blessings and predicts terrible military defeat, loathsome diseases, agricultural disaster, and finally return to slavery in Egypt.

These promises in the Torah are conditional. In a striking way these promises connect fertility in the field with obedience to the commandments of God. In modern parlance this is to link ecology and ethics.[4]

In the Prophets

We turn to an oracle (Hos. 2:18–23) embedded in the story of Hosea's unfaithful wife, whose children Hosea named Not-pitied and Not-my-people. Israel is Yahweh's unfaithful wife, yet Yahweh promises to remarry her, to be reconciled to her children, and to give her *shalom.*

I will make for you a covenant on that day with the wild animals, the birds of the air, and the creeping things of the ground; and I will abolish the bow, the sword, and war from the land; and I will make you lie down in safety. (Hos. 2:18)

The familiar themes are here: peace with the animals, the abolition of war. In the verses that follow we meet agricultural fruitfulness: "the earth shall answer the grain, the wine, and the oil" (v. 22), and personal reconciliation: the wife is rewed forever (vs. 19–20); Lo-ruhamah is pitied and Lo-ammi becomes God's people (v. 23). For further promises of agricultural fruitfulness, see Hos. 14:4–7 and Joel 2:21–27.

In Isa. 29:17–21 we find a promise that begins with these words:

> Shall not Lebanon in a very little while
> become a fruitful field,
> and the fruitful field be regarded as a forest?

In the following verses it is promised that the deaf will hear, the blind will see, the meek and the needy will obtain joy; but the tyrants who deny them justice will be no more. Beginning with the agricultural note, this vision of peace goes on to include healing and justice—all parts of *shalom*. We are again in the presence of a linkage between ecology and ethics.

Promises of a Righteous Ruler

The kings of Israel and Judah did not do too well as managers and preservers of *shalom*, but hope sprang eternal that in the future there would be a king who would fulfill Israel's yearning and expectation. Many of the visions centered around a righteous ruler who would actually bring peace to Israel.[5] When new kings came to the throne, the psalmists expressed this hope in coronation odes. Psalm 72 is the most explicit:

> Give the king your justice, O God,
> and your righteousness to a king's son.
> May he judge your people with righteousness,
> and your poor with justice.
> May the mountains yield *shalom* for the people,
> and the hills, in righteousness.
> May he defend the cause of the poor of the people,
> give deliverance to the needy,
> and crush the oppressor.
> May he live while the sun endures,
> and as long as the moon, throughout all generations.
> May he be like rain that falls on the mown grass,
> like showers that water the earth.

> In his days may righteousness flourish
>   and *shalom* abound, until the moon is no more.
>   (Ps. 72:1–7)

Here is the familiar combination of agricultural fruitfulness and civic justice in accordance with the Torah. In what follows we see power over all enemies, the prayerful support of all his people, repeated emphasis on concern for the needy, the weak, those who have no helper, and once again "abundance of grain in the land" (v. 16).

In Isaiah, more than in any other prophet, the dream of peace centered around a righteous ruler who would break the rod of Israel's oppressors and reign in peace:

> For a child has been born for us,
>   a son given to us;
> authority rests upon his shoulders;
>   and he is named
> Wonderful Counselor, Mighty God,
>   Everlasting Father, Prince of *Shalom*.
> His authority shall grow continually,
>   and there shall be endless *shalom*
> for the throne of David and his kingdom.
>   He will establish and uphold it
> with justice and righteousness
>   from this time onward and forevermore.
> The zeal of the LORD of hosts will do this.
>   (Isa. 9:6–7)

The biblical ambiguity haunts this promise, for the immediately preceding verses mention the breaking of the rod of Israel's oppressor, the boots of tramping warriors, the garments rolled in blood. David, although a warlike king, is named in this dream of peace. We shall see this again and again.[6]

Another familiar promise in Isaiah 11:1–9 is a case in point. It speaks of a shoot from the stump of Jesse (David's father), a branch from his roots.[7] Endowed with the spirit of the LORD, he shall rule in equity—so far a picture of *shalom*. But then "he shall strike the earth with the rod of his mouth, and with the breath of his lips he shall kill

the wicked." This warlike note is followed by an extraordinarily
peaceful vision:

> The wolf shall live with the lamb,
>   the leopard shall lie down with the kid,
> the calf and the lion and the fatling together,
>   and a little child shall lead them.
> The cow and the bear shall graze,
>   their young shall lie down together;
>   and the lion shall eat straw like the ox.
> The nursing child shall play over the hole of the asp,
>   and the weaned child shall put its hand on the adder's den.
> They will not hurt or destroy
>   on all my holy mountain;
> for the earth will be full of the knowledge of the LORD
>   as the waters cover the sea.
>
>   (Isa. 11:6–9)

At last there will be a king who listens to Torah and rules by its
principles, and great peace will be the result. We have already met
the idea that *shalom* will involve a truce between the wild animals
and humankind. Here the truce will hold even among the animals,
between predators and prey. For other visions of the prince of
shalom in Isaiah, see 32:1–8 and 33:17–22.[8]

In Micah also there is a promise of peace that centers around a
just ruler:

> But you, O Bethlehem of Ephrathah,
>   who are one of the little clans of Judah,
> from you shall come forth for me
>   one who is to rule in Israel,
> whose origin is from of old,
>   from ancient days.
> [Therefore he shall give them up until the time
>   when she who is in labor has brought forth;
> then the rest of his kindred shall return
>   to the people of Israel.]
> And he shall stand and feed his flock in the strength of
>   the LORD,

> in the majesty of the name of the LORD his God.
> And they shall live secure, for now he shall be great
> to the ends of the earth;
> and he shall be the one of peace.
>
> (Micah 5:2–5a)

This oracle, so familiar to us from the story of the Magi in Matthew 2, contains some difficulties. If the lines I have bracketed are allowed to stand, they might indicate that this promise belongs in the time of the exile, long after Micah; but the bracketed lines are such an obvious interruption to the flow of the poem that they must belong elsewhere. The final line, literally "this one shall be *shalom*," is very strong, reminding us of Gideon's altar, "Yahweh is *shalom*."

Micah is even clearer than Isaiah 11 that Yahweh will reject the current line of David. Yahweh will go back to Bethlehem and start over.[9] The differences between the vision of Micah, who speaks for the peasants who live on the land, and that of Isaiah, who speaks for the sophisticated citizens of Jerusalem, are noteworthy, but both look for peace through a righteous ruler whom God will raise up.

Promises of Return

When Jerusalem was burned and the people were carried captive and Israel became a nation of have-nots, the yearning for *shalom* was a yearning for liberation and return.[10]

There is one remarkable promise of return in the Torah (Deut. 30:1–10). In the prophets it becomes a constant hope and dream.

Such a dream of return has been attached to the prophecy of Amos:

> On that day I will raise up
>   the booth of David that is fallen,
> and repair its breaches,
>   and raise up its ruins,
>   and rebuild it as in the days of old;
> in order that they may possess the remnant of Edom
>   and all the nations who are called by my name,

> says the LORD who does this.
> The time is surely coming, says the LORD,
>> when the one who plows shall overtake the one who reaps,
>> and the treader of grapes the one who sows the seed;
> the mountains shall drip sweet wine,
>> and all the hills shall flow with it.
> I will restore the fortunes of my people Israel,
>> and they shall rebuild the ruined cities and inhabit them;
> they shall plant vineyards and drink their wine,
>> and they shall make gardens and eat their fruit.
> I will plant them upon their land,
>> and they shall never again be plucked up
>> out of the land that I have given them,
>>>>>>> says the LORD your God.
>>>>>>> (Amos 9:11–15)

Return, rebuilding, agricultural abundance, security are all parts of this vision of peace from the place of exile (cf. Zeph. 3:14–20).

The prophecy of Jeremiah, coming from the last days of Judah, is an almost uninterrupted prediction that the people will lose their land and go into captivity. But these predictions are punctuated by dreams of return. See Jeremiah 16:14–15; 23:7–8; 24:4–7; 29:10–14. The hope of return reaches a climax in chs. 30–33, the Book of Consolation. These chapters contain striking visions of *shalom.*

In Jeremiah 30 the theme is announced, "The days are surely coming, says the LORD, when I will restore the fortunes of my people, Israel and Judah, says the LORD, and I will bring them back to the land that I gave to their ancestors and they shall take possession of it" (v. 3). They will no longer serve foreigners, but a king of the line of David will rule over them (vs. 8–9, 21). When they return they will have *shalom:* "quiet and ease, and no one shall make them afraid" (v. 10). Their captors will be punished (vs. 11, 16). Their health will be restored (v. 17). The city will be rebuilt (v. 18), a place of thanksgiving and merrymaking (v. 19).

The whole of Jeremiah 31 can be read as a vision of *shalom.* The people will be brought back to their land (vs. 7–11, 16–17, 21). There will be rebuilding (vs. 4, 38–39), dancing (vs. 4, 13), singing (v. 12), planting (vs. 5, 27–28), abundance (vs. 5, 12), a new covenant (vs. 31–34) which will be irrevocable (vs. 35–37). Compare 33:19–26.

The hope for a righteous ruler persisted, even after the land was lost. That is a central theme of Jeremiah 33. After repeating promises of healing, prosperity, security, rebuilding, cleansing, forgiveness, and celebration—"the voice of mirth and the voice of gladness, the voice of the bridegroom and the voice of the bride, the voices of those who sing" (v. 11)—the prophet declares this promise of Yahweh:

> In those days and at that time I will cause a righteous Branch to spring up for David; and he shall execute justice and righteousness in the land. (Jer. 33:15)

As a result, Judah will be saved and Jerusalem will live in safety, a shorthand description of *shalom* (v. 16). The covenant with David will be irrevocable (vs. 19–26). Compare 31:35–37.

Isaiah 35 is a notable vision of the return of Israel to Zion. The desert shall rejoice and blossom (vs. 1–2). It shall be abundantly watered (vs. 6–7). Across it shall be a highway for the returning exiles (vs. 8–10). Wild beasts will not harm them (v. 9). The weak, feeble, and fearful will be strengthened and reassured (vs. 3–4). The deaf, blind, lame, and speechless shall be healed (vs. 5–6). There will be singing, joy, and gladness (v. 10).

Isaiah 40–55 is punctuated by visions of the return. God's warfare against his people is ended and a highway is being prepared across the desert (40:1–5; 49:11). Like a shepherd, God is leading his flock back to Zion (40:9–11; 49:9–10). God will assuage the thirst of the poor and needy travelers by providing abundant water in the wilderness (41:17–20; 43:19–20; 44:3; 49:10). God will make a way through the sea, as at the time of the exodus (43:2, 16–17). God will make a way even through fire (43:2). God will send to Babylon and break down all the bars (43:14; 52:11–12). Yahweh's sons and daughters will be gathered from east and west and north and south, from the end of the earth (43:5–7; 49:12). The return is an occasion for joy and singing (52:8–9; 55:12). The return is *shalom* (52:7; 55:12).

Ezekiel likewise has visions of the return and of a life of peace when Israel is resettled in the land. The Lord GOD will be their shepherd, bringing the lost and scattered flock of Judah back to its own land, feeding them, healing them, giving them rest, establishing justice (Ezek. 34:11–16).

In a slightly different vein, a king of David's line will be their shepherd and Yahweh will be their God. Yahweh will make with them a covenant of *shalom*, which will include the banishment of wild animals, abundant showers, splendid vegetation. They will live in safety and none shall make them afraid (Ezek. 34:23–31).

More than any other prophet, Ezekiel stresses the inward renewal that is part of *shalom*.

> I will sprinkle clean water upon you, and you shall be clean from all your uncleannesses, and from all your idols I will cleanse you. A new heart I will give you, and a new spirit I will put within you; and I will remove from your body the heart of stone and give you a heart of flesh. I will put my spirit within you, and make you follow my statutes and be careful to observe my ordinances. (Ezek. 36:25–27)

Liberation, return, safety, healing, cleansing, new hearts, justice, freedom from hunger, freedom from depredations by wild animals, rule by David—the whole picture of *shalom* is here. The vision comes again and again in Ezek. 36:8–12, 33–38; 37:24–28; 39:25–29.

Where did the prophets get the materials for their dreams of a future return? From the past action of God, from the exodus. Ezekiel 20:33–44 uses exodus rhetoric: a mighty hand and an outstretched arm (vs. 33–34). It speaks of face-to-face judgment in the wilderness (vs. 35–36); of the bond of the covenant (v. 37); of rebels who will not be permitted to enter the land (v. 38). There are echoes of the golden calf (v. 39) and the great offering for the tabernacle (v. 40). Isaiah 35 and 40–55 are filled with such memories as water in the wilderness (35:6; 41:17–18; 43:19–20; 48:21; 49:10; 55:1) and passing through the Red Sea (43:2, 16–17; 44:17; 50:2; 51:10).

Apocalyptic Promises

The return was obviously a disappointment. The soaring dreams of the exiles were not realized. Rebuilding the temple was difficult, and when it was finally accomplished, it hardly resembled the former glory. The hopes that Zerubbabel would be the promised righteous ruler of the line of David came to naught. In a struggle for power in the tiny restoration community, the Zadokite priests came out on top and disenfranchised the disciples of the great prophet who wrote Isaiah 40–55.[11] History held no hope for the disenfranchised. They were in an apocalyptic situation. Yet they continued to envision an intervention by God which would bring *shalom.*

One of the most notable visions of *shalom* is the vision of the new Jerusalem in Isaiah 65:17–25. The poetry is so beautiful that I quote it at length:

> For I am about to create new heavens
>   and a new earth;
> the former things shall not be remembered
>   or come to mind.
> But be glad and rejoice forever
>   in what I am creating;
> for I am about to create Jerusalem as a joy,
>   and its people as a delight.
> I will rejoice in Jerusalem,
>   and delight in my people;
> no more shall the sound of weeping be heard in it,
>   or the cry of distress.
> No more shall there be in it
>   an infant that lives but a few days,
>   or an old person who does not live out a lifetime;
> for one who dies at a hundred years will be considered
>   a youth,
>   and one who falls short of a hundred will be considered
>   accursed.
> They shall build houses and inhabit them;
>   they shall plant vineyards and eat their fruit.
> They shall not build and another inhabit;
>   they shall not plant and another eat;
> for like the days of a tree shall the days of my people be,

and my chosen shall long enjoy the work of their hands.
They shall not labor in vain,
    or bear children for calamity;
for they shall be offspring blessed by the LORD—
    and their descendants as well.
Before they call I will answer,
    while they are yet speaking I will hear.
The wolf and the lamb shall feed together,
    the lion shall eat straw like the ox;
    but the serpent—its food shall be dust!
They shall not hurt or destroy
    on all my holy mountain.

(Isa. 65:17–25)

There are several interesting developments here. The picture of agricultural plenty in blessed fields, with which we have become familiar, gives way to a focus on the city.[12] The city is the new Jerusalem, the center of new heavens and a new earth. Infant mortality is zero. Longevity is the rule. It is a very stable city; people do not lose their property. The ideal which the Torah sought to protect is a reality. God is never distant, always available. The vision ends with peace among the animals, quoting Isaiah 11.[13]

Zechariah 8, stemming also from the distress of Jerusalem in postexilic times, is a series of promises of peace. We cite the most notable one, where the city is again the focus:

Thus says the LORD: I will return to Zion, and will dwell in the midst of Jerusalem; Jerusalem shall be called the faithful city, and the mountain of the LORD of hosts shall be called the holy mountain. Thus says the LORD of hosts: Old men and old women shall again sit in the streets of Jerusalem, each with staff in hand because of their great age. And the streets of the city shall be full of boys and girls playing in its streets. (Zech. 8:3–5)

Zechariah 9 is a poetic oracle of judgment on the enemies of postexilic Jerusalem and of Judah's rescue from them by the monergistic action of Yahweh. It takes the form of a Divine Warrior Hymn (note the language of vs. 13–14),[14] but it is interrupted by this vision of peace:

Rejoice greatly, O daughter Zion!
  Shout aloud, O daughter Jerusalem!
Lo, your king comes to you;
  triumphant and victorious is he,
humble and riding on a donkey,
  on a colt, the foal of a donkey.
He will cut off the chariot from Ephraim
  and the war horse from Jerusalem;
and the battle bow shall be cut off,
  and he shall command *shalom* to the nations;
his dominion shall be from sea to sea,
  and from the River to the ends of the earth.
                                        (Zech. 9:9–10)[15]

Whatever its origin, this insertion into Zechariah 9 is an extraordinary vision of peace. The ancient hope that a king would arise as the manager and guarantor of peace is revived, but this king differs from the king in Isaiah 9, 11, 32, or 33; in Micah 5 or Jeremiah 30 or Ezekiel 34 or 37. The name of David, so frequently mentioned in the earlier visions, is not mentioned in connection with this king. In the earlier visions, though the king is just and rules by Torah, he maintains peace by the exercise of royal power. This king is humble and lowly, and it is through that humility and lowliness that he is triumphant and victorious. The extent of his dominion exceeds that of Solomon (cf. 1 Kings 4:24), but he does not have Solomon's horses and chariots. He has intentionally disarmed.

A Promise of Universal Peace

The foregoing is enough to demonstrate that the familiar swords into plowshares vision is not the only vision of peace in the Hebrew scriptures. Nevertheless, it has a unique place. The visions we have cited mainly promise peace to Israel. There is a hint in Zechariah 9 that the peace may be shared with other nations, but the swords into plowshares vision is clearly a vision of worldwide peace, of the abolition of war.

This vision is found in both Isa. 2:2–4 and Micah 4:1–4. These two prophets were roughly contemporaries. We shall probably never know whether one copied the other, or whether both copied a vision older than either, or whether a later hand inserted a later vision in both. We shall cite the version of Micah, which has a final verse that is lacking in Isaiah:

> In days to come
>> the mountain of the LORD's house
> shall be established as the highest of the mountains,
>> and shall be raised up above the hills.
> Peoples shall stream to it,
>> and many nations shall come and say:
> "Come, let us go up to the mountain of the LORD,
>> to the house of the God of Jacob;
> that he may teach us his ways
>> and that we may walk in his paths."
> For out of Zion shall go forth *torah*,
>> and the word of the LORD from Jerusalem.
> He shall judge between many peoples,
>> and shall arbitrate between strong nations far away;
> they shall beat their swords into plowshares,
>> and their spears into pruning hooks;
> nation shall not lift up sword against nation,
>> neither shall they learn war any more;
> but they shall all sit under their own vines and under their
>> own fig trees,
> and no one shall make them afraid;
>> for the mouth of the LORD of hosts has spoken.
>
>   (Micah 4:1–4)

In this passage, actions of Yahweh and actions of the world's peoples alternate. The first action of Yahweh is the exaltation of the Temple Mount. Physically speaking, Mount Zion is far from the highest mountain in the world. This may be a trace of apocalyptic, or it may simply be a prophetic figure for the exaltation of Zion in spiritual importance.

Now the peoples and nations of the world act. They come streaming to Zion, not bringing tribute or bringing back captives, as in so many prophetic oracles, but seeking instruction, Torah, from Yahweh, the God of Jacob.

Yahweh's second action is to judge and arbitrate between the nations. This does not seem to be "the final judgment," but a settling of the conflicting interests and disputes that lead to war. On the basis of Torah, these can be resolved.

The peoples and nations act again. The weapons of war are converted into the instruments of peace. The practice of war is abolished and the study of war comes to an end. Is war an ineradicable part of human nature, as some recent anthropologists maintain? Or is it a learned activity, as our passage suggests? Do we "have to be taught to hate"? And can war be unlearned?

The resultant picture is breathtaking. Not in Israel alone, but in all nations, the *shalom* envisioned in the Torah becomes a reality. People sit under their own vines and fig trees.[16] No one loses land or houses or crops by the military invasion of enemy nations, or by the draft and taxation demanded by their own nation for its military defense. Every family possesses a stake in the commonwealth and access to the means of production. The familiar agricultural description of *shalom* makes this vision earthy, material, far removed from "pie in the sky by and by." And the terrible fear, dread, and insecurity in which so many of earth's people live and die, is gone. "No one shall make them afraid."

Is this promise of universal peace a deliberate refutation of Joel's call to universal war, "Beat your plowshares into swords, and your pruning hooks into spears" (Joel 3:10)? Or was Joel intentionally refuting this as an unrealistic dream? We have no way of knowing, but we could not find a better illustration of the ambiguity that marks the Hebrew Bible. Not only in its litanies of worship, not only in its understanding of the nature and character of God, but in its vision of the future, the Old Testament is ambiguous. Its pages, over which Jesus pored as a boy, drip with the blood of battle, but also with the sweet wine of peace.

9

Jesus Revisited

Our preliminary examination of Jesus' actions and teachings in chapters 1 and 2 led to these questions: How could Jesus be a peacemaker when he was raised on the Old Testament and when he accepted its authority? Did he have a way of reading it that permitted him or even demanded of him that he be a peacemaker, even at the cost of his life? We need to revisit Jesus at this point to see what light our explorations in the Old Testament have shed on this central riddle.

The Way of the Prophets

Jesus did not, it seems to me, reconcile the ambiguity of the Old Testament. He did not, like a good Hegelian, move from the thesis of a Warrior God through the antithesis of a Giver of Peace to some shining synthesis of the two. He made a choice. From the great diversity of the Old Testament, he chose the prophetic strain as that which is closest to the truth, as that in the light of which all the rest must be interpreted.

He did not hesitate to identify himself as belonging to that strain. It was of himself he spoke when he said, "Prophets are not without honor, except in their hometown, and among their own kin, and in their own house" (Mark 6:4; cf, Matt. 13:57; Luke 4:24; John 4:44). It was of himself he spoke when he said: "It is impossible for a prophet to be killed outside of Jerusalem" (Luke 13:33).

His words and actions were such that he was widely recognized by his contemporaries as belonging to the prophetic line. The Samaritan woman at the well said, "Sir, I see you are a prophet" (John 4:19). When Jesus raised the son of the widow of Nain, the people said, "A great prophet has risen among us!" (Luke 7:16). Simon the Pharisee had heard the report, for he said, "If this man were a prophet, he would have known who and what kind of woman this is who is touching him" (Luke 7:39). The five thousand who were fed said, "This is indeed the prophet who is to come into the world" (John 6:14; cf. 7:40). When the Pharisees asked the man born blind what he had to say about Jesus, he replied, "He is a prophet" (John 9:17). There was widespread discussion as to who Jesus really was, and some said, "A prophet, like one of the prophets of old" or "one of the ancient prophets" who had risen from the dead (Mark 6:15; Luke 9:8). This was reported to Jesus by the disciples when he asked, "Who do people say that I am?" (Mark 8:27–28; Matt. 16:13–14; Luke 9:18–19). At the triumphal entry into Jerusalem, he was hailed as "the prophet Jesus from Nazareth in Galilee" (Matt. 21:11). When the Jerusalem authorities wanted to arrest him, they hesitated because the crowds regarded him as a prophet (Matt. 21:46). The popular belief that he was a prophet was known to the temple guards, who after his arrest mocked him and beat him and said, "Prophesy!" (Matt. 26:68; Mark 14:65; Luke 22:64). The two disciples on the way to Emmaus on Easter evening described him as "Jesus of Nazareth, who was a prophet mighty in deed and word before God and all the people" (Luke 24:19).

Jesus' approach to *shalom* was in many respects quite similar to that of the prophets. He carried matters further, but along lines that he found in their actions and writings.

The Defense of *Shalom*

The prophets, we remember, defended the Torah principles on which *shalom* rests, against rulers who sought to take advantage of the poor. Jesus chose to stand in that line, criticizing the scribes who "devour widows' houses and for the sake of appearance say long

prayers" (Mark 12:40; Luke 20:47; cf. Isa. 1:10–17). He condemned
the temple authorities for making it "a den of robbers," robbing the
poor by the rate of exchange on money and the cost of sacrificial
animals (Mark 11:17; Matt. 21:13; Luke 19:46; cf. Jer. 7:11). He
defended the ancient right of gleaning, even on the Sabbath (Matt.
12:1–6; Mark 2:23–28; Luke 6:1–5; cf. Lev. 19:9–10). He emphasized that justice and mercy and faith were the weightier matters of
the law (Matt. 23:23; cf. Micah 6:8).

Was the revival of the sabbatical year and the year of jubilee a
feature of Jesus' prophetic ministry? André Trocmé, pastor at Le
Chambon[1] and later a secretary for the Fellowship of Reconciliation, has developed an interesting argument. Jesus, we remember,
launched his ministry in the synagogue at Nazareth by reading
Isaiah 61:1–2 (see Luke 4:16–19). The last phrase that he read was,
"to proclaim the year of the Lord's favor." That was, says Trocmé,
the sabbatical year, the year for freeing slaves (Ex. 21:1–3; Deut.
15:12–18) and forgiving debts (Deut. 15:1–10) and letting land lie
fallow (Lev. 25:1–7). It may also have been the fiftieth year, the year
of jubilee, after seven sevens, when all land was to be returned to
the original owners (Lev. 25:18–24). Trocmé relates Jesus' teaching
about debts in the Sermon on the Mount (Matt. 5:42; cf. Luke
6:30), in the Lord's Prayer, in the parable of the unforgiving servant
(Matt. 18:23–35), in the parable of the dishonest manager (Luke
16:1–9) to his proclamation of the sabbatical year. He relates Jesus'
teaching about being fed and clothed by God (Matt. 6:25–33; cf.
Luke 12:22–31) to the fields lying fallow. This was especially disturbing to the Roman authorities who relied on steady production
and the resultant taxes to support their regime.[2] If this is correct, it
is a striking example of Jesus' concern for the foundational principles of *shalom*.

Like the prophets, Jesus took the side of the marginal, the excluded, the powerless: lepers (Luke 5:12–15; 7:22; 17:11–19); tax
collectors (5:27–32; 15:1; 18:9–14; 19:1–9); the disabled (6:6–11;
7:22; 13:10–17; 18:35–42); the poor (6:20; 7:22; 14:21; 16:19–22;
18:22); the hungry (6:21; 9:12–17); the grief-stricken (6:21; 7:13); the
reviled and defamed (7:22); slaves (7:1–10); widows (7:11–17; 18:1–8;

21:1–2); prostitutes (7:36–50); women (8:1–3, 43–48; 10:38–42; 13:10–17); children (8:49–56; 9:46–48; 17:2; 18:15–17). We have not cited all the instances here; there are additional stories in the other Gospels, as well as parallels to the Lukan accounts. Not to be omitted is Jesus' complete identification with the hungry, the thirsty, the stranger, the naked, the sick, the prisoner in Matt. 25:31–46.

The powerful among the Jews of Jesus' day were not ultimately powerful, because they were subject to Rome. Nevertheless, Jesus' words to them are severe. In this, too, Jesus stood in the line of the prophets:

> Woe to you who are rich . . .
> Woe to you who are full now . . .
> Woe to you who are laughing now . . .
> Woe to you when all speak well of you.
> (Luke 6:24–26)

> Woe to you Pharisees! . . .
>   you tithe, but you neglect justice and the love of God . . .
>   you love seats of honor . . .
>   you are like unmarked graves . . .
> Woe to you lawyers! . . .
>   you load people with burdens hard to bear . . .
>   you build the tombs of the prophets . . .
>   you have taken away the key of knowledge.
> (Luke 11:42–52)

> Woe to you, scribes and Pharisees, hypocrites! . . .
>   you lock people out of the kingdom of heaven . . .
>   you make the new convert twice as much as a child of hell . . .
>   you are blind guides . . .
>   you clean the outside, but inside are full of greed . . .
>   you are like whitewashed tombs . . .
>   you are descendants of those who murdered the prophets.
> (Matt. 23:13–31)

This is prophetic rhetoric in defense of the underlying foundations of *shalom*. We have only to compare it with Isaiah 5:8–23; 10:1–4; or Habakkuk 2:6–20.

A lawyer asked Jesus which commandment in the Torah is the greatest. Jesus replied, " 'You shall love the Lord your God with all your heart, and with all your soul, and with all your mind.' This is the greatest and first commandment. And a second is like it: 'You shall love your neighbor as yourself.' On these two commandments hang all the Torah and the prophets" (Matt. 22:37–40). You cannot stop with one commandment, said Jesus. The second must always immediately follow. And the second is drawn from the heart of those provisions which concern the maintenance and management of *shalom* (Lev. 19:18).

The Extension of *Shalom*

The lawyer could not let it go. "Who is my neighbor?" he asked (Luke 10:29). How widely do the foundational principles of *shalom* apply? It is our long tradition that they do not apply to those who are not part of the people of Israel. We even wonder if they apply to the accursed crowd within Israel which does not know the law (John 7:46).

In reply, Jesus told the familiar parable of the Good Samaritan (Luke 10:30–37), where the neighbor who must be loved is clearly one whom strict Jews would regard as a half-breed and a heretic. John records a tradition that Jesus had a ministry among the Samaritans (John 4:4–42), and that his enemies as a result accused him of being a Samaritan himself (8:48).

Jesus visited the Greek region of Decapolis and performed healings there (Mark 5:1–20; 7:31–37). He visited the Phoenician region of Tyre and Sidon, and though he expressed there a typical Jewish attitude of exclusion,[3] a Gentile woman's salty reply won him over and he extended *shalom,* healing, to her daughter (7:24–30).

Jesus praised a Roman centurion for faith such as he had not found in Israel (Matt. 8:5–10; Luke 7:1–10). It was in this connection that he spoke of many from east and west who would eat with Abraham, Isaac, and Jacob in the kingdom of heaven (Matt. 8:11; cf. Luke 13:29).

In the sermon at Nazareth which Luke sets forth as the grand opening of Jesus' ministry, he reminded his hearers of how the prophets of old extended *shalom* to Phoenicians and Syrians, and was nearly killed for what he said (Luke 4:16–30; cf. 1 Kings 17:8–24; 2 Kings 5). And at the end of his ministry he quoted the prophetic word that the temple should be a house of prayer for all nations (Mark 11:17; cf. Isa. 56:6–7), and was killed soon afterward.

The prophets, we remember, stood for the extension of *shalom* beyond the boundaries of Israel, even to Israel's worst enemies. Here, too, Jesus stands with the prophets.

Predictions of Antagonistic Warfare

Jesus' predictions of wars have been troublesome to those who wish to claim him for the peace movement. In this he stands squarely in the prophetic line; we remember their constant predictions of wars in which Yahweh would fight against Israel, or against the nations, as a punishment for their breaches of *shalom.*

Jesus seems to have foreseen that the Romans would continue to use military force against the Jews, and that this would be God's punishment for their sins. When asked about Pilate's brutal slaughter of some Galileans who were offering their sacrifices as a part of their worship, Jesus warned, "Unless you repent, you will all perish as they did" (Luke 13:3).

Jesus went on to predict the destruction of Jerusalem because it did not know or practice the things that belong to peace. "Your house," he said, "is left to you, desolate" (Matt. 23:38; Luke 13:35). He describes the siege of the city:

> Indeed, the days will come upon you, when your enemies will set up ramparts around you and surround you, and hem you in on every side. They will crush you to the ground, you and your children within you, and they will not leave within you one stone upon another; because you did not recognize the time of your visitation from God. (Luke 19:43–44)
>
> When you see Jerusalem surrounded by armies, then know that its desolation has come near. . . . They will fall by the edge of the

sword and be taken away as captives among all nations; and Jerusalem will be trampled on by the Gentiles, until the times of the Gentiles are fulfilled. (Luke 21:20, 24)[4]

The temple itself will be destroyed, says Jesus. It will be polluted by a terrible sacrilege (Matt. 24:15; Mark 13:14). Then, "Truly I tell you, not one stone will be left here upon another; all will be thrown down" (Matt. 24:2; Mark 13:2; Luke 21:6).[5]

God's hand will be in all this, punishing Israel for its sins. This seems to be the point of the parable of the vineyard and its wicked tenants (Matt. 21:33–46; Mark 12:1–12; Luke 20:9–19; cf. Isa. 5:1–7; Ps. 80:6–13).[6] The prediction of God's punishment of Israel by warfare is quite clear in the saying that upon this generation will come "all the righteous blood shed on earth, from the blood of righteous Abel to the blood of Zechariah son of Barachiah, whom you murdered between the sanctuary and the altar" (Matt. 23:35–36; Luke 11:50–51).

Apocalyptic Predictions

We have seen how in the Old Testament, prophecy flowed into apocalyptic, with its predictions of universal war, of universal peace, of divine intervention at the end of time. This same movement occurs in the sayings attributed to Jesus.[7] In Mark 13, often called the little Apocalypse (cf. Matt. 24; Luke 21), the prediction of the destruction of the temple flows easily into an apocalyptic scenario. There will be wars and rumors of war, nation will rise against nation and kingdom against kingdom, but that will not be the end (Mark 13:6–7). This reminds us of the long description in Daniel of centuries of warfare that will precede the final conflict that brings history to a close. There will be false messiahs and prophets, earthquakes, famines, persecutions, trials, the proclamation of the gospel to all nations. It is after all this that the heavenly bodies will be in commotion and the Human One will come in clouds with great power and glory (cf. Dan. 7:13–14).[8]

It is to this apocalyptic view of God's final victory and judgment that the following sayings belong:

Woe to you, Chorazin! Woe to you, Bethsaida! For if the deeds of power done in you had been done in Tyre and Sidon, they would have repented long ago in sackcloth and ashes. But I tell you, on that day of judgment it will be more tolerable for Tyre and Sidon than for you. And you, Capernaum,
will you be exalted to heaven?
No, you will be brought down to Hades.
For if the deeds of power done in you had been done in Sodom, it would have remained until this day. But I tell you that on the day of judgment it will be more tolerable for the land of Sodom than for you. (Matt. 11:21–24; cf. Luke 10:13–15)

There are striking similarities here to Isaiah's taunt song regarding the king of Babylon (Isaiah 14, esp. vs. 13–15).

The apocalyptic bent of Jesus becomes more evident when we look among his teachings for promises of peace. We find few if any predictions of peace within history. Jesus concentrates on a final and universal peace which he calls "the kingdom of heaven" (Matthew) or "the kingdom of God" (Mark and Luke).

The "kingdom of God" is recognized as a central idea in Jesus' teaching. Indeed, it is central in the whole Bible.[9] God was proclaimed as king of Israel in the great hymn about the crossing of the Red Sea (Ex. 15:18). As the sole victor over the Egyptian army, Yahweh was to be the sole ruler in Israel.[10] When Israel was settled in the land that had been promised, there were those who hoped that the kingdom of God was now present reality. The tribal confederacy, with no human king, was to be the form of that kingdom. But, alas, it was often more anarchy than kingdom. "There was no king in Israel; all the people did what was right in their own eyes" (Judg. 21:25). When the Davidic monarchy was established, there were those who were sure that the kingdom of God had arrived in history. Solomon declared, "To David, and to his descendants, and to his house, and to his throne, there shall be *shalom* from the LORD forevermore" (1 Kings 2:33). But the reality was better predicted by Nathan, "The sword shall never depart from your house" (2 Sam. 12:10). When the Davidic kingdom fell and Judah went into exile, some began to dream of a restoration of the kingdom of God. In Ezekiel 34, Yahweh condemns the shepherds (kings) of Israel who have been feeding themselves at the expense of the flock. I myself will now become the Shepherd (king) of Israel, says Yahweh.[11] But the restoration community in Jerusalem was no kingdom of God. It was a tiny corner of the vast Persian Empire, hated by its neighbors and torn by internal dissension.

It was in this time of utter hopelessness that Israel ceased to dream of a realization of the kingdom of God within history. The dawn of apocalyptic came, with its hopes for an action by God which human beings could neither delay nor hasten, an action that would end history and bring in an entirely new age, the age of the kingdom of God. In the mature apocalyptic of Daniel, the kingdom of God is that stone, not cut by human hands, that falls on all earthly kingdoms and demolishes them, supplanting them by an everlasting kingdom (Dan. 2:44–45). It is the human and humane kingdom that replaces all the bestial kingdoms of history and is given beyond history by the Ancient One to the Human One, to be his forever (7:9–14).

Jesus, as we said, stood in the apocalyptic tradition and devoted a great portion of his teaching to "the kingdom of God," the kingdom that God would bring in; "the kingdom of heaven," qualitatively different from all earthly kingdoms. This would clearly not be the Zealots' dream of a Jewish kingdom restored by a military coup against Roman power. It would be characterized by many of the marks of *shalom* with which we are familiar:

Abundance. Having enough: "Strive first for the kingdom of God and its righteousness, and all these things [food, drink, clothing] will be given to you as well" (Matt. 6:33). "Truly I tell you, there is no one who has left house or brothers or sisters or mother or father or children or fields, for my sake and for the sake of the good news, who will not receive a hundredfold now in this age—houses, brothers and sisters, mothers and children, and fields with persecutions—and in the age to come eternal life" (Mark 10:29–30; cf. Matt. 19:29; Luke 18:29–30). One of Jesus' favorite pictures of the kingdom is a feast: "Then people will come from east and west, from north and south, and will eat in the kingdom of God" (Luke 13:29; cf. Matt. 8:11; 22:2; Luke 22:28–30; Isa. 25:6).

Healing. "Then Jesus went about all the cities and villages, teaching in their synagogues, and proclaiming the good news of the kingdom, and curing every disease and every sickness" (Matt. 9:35). To his disciples he said: "As you go, proclaim the good news, 'The kingdom of heaven has come near.' Cure the sick, raise the dead, cleanse the lepers, cast out demons" (Matt. 10:7–8).

Security. "Do not worry about your life, what you will eat or what you will drink, or about your body, what you will wear. . . . Do not worry about tomorrow. . . . Ask, and it will be given you; search, and you will find; knock, and the door will be opened for you" (Matt. 6:25, 34; 7:7). "Do not be afraid, little flock, for it is your Father's good pleasure to give you the kingdom" (Luke 12:32).

The Great Reversal. In the prophetic promises of *shalom* there was usually the element of the reversal of the present situation: plenty instead of want, healing instead of disease, security instead of constant danger, return to the land instead of being scattered over the earth, plowshares instead of swords. In Jesus' vision of the kingdom of God, the reversal is dramatic. The kingdom will belong to the poor instead of to the rich (Luke 6:20, 24; Matt. 19:23–26; Mark 10:23–27; Luke 18:24–27); to little children instead of to adults (Matt. 19:14; Mark 10:14–15; Luke 18:16–17); to infants instead of to the wise and intelligent (Matt. 11:25; Luke 10:21). The last will be first and the first will be last (Matt. 19:30; 20:6; Mark 10:31; Luke 13:30). The great ones in the kingdom will be humble as a little child instead of ambitious and proud (Matt. 18:1–4); they will be servants and slaves instead of lords and tyrants (Matt. 20:25–27; 23:11; Mark 10:43–44). Tax collectors and prostitutes will go into the kingdom ahead of proper religious people (Matt. 21:31). Those who exalt themselves will be humbled, and those who humble themselves will be exalted (Matt. 23:12; Luke 14:11; 18:14). All this is very disturbing; can it be a vision of *shalom?* Upon reflection, without such reversals there can be no *shalom.*

We are clearly in the realm of apocalyptic here—a new age beyond history as we know it, when the abundance, the healing, the security, the astounding reversals of the kingdom will finally come. Jesus does something no prophet or apocalyptic visionary had ever done. He announces that the kingdom is already present! It is obviously not fully and publicly present, for we are bidden to pray for it (Matt. 6:10; Luke 11:2), to watch for it (Matt. 24:36–25:13; Mark 13:32–37; Luke 12:35–40); but in the person of Jesus and in his ministry and the ministry of his followers, the kingdom is at hand (Matt. 4:17; 10:7; Mark 1:14–15; Luke 10:9, 11). It has in some sense already come (Matt. 12:28; Luke 11:20; 17:20–21). It is present in a hidden and dynamic way, like seed sown in the soil or yeast mixed in the dough (Matt. 13:31–33; Mark 4:26–32; Luke 13:18–21). The seed will sprout, the dough will rise. Even so, the kingdom of God, the promised time of *shalom*, is already at work in the world and will surely come!

Prophetic Actions

Another evidence that Jesus chose the prophetic way is his performance of prophetic actions. The prophets sometimes did bizarre and attention-arousing things, acted out parables as it were, to get their message across, to demand decisions from their hearers. Thus Isaiah walked naked and barefoot, like a captive of war, for three years, as a sign and a portent against Egypt and Ethiopia, rebuking the party in court that advised trust in them against the Assyrian threat (Isaiah 20). Jeremiah buried a linen loincloth in a cleft of rock near the Euphrates and took it out ruined as a symbol of the impending ruin of the pride of Judah (Jer. 13:1–11). He broke a potter's earthenware jug as a sign that God would break the people and city of Jerusalem (Jeremiah 19). He wore a yoke as a sign that Judah should accept the overlordship of Nebuchadnezzar (Jeremiah 27). Ezekiel lay on his side to portray the coming siege of Jerusalem (Ezekiel 4). He shaved himself with a sword and used the hair to portray how the people would die of pestilence or famine, be slaughtered by the sword, or be scattered in exile (Ezekiel 5). He carried baggage out through a hole in the wall to portray going into exile (Ezekiel 12).

Jesus did several things that may be interpreted as prophetic actions: the feeding of the five thousand, the cleansing of the temple, the washing of the disciples' feet. The one that rivets our attention and speaks volumes about *shalom* is the triumphal entry into Jerusalem (Matt. 21:1–11; Mark 11:1–10; Luke 19:28–40; John 12:12–19). In all four accounts, Jesus deliberately enacts the coming of the peaceful, disarmed king promised in Zech. 9:9–10.[12] According to Matthew and Mark, the crowd does not understand and hails him as Son of David, the king who will establish *shalom* by military might. According to Luke, "the multitude of the disciples" do understand and sing a song of *shalom:*

> Blessed is the king
> who comes in the name of the Lord!
> Peace in heaven,
> and glory in the highest heaven!
>   (Luke 19:38)

According to John, the crowd was already hailing him as king and Jesus enacted the Zechariah prophecy in response. It was only later, after the resurrection, that the disciples understood the meaning of his action (John 12:16). This may be one of those mystifying instances where the Fourth Gospel is the most accurate one. In any event, Jesus' intention in this prophetic action is quite clear. For him, the choice of the prophetic way was the choice of the way of *shalom.*

The Servant of the Lord

The suffering and death of Jesus seemed to Peter an absurdity. "God forbid it, Lord!" he said. "This must never happen to you" (Matt. 16:22; Mark 8:32). To Jesus this was a suggestion of Satan. He moved persistently toward Jerusalem, repeatedly predicting his death to his uncomprehending disciples (Matt. 17:12, 22–23; 20:28; Mark 9:12, 31–32; 10:32–34; Luke 9:22, 44–45, 51; 13:33; 18:31–34). He said that all this was necessary to fulfill what was written in the prophets. "See, we are going up to Jerusalem, and everything that is written about the [Human One] by the prophets will be accomplished" (Luke 18:31).

Where is it written by the prophets that the Human One will suffer and die? This is what is predicted of the Servant of the Lord in Isaiah 40–55. There are at least hints that Jesus identified the Human One (himself) with the Servant of the Lord. In Mark 9:12 he says, "How then is it written about the [Human One], that he is to go through many sufferings and be treated with contempt?" (cf. Isa. 50:6; 53:3). In Mark 10:45 = Matthew 20:28 he says, "For the [Human One] came not to be served but to serve, and to give his life a ransom for many" (cf. Isa. 53:11–12). Jesus' decision to engage in "reverse fighting," to win by enduring suffering rather than by imposing suffering on others, seems to have been profoundly influenced by the Servant songs in Isaiah 40–55.[13]

Jesus' choice of the prophetic way ultimately led to the way of the cross.

The Son of David?

Even within the prophetic way, Jesus seems to have made a narrower choice. We saw in chapter 8 that there is a considerable body of prophetic promises where *shalom* will be won and managed by a true and just king in David's line. By Jesus' time these promises had coalesced into the messianic hope, the hope for an Anointed One (Hebrew: Messiah; Greek: Christ). Did Jesus come to see himself as the fulfillment of that hope? This is a very difficult question.

Jesus' preferred title for himself was "the Human One" (lit. Greek: Son of Man). He preferred to see himself as the apocalyptic figure of Daniel 7, whose coming would spell the end of the bestial earthly kingdoms, and to whom the Ancient of Days would give the kingdom of God, rather than seeing himself a king in David's line, even an apocalyptic one. The danger was the popular understanding that the Messiah would free Israel and usher in the age of peace by Davidic methods, that is, by a victorious military campaign.

Peter's confession, "the turning point of the Synoptic Gospels," was that Jesus is the Messiah (Matt. 16:16; Mark 8:29; Luke 9:20). In Matthew's account, Peter is praised for this, but in Mark and

Luke there are only stern orders not to tell this to anybody. In all three there is an immediate emphasis on the Suffering Servant, on Jesus' suffering and death.

The matter came up again at Jesus' trial. In all three Synoptic Gospels he is asked point-blank: Are you the Messiah? (Matt. 26:63; Mark 14:62; Luke 22:67). In Mark, Jesus replies, "I am." In Matthew and Luke his answer is evasive. In all three he immediately moves to the vision of the Human One coming on the clouds of heaven. And in all three he is judged guilty of blasphemy. This charge is related to Pilate (Luke 23:2), who later uses the title in his shouting match with the mob (Matt. 27:17, 22).

The question of Jesus' self-understanding is further complicated by his difficult argument that the Messiah is not David's son, but David's Lord (Matt. 22:41–46; Mark 12:35–37; Luke 20:41–44). While this may well reflect christological controversies in the early church, it may also indicate Jesus' resistance to the title often given him and to the interpretation of the Messiah as military leader that was implicit in it.

To add to the ambiguity, there are scattered sayings in the Gospels where without argument Jesus refers to himself as the Messiah: Matt. 23:8, 10; and Mark 9:41.

On balance we can say that in choosing the way of the prophets Jesus was more comfortable with visions of the future that pictured the direct rule of God (the kingdom of God), or the gift of that rule to an apocalyptic Human One, than with the vision of a kingdom ruled by an earthly king of David's line.

The Divine Warrior?

Finally we need to ask whether, in choosing the way of the prophets, Jesus totally laid aside the idea of the Divine Warrior which is so strong in the Hebrew scriptures. We have seen that the prophetic idea of God's antagonistic warfare against God's own sinful and rebellious people and the apocalyptic idea of final, universal victory survive in Jesus' teaching. Is there anything else? Did Jesus himself engage in anything we could call warfare?

The Struggle with the Demons

Jesus' most obvious "warfare" was his struggle with the demons or unclean spirits that he encountered again and again in his ministry.[14] Ulrich Mauser sees Jesus' statement "I have not come to bring peace, but a sword" (Matt. 10:34) as belonging to this struggle.[15]

Jesus' very presence provoked the unclean spirits into hostile action. The man in the synagogue at Capernaum cried out, "Let us alone! . . . Have you come to destroy us?" (Luke 4:34; cf. Mark 1:24). The Gadarene demoniac came running out of the tombs to confront him, crying, "I adjure you by God, do not torment me" (Mark 5:1–7; cf. Matt. 8:28–29; Luke 8:26–28). They recognized Jesus as their enemy. "He would not permit the demons to speak, because they knew him" (Mark 1:34). "He sternly ordered them not to make him known" (3:12).

Jesus did not deal gently with the demons. He rebuked them (Mark 1:25; 5:8; 9:25). He cast them out (an active, forceful word; 1:34, 39). Their departure was often violent. "The unclean spirit, convulsing him and crying with a loud voice, came out of him" (1:26). "After crying out and convulsing him terribly, it came out, and the boy was like a corpse, so that most of them said, 'He is dead'" (9:26). In the case of the Gadarene demoniac the egress of the demons destroyed a valuable herd of swine (5:13).

This continuous battle with hostile, demonic powers was one of the strongest signs of the kingdom's presence. "If it is by the finger of God that I cast out the demons, then the kingdom of God has come to you" (Luke 11:20; cf. Matt. 12:28).

Jesus' enemies said that it was by the power of Beelzebul, the prince of demons, that he cast out demons. To which Jesus replied that such an explanation meant that the demonic kingdom was divided and would fall (Matt. 12:24–26; Mark 3:22–26; Luke 11:15–18). He went on with this parable:

> When a strong man, fully armed, guards his castle, his property is safe. But when one stronger than he attacks him and overpowers him, he takes away his armor in which he trusted and divides his plunder. (Luke 11:21–22; cf. Matt. 12:29; Mark 3:27)

The true explanation of the exorcisms is that he, Jesus, is the stronger One who enters the castle of Satan, the strong one, overpowers him, takes away his armor, ties him up, and plunders his property, that is, sets free the human victims whom he "owns."

Jesus sent his disciples out to engage in the same battle. He gave them authority to cast out demons (Matt. 10:8; Mark 3:15; 6:7, 13; Luke 9:1). When seventy of them returned with accounts of their success, Jesus was ecstatic. "I watched Satan fall from heaven like a flash of lightning," he said (Luke 10:18).

All this is passing strange to modern people who do not think in terms of a kingdom of Beelzebul or Satan, whose minions are myriads of demons or unclean spirits who "possess" and torment helpless human beings.

Two explanations are often given for the phenomena attributed to demons in these stories. Many writers treat them as symptoms of physical diseases like epilepsy or mental diseases like schizophrenia. On the other hand, liberation theologians treat them as reactions to oppressive, demeaning, unbearable social situations.[16]

Do we really need to explain them away? Anyone who has witnessed a mob in action has a sense of some kind of inhuman power that does indeed "possess" people and lead them to do things they would never do on their own. Mass psychosis is an inadequate description for the raw evil that one feels in such a situation. Anyone who looks with sensitivity at the suffering of the poor and powerless, suffering that most of us do not deliberately intend, has a sense that some kind of cunning evil that is too strong for us and dehumanizes us has captured and controls the systems and structures in which we live.

The Struggle with the Establishment

There may be another "war." In chapter 1 we noted briefly that Jesus was in continuing conflict with the religious leaders of his own people, a conflict that burst into action with the cleansing of the temple. Earlier in this chapter we cited some of Jesus' prophetic rhetoric in condemning the rich, the Pharisees, the lawyers. Is this a transformation of the holy war motif, with Jesus as the Divine Warrior, doing battle for God's little people, the marginalized whom we also described earlier?

Ched Myers has written a massive socioliterary commentary on Mark,[17] in which Jesus' struggle against the "establishment" is the central theme of the Gospel from beginning to end. There is a Jerusalem establishment, the priestly families who control the temple, and a Galilean establishment, the Pharisees who are seeking a power base among the populace. Neither is for a radical change in the status quo. Both the way of the Essenes (withdrawal) and the way of the Zealots (violence) are reformist, seeking to purify the system, not to replace it. The real radical is Jesus. In his nonviolent way, he challenges the very foundations of the system. The system understands this and declares war on him.[18]

There is, then, in the Gospel accounts a transformation of holy war. Jesus is not a passive victim. He is a warrior, constantly on the attack. But he fights by "reverse fighting," accepting the punishment and death that the establishment dishes out.

John Howard Yoder pictures Jesus as seriously tempted to follow the holy war pattern, to exercise "the Zealot option." He confronted it in the wilderness, when he was tempted to make league with "the strong one" and conquer the world (Matt. 4:8–9; Luke 4:6–7). He confronted it again when the five thousand were fed (John 6:15); again at the triumphal entry (Mark 11:1–10 and par.); finally when Peter drew his sword in the garden and Jesus spoke his strange words about the possibility of the heavenly hosts fighting in his defense (Matt. 26:53).[19] Jesus made an ethical, political decision for the way of the cross, a way that avoided the violence of the Zealots and the withdrawal of the Essenes and the compromise of the Sadducees and Pharisees. In choosing the way of the cross, Jesus followed his own teaching in the Sermon on the Mount. "Here at the cross is the man who loves his enemies, the man whose righteousness is greater than that of the Pharisees, who, being rich became poor, who gives his robe to those who took his cloak, who prays for those who despitefully use him."[20]

Summary

The ambiguity of Jesus' teaching regarding war and peace remains. Although he made a clear choice, choosing the way of the prophets over the royal pursuit of empire, the ambiguity which is heavy in the prophets remains in him. On the one hand, he teaches as they taught that God uses war as an instrument to punish and correct God's wayward, rebellious people who have breached the *shalom* that God intends. On the other hand, he teaches that God forgives God's enemies and makes the sun rise on the evil and the good, sends rain on the righteous and the unrighteous. The ambiguity between the wrath and the love of God remains. Perhaps it always will. Perhaps it is part of the divine mystery, the divine abyss which human intelligence cannot plumb. The God of the Bible is free and dangerous, offending our human sense of propriety and our human ideas of justice both negatively and positively.

Nevertheless, Jesus is very clear about how his followers are to behave. He does not encourage them to participate in the divine wrath. There is no "arise and thresh, O daughter Zion . . . beat in pieces many peoples," as in the prophets (Micah 4:13); no "let the high praises of God be in their throats and two-edged swords in their hands, to execute vengeance on the nations," as in the Psalms (Ps. 149:6–7). It is the other side of the divine ambiguity which they are to imitate. If they wish to be children of God, they are to love their enemies and pray for those who persecute them (Matt. 6:44–45). If they wish to be children of God, they are to be peacemakers (Matt. 5:9).

The war that is open to Jesus' followers is not war against other nations, but war against hypocrisy and greed and cruelty and injustice, war against all the demonic systems and powers that cripple and cramp and pervert the humanity of human beings. The method of that warfare is "reverse fighting," the acceptance of injustice done to oneself, of pain and suffering and even death.

Part Three

The Ambiguity of the Church

Then I saw heaven opened, and there was a
white horse! Its rider is called Faithful and
True, and in righteousness he judges and
makes war.

(Rev. 19:11)

Christ also suffered for you, leaving you
an example, so that you should follow
in his steps. . . . When he was abused,
he did not return abuse; when he
suffered, he did not threaten; but he
entrusted himself to the one who
judges justly.

(1 Peter 2:21, 23)

10

The Church: Part of a Violent World

We have already been in touch with the apostolic church to an undetermined extent. As we have said before, the picture of Jesus we find in the Gospels is the product of that church, touched by the faith of that church and by its immediate concerns. There is no foolproof way of separating out the Jesus of history from the Christ of the church's faith.

Acknowledging that, we move on to the letters of the church, most of them earlier than the Gospels, to the Acts of the Apostles, and to those parts of the Gospels where Jesus does not speak, notably the infancy narratives. (We shall delay a consideration of the Revelation until chapter 12.) Here we can test whether the understanding of Jesus as a peacemaker we have developed thus far accords with the understanding of his contemporaries and the next succeeding generation. Here we can try to see, as honestly as we can, how far the biblical ambiguity regarding war and peace continued in the life and writings of the early Christian community. We look first at the church's involvement with violence.

Compromise with Roman Violence

As we began our study of Jesus by examining those parts of the record that showed him as situated in a highly conflicted situation and making certain adaptations to it, so we begin here with a look at the church as situated in the Roman Empire, founded on violence, and making certain adaptations to that.

The Pax Romana

When Paul had his hearing before the governor Felix, the attorney for his accusers, one Tertullus, began his speech with this piece of calculated flattery: "Your Excellency, because of you we have long enjoyed peace" (Acts 24:2). This is a clear reference to the Pax Romana, the "peace" in which Roman writers and rulers took great pride.[1] The Pax Romana (the peace of Rome) has often been hailed as a uniquely peaceful period in world history. For example, Paul was able to travel the Mediterranean world on good roads, without changing language, without changing currency, without showing his passport at a single border crossing—something that has been impossible ever since the Roman peace collapsed. There was indeed *eirēnē* in the Greek sense: the absence of large-scale war (except far away on the empire's borders). But there was no *shalom*. There was no absence of violence. We have seen the presence of violence in the story of Jesus' life and death. The Roman Empire was an example of institutionalized violence, held in place by military might, legions stationed everywhere, and met by outbreaks of violent resistance year after year after year. Several are mentioned in the book of Acts (5:36, 37; 21:38).

Loyalty to the State

The early church practiced and urged loyal obedience to this tyrannical military state.

> First of all, then, I urge that supplications, prayers, intercessions, and thanksgivings be made for everyone, for kings and all who are in high positions, so that we may lead a quiet and peaceable life in all godliness and dignity. (1 Tim. 2:1–2)

> Remind them to be subject to rulers and authorities, to be obedient, to be ready for every good work, to speak evil of no one, to avoid quarreling, to be gentle, and to show every courtesy to everyone. (Titus 3:1)

> For the Lord's sake accept the authority of every human institution, whether of the emperor as supreme, or of governors, as sent by

him to punish those who do wrong and to praise those who do right. For it is God's will that by doing right you should silence the ignorance of the foolish. As servants of God, live as free people, yet do not use your freedom as a pretext for evil. Honor everyone. Love the family of believers. Fear God. Honor the emperor. (1 Peter 2:13–17)

The most famous passage, which has had an enormous impact on European history, is in Romans:

Let every person be subject to the governing authorities; for there is no authority except from God, and those authorities that exist have been instituted by God. Therefore whoever resists authority resists what God has appointed, and those who resist will incur judgment. For rulers are not a terror to good conduct, but to bad. Do you wish to have no fear of the authority? Then do what is good, and you will receive its approval; for it is God's servant for your good. But if you do what is wrong, you should be afraid for the authority does not bear the sword in vain! It is the servant of God to execute wrath on the wrongdoer. Therefore one must be subject, not only because of wrath but also because of conscience. For the same reason you also pay taxes, for the authorities are God's servants, busy with this very thing. Pay to all what is due them—taxes to whom taxes are due, revenue to whom revenue is due, respect to whom respect is due, honor to whom honor is due. (Rom. 13:1–7)[2]

Early Christians clearly resisted Jewish authorities who sought to prevent them from preaching about Jesus:

Whether it is right in God's sight to listen to you rather than to God, you must judge; for we cannot keep from speaking about what we have seen and heard. (Acts 4:19–20)

We must obey God rather than any human authority. (Acts 5:29)

But at first there was no recorded resistance to the Roman state. For one thing, Rome did not prevent preaching. For another, it did not draft Christians to fight in its wars.

The church was, however, confronted with new converts from the Roman military who did fight wars for Rome. Cornelius (Acts

10) was a case in point. Apparently no question was ever raised regarding a possible conflict between his daily occupation and his profession as a Christian.

Accepting the State's Protection

Paul, who was a Roman citizen, asserted his rights when he had been beaten at Philippi (Acts 16:35–39), when he was about to be beaten in Jerusalem (22:25–29), and when he appealed to Caesar (25:10–12; 26:32). He accepted military protection when the Jerusalem mob was trying to kill him (21:30–32), when the dissension in the Sanhedrin became violent (23:10), and when a band of sworn assassins planned to ambush him (23:12–35). In the latter case the force was massive: two hundred soldiers, seventy horsemen, and two hundred spearmen![3]

Internal Strife

The apostolic church was not free from the internal tension, dissension, and strife that seem to mark all human communities. Although the descriptions of Christian unity and harmony in Acts 2:41–47 and 4:32–37 are almost lyrical, trouble soon emerged. There was difficulty between the Greek-speaking Hellenists and the Aramaic-speaking Hebrews (Acts 6:1). The long struggle over table fellowship with Gentiles and whether to require circumcision of them began early and lasted late.

The church at Corinth was a microcosm of the tensions in the larger church. There were factions: "I belong to Paul," or "I belong to Apollos," or "I belong to Cephas," or "I belong to Christ" (1 Cor. 1:10–13). There were lawsuits between members (6:1). There was friction between "the strong" who exercised their freedom from superstition by eating meat that had been offered to idols and "the weak" who felt compromised in their faith by eating (8:1–13). Even at the Lord's Supper people gathered in little cliques and the rich did not share with the poor (11:17–22). Those who had certain "spiritual gifts" looked down on others whose gifts were different (chs. 12–14).

Violent Language

Use of Military Expressions and Metaphors

Early Christian writers did not hesitate to use expressions and metaphors drawn from warfare. Two passages picture Christ at the head of a typical Roman triumph, in which Roman commanders would display prisoners taken captive in war, while crowds cheered and incense wafted over the procession:

> But thanks be to God, who in Christ always leads us in triumphal procession, and through us spreads in every place the fragrance that comes from knowing him. (2 Cor. 2:14)

> He disarmed the rulers and authorities and made a public example of them, triumphing over them in it [the cross]. (Col. 2:15)

"Fighting the good fight" is a frequent expression in the pastoral epistles (1 Tim. 1:18; 6:12; 2 Tim. 4:7). Service in the church is compared with service in the army:

> Share in suffering like a good soldier of Christ Jesus. No one serving in the army gets entangled in everyday affairs; the soldier's aim is to please the enlisting officer. (2 Tim. 2:3–4; see also 1 Cor. 9:7; Phil. 2:25; Philemon 2)

The weapons of Christian warfare are described in several passages: 2 Corinthians 6:6–7; 10:3–6; 1 Thessalonians 5:8; and the famous passage about the whole armor of God in Ephesians 6:10–17. We shall be discussing the Ephesians passage in detail in chapter 11.

Condemnation of False Teachers

Just as the prophets condemned the false prophets in scathing diatribes, just as Jesus condemned the hypocritical religious leaders of his people in unsparing language, so the early church condemned false teachers that arose in its midst.

It is clear that Paul expended considerable energy in condemning those whom he calls false apostles, ministers of Satan. He says that their end will match their deeds (2 Cor. 11:1–15). He wishes they would castrate themselves (Gal. 5:12). They are "enemies of the cross. . . . Their end is destruction; their god is the belly; . . . their minds are set on earthly things" (Phil. 3:18–19).

The pastoral epistles declare that the false teachers' teaching is meaningless talk because they do not understand what they are talking about (1 Tim. 1:6–7). They are deceitful spirits, demons, liars whose consciences are seared with a hot iron (1 Tim. 4:1–2). They are conceited, understanding nothing, having a morbid craving for controversy and for disputes about words (1 Tim. 6:3–6). They are people of corrupt mind and counterfeit faith, who oppose the truth (2 Tim. 3:1–8). They are "idle talkers and deceivers, . . . teaching for sordid gain what it is not right to teach. . . . Their very minds and consciences are corrupted. They profess to know God, but they deny God by their actions. They are detestable, disobedient, unfit for any good work" (Titus 1:10–11, 15–16).

Later writers warm to the invective:

> These are waterless springs and mists driven by a storm; for them the deepest darkness has been reserved. For they speak bombastic nonsense, and with licentious desires of the flesh they entice people who have just escaped from those who live in error. They promise them freedom, but they themselves are slaves of corruption; for people are slaves to whatever masters them. For if, after they have escaped the defilements of the world through the knowledge of our Lord and Savior Jesus Christ, they are again entangled in them and overpowered, the last state has become worse for them than the first. For it would have been better for them never to have known the way of righteousness than, after knowing it, to turn back from the holy commandment that was passed on to them. It has happened to them according to the true proverb,
> "The dog turns back to its own vomit,"
> and,
> "The sow is washed only to wallow in the mud."
> (2 Peter 2:17–22; cf. 2:1–16
> and Jude 5–16.)

This is hardly language that makes for peace or illustrates love for enemies.

The Wrath of God

Again, like the prophets and like Jesus, the early church preserves the ancient idea of God's antagonistic warfare against his own rebellious people and against all who are sinful.

"For the wrath of God is revealed from heaven against all ungodliness and wickedness of those who by their wickedness suppress the truth" (Rom. 1:18). With those words Paul opens a lengthy discussion of God's wrath that runs all the way to Romans 3:20. The objects of God's wrath have no excuse (1:20; 2:1). Both Jews and Gentiles are included in this condemnation (2:9–24). God's way of punishing is simply to give them up to their lusts, passions, and debased minds (1:24, 26, 28).

Briefer statements are found all through the New Testament: "The wrath of God is coming on those who are disobedient" (Col. 3:6; cf. 1 Thess. 1:10). "Our God is a consuming fire" (Heb. 12:29). "For judgment will be without mercy to anyone who has shown no mercy" (James 2:13).

Who can forget the passage made famous by Jonathan Edwards?

> For if we willfully persist in sin after having received the knowledge of the truth, there no longer remains a sacrifice for sins, but a fearful prospect of judgment, and a fury of fire that will consume the adversaries. Anyone who has violated the law of Moses dies without mercy "on the testimony of two or three witnesses." How much worse punishment do you think will be deserved by those who have spurned the Son of God, profaned the blood of the covenant by which they were sanctified, and outraged the Spirit of grace? For we know the one who said, "Vengeance is mine, I will repay." And again, "The Lord will judge his people." It is a fearful thing to fall into the hands of the living God. (Heb. 10:26–31)

The New Testament even dares to picture Jesus as the executor of God's vengeance. The Lord Jesus will be

> revealed from heaven with his mighty angels in flaming fire, inflicting vengeance on those who do not know God and on those who do not obey the gospel of our Lord Jesus. These will suffer the

punishment of eternal destruction, separated from the presence of the Lord and from the glory of his might. (2 Thess. 1:7–9)

We shall see more of this when we come to the book of Revelation, but this is enough to show that to the early church God is not unambiguous love and mercy, nor is Jesus "gentle Jesus, meek and mild."

Looking at this side of the ambiguity, we see a church in which many first-world Christians of our day could feel comfortable and undisturbed: a church that lives without question or resistance in a state founded on violence and made prosperous by the exploitation of less fortunate nations; a church that accepts various perquisites from that state as its due; a church where changing jobs for the sake of peace and justice is seldom considered; a church that constantly speaks in the language of war; a church given to eloquent invective in its internal disputes and against outside opponents; a church quite sure that God will punish the wicked.

But there is another side of the ambiguity, which we shall find quite uncomfortable and disturbing.

11

The Church: Christ's Peaceful People

When we turn to the other side of the ambiguity we find a church that taught and tried to obey Jesus' commands for peaceful living, even the hard ones; a church that continued resolutely Jesus' peacemaking ministry; a church that meditated deeply and seriously on the meaning of Jesus, and especially of his death and resurrection, for the proper understanding of peacemaking.[1]

Remembering Jesus' Commands

As we saw in chapter 2, Jesus could be recognized during his lifetime as a man of peace, who refused to take revenge when mistreated, who did not fight in his own defense or permit others to fight for him, who commanded his disciples to follow his example of nonviolence, who wept because his nation would not follow "the things that make for peace." The apostolic church kept that memory alive, tried to follow that example and obey those commands.

Love One Another

Jesus was concerned with the internal peace of the apostolic band. "Have salt in yourselves, and be at peace with one another," he said (Mark 9:50). The Johannine form of this command is "I give you a new commandment, that you love one another. Just as I have loved you, you also should love one another" (John 13:34).

The church tried and often failed. We reviewed some of those failures in chapter 10. But it never ceased to repeat the command, to remind itself of its destiny and goal: to be a peaceful community.

By giving up the privilege of eating meat for the sake of the weaker brother or sister, "let us then pursue what makes for peace" (Rom. 14:19). In marital disputes, "it is to peace that God has called you" (1 Cor. 7:15). In the excitement of charismatic worship, "God is a God not of disorder but of peace" (1 Cor. 14:33). Where there have been disputes, "put things in order, listen to my appeal, agree with one another, live in peace" (2 Cor. 13:11). If you claim to have the Holy Spirit, remember that "the fruit of the Spirit is love, joy, peace" (Gal. 5:22). Make every effort "to maintain the unity of the Spirit in the bond of peace" (Eph. 4:3). Let those tempted by youthful passions "pursue righteousness, faith, love, and peace" (2 Tim. 2:22). As you wait for new heavens and a new earth, "strive to be found by him at peace" (2 Peter 3:14).

A passage to ponder is this one:

> As God's chosen ones, holy and beloved, clothe yourselves with compassion, kindness, humility, meekness, and patience. Bear with one another and, if anyone has a complaint against another, forgive each other; just as the Lord has forgiven you, so you also must forgive. Above all, clothe yourselves with love, which binds everything in perfect harmony. And let the peace of Christ rule in your hearts, to which indeed you were called in the one body. And be thankful. (Col. 3:12–15)

There is almost no end to the passages that urge the internal peace, the mutual love of the church, including 1 Corinthians 12 on the mutual concern of the members of the body of Christ; 1 Corinthians 13 on love as the highest spiritual gift; Philippians 2 on the mind of Christ; 1 John 4 on the interconnection between love of God and love of brothers and sisters.[2]

Love Your Enemies

What are often spoken of as Jesus' hard commands are those that concern his followers' dealings with those who persecute and malign them, their enemies. The apostolic church remembered those, too.

> Bless those who persecute you; bless and do not curse them. . . .
> Do not repay anyone evil for evil, but take thought for what is
> noble in the sight of all. Beloved, never avenge yourselves, but
> leave room for the wrath of God; for it is written, "Vengeance is
> mine, I will repay, says the Lord." No, "if your enemies are
> hungry, feed them; if they are thirsty, give them something to
> drink, for by doing this you will heap burning coals on their
> heads." Do not be overcome by evil, but overcome evil with
> good. (Rom. 12:14, 17–21)

The close agreement of this passage with Matthew 5:38–48 and
Luke 6:27–36 is remarkable. The agreement is not verbal. Romans
was written before the publication of the Gospels and is not quoting
the Sermon on the Mount. Rather, it cites two Old Testament
passages as its authority (Deut. 32:35; Prov. 25:21–22). But the
Romans passage is striking evidence that the loving, forgiving,
nonretaliatory posture recommended by Jesus was a living, active
memory within the apostolic church.

There is further evidence: "When reviled, we bless; when persecuted, we endure; when slandered, we speak kindly" (1 Cor. 4:12–
13). "See that none of you repays evil for evil, but always seek to do
good to one another and to all" (1 Thess. 5:15). "Do not repay evil
for evil or abuse for abuse; but, on the contrary, repay with a
blessing. It is for this that you were called—that you might inherit a
blessing" (1 Peter 3:9; cf. Matt. 5:11–12; Luke 6:22–23).

Perhaps the most moving evidence that the apostolic church
remembered and tried to live by the hard sayings and harder
example of Jesus is the "imitation of Christ" by Stephen:

> They covered their ears, and with a loud shout all rushed together
> against him. Then they dragged him out of the city and began to
> stone him. . . . While they were stoning Stephen, he prayed, "Lord
> Jesus, receive my spirit." Then he knelt down and cried out in a
> loud voice, "Lord, do not hold this sin against them." When he
> had said this, he died. (Acts 7:57–60; cf. Luke 23:34)

The apostolic church was far from perfect, riddled with internal
dissension and conflict. But there is no record that they ever

resorted to force of arms to settle their disputes or that they ever used weapons to defend themselves against external enemies. They remembered the commands of Jesus.

Continuing Jesus' Ministry

In chapter 9 we saw that Jesus interpreted the Old Testament in the light of the prophetic movement, and that his peacemaking ministry was a continuation and deepening of the ministry of the prophets. In like manner, the ministry of the apostolic church was a continuation of the peacemaking ministry of Jesus.

The Defense of *Shalom*

The prophets had seen the Torah, particularly in its provisions for the poor and landless, as instruction as to how *shalom* could be maintained and managed. Jesus had championed the same instructions as the primary defense of *shalom*. The early church continued this.

Care for the Poor

In the church at Jerusalem, care for the poor assumed the radical form of a community of goods! "All who believed were together and had all things in common; they would sell their possessions and goods and distribute the proceeds to all, as any had need" (Acts 2:44–45; cf. the expanded description in 4:32–37). This policy does not seem to have spread beyond Jerusalem, and is not mentioned after Acts 6. Yet it survives in monasticism to the present day.

A particular constituency among the poor continued to receive special attention in the church: widows. They received a daily distribution of food in Jerusalem (Acts 6:1). They were a recognized group in the church at Joppa (9:39, 41). James writes, "Religion that is pure and undefiled before God, the Father, is this: to care for orphans and widows in their distress, and to keep oneself unstained by the world" (James 1:27). By the time of the pastoral epistles, widows were almost an "order" in the church, with definite rules as to who should be enrolled as a widow. It seems clear that those properly enrolled received the financial support of the church (1 Tim. 5:3–16).

A less formal sharing of goods is pictured in the following passages:

> If a brother or sister is naked and lacks daily food, and one of you says to them, "Go in peace; keep warm and eat your fill," and yet you do not supply their bodily needs, what is the good of that? (James 2:15–16)

> How does God's love abide in anyone who has the world's goods and sees a brother or sister in need and yet refuses help? (1 John 3:17)

There was sharing of goods from church to church. This became urgent in time of famine (Acts 11:27–30), but was welcome at any time. Paul recalls the final action of an important conference between himself (and Barnabas) and the leaders of the church at Jerusalem: "They asked only one thing, that we remember the poor, which was actually what I was eager to do" (Gal. 2:10). The purpose of the trip to Jerusalem during which Paul was arrested was to deliver an offering that had been taken up from many churches for the relief of the poor in Jerusalem (Acts 24:17; 1 Cor. 16:1–4; 2 Cor. 8–9).

The sharing of goods extended beyond the bounds of the church. This is implied in the frequent occurrence of the word "hospitality." The word means "love of strangers." It echoes the old Torah provisions for "sojourners" and aliens. Persons away from home or without means of support could expect and receive hospitality from the apostolic church (Rom. 12:13; 1 Tim. 3:2; Titus 1:8; Heb. 13:2; 1 Peter 4:8).

Injunctions to the Rich

The writer of James became incensed when he saw the church forgetting God's "tilt" toward the poor, giving great honor to the rich in their assemblies, and asking the poor to stand aside.

> Listen, my beloved brothers and sisters. Has not God chosen the poor in the world to be rich in faith and to be heirs of the kingdom

that he has promised those who love him? [cf. Matt. 5:3; Luke 6:20]. But you have dishonored the poor. Is it not the rich who oppress you? Is it not they who drag you into court? Is it not they who blaspheme the excellent name that was invoked over you? (James 2:5–7)

Let the believer who is lowly boast in being raised up, and the rich in being brought low, because the rich will disappear like a flower in the field. For the sun rises with its scorching heat and withers the field; its flower falls, and its beauty perishes. It is the same way with the rich, in the midst of a busy life, they will wither away. (James 1:9–11)

Just as the prophets and Jesus condemned the rich for undermining *shalom* by taking advantage of the poor, so do writers in the apostolic church:

Come now, you rich people, weep and wail for the miseries that are coming to you. Your riches have rotted, and your clothes are moth-eaten. Your gold and silver have rusted, and their rust will be evidence against you, and it will eat your flesh like fire. You have laid up treasure for the last days. Listen! The wages of the laborers who mowed your fields, which you kept back by fraud, cry out, and the cries of the harvesters have reached the ears of the Lord of hosts. You have lived on the earth in luxury and in pleasure; you have fattened your hearts in a day of slaughter. You have condemned and murdered the righteous one, who does not resist you. (James 5:1–6)

Those who want to be rich fall into temptation and are trapped by many senseless and harmful desires that plunge people into ruin and destruction. For the love of money is a root of all kinds of evil, and in their eagerness to be rich some have wandered away from the faith and pierced themselves with many pains. (1 Tim. 6:9–10)

As for those who in the present age are rich, command them not to be haughty, or to set their hopes on the uncertainty of riches, but rather on God who richly provides us with everything for our enjoyment. They are to do good, to be rich in good works, generous, and ready to share, thus storing up for themselves the treasure of a good foundation for the future, so that they may take hold of the life that really is life. (1 Tim. 6:17–18)

There is no peace without justice, without economic justice in particular. The apostolic church understood this and tried to practice it.

Love of Neighbor

Jesus felt that the principles of Torah on which *shalom* rests were summed up in Leviticus 19:18: "You shall love your neighbor as yourself." This was alive and working in the apostolic church:

Owe no one anything, except to love one another; for the one who loves another has fulfilled the law. The commandments, "You shall not commit adultery; You shall not murder; You shall not steal; You shall not covet"; and any other commandment, are summed up in this word, "Love your neighbor as yourself." Love does no wrong to a neighbor; therefore, love is the fulfilling of the law. (Rom. 13:8–10)

For the whole law is summed up in a single commandment, "You shall love your neighbor as yourself." (Gal. 5:14)

You do well if you really fulfill the royal law according to the scripture, "You shall love your neighbor as yourself." But if you show partiality, you commit sin and are convicted by the law as transgressors. (James 2:8–9)

The Extension of *Shalom*

Jesus' extension of *shalom* beyond the borders of Israel was quiet and at times ambiguous, but the church heard the risen Lord say, "Go therefore and make disciples of all nations" (Matt. 28:19). In the old tradition of *shalom* for Israel only, the apostles asked him, "Lord, is this the time when you will restore the kingdom to Israel?" He replied, "It is not for you to know the times or periods that the Father has set by his own authority. But you will receive power when the Holy Spirit has come upon you; and you will be my witnesses in Jerusalem, in all Judea and Samaria, and to the ends of the earth" (Acts 1:6–8).

Carrying out that commission involved the apostolic church in a severe internal struggle: should Gentiles become Christians? And if so, should they become Jews first, by the rite of circumcision?

This struggle is a central theme of the book of Acts. The Holy Spirit indicated that Samaritans (Acts 8:4–25) and an Ethiopian (vs. 26–40) were to be included in the church. Then came the crucial conversion of Cornelius, a Roman centurion, and members of his household (10:1–48). This was strongly challenged by the Jerusalem church, but successfully defended by Peter (11:1–15). The church at Antioch became the first fellowship where Jews and Greeks regularly worshiped together (vs. 19–26).[3]

The church at Antioch sent out Saul (Paul) and Barnabas to spread the gospel (Acts 13:1–3). They went first to Jewish synagogues, but when they were rejected there, they turned to the Gentiles (vs. 44–52). The success of the Gentile mission led to a head-on confrontation on the question whether they must first become Jews by the rite of circumcision. This was debated and presumably settled in Jerusalem in favor of a church that would include both Jews and Gentiles, without requiring circumcision of the latter (ch. 15).

But the issue did not die. Jewish opponents hounded Paul on his subsequent journeys. Again and again he "turned to the Gentiles" (Acts 18:5–8; 19:8–10). The circumcision issue marks his letters (Galatians, passim; Romans 2–4, 15; 1 Cor. 7:19; Philippians 3; Col. 2:11; 3:11). Nevertheless he clung to a vision of one church, embracing Jews and Gentiles in gracious *shalom* (Romans 9–11).

Paul hoped to extend the *shalom* of the church by action, even though words failed. The action was the great offering referred to above, raised among the Gentile churches, to be taken to the church at Jerusalem. Paul dreamed that the delivery of this offering would lead the Jewish Christians to long for their Gentile brothers and sisters, to pray for them because of the surpassing grace of God that they could now see had been given to them (2 Cor. 9:14). It did not turn out that way. Delivery of the gift led to Paul's arrest and ultimately to his journey to Rome as a prisoner. There in Rome there was one more "turning to the Gentiles" (Acts 28:17–28). The attempt to extend *shalom* experienced more failure than success, but it had been earnestly pursued.

The Promise of the Kingdom

Jesus in his ministry held out to his hearers the promise of *shalom* in the form of the kingdom of God. The common impression that this dropped out of the teaching of the early church is not accurate. The record states that Philip preached the kingdom in Samaria (Acts 8:12); and Paul preached it in Ephesus (19:8; 20:25) and at Rome (28:23, 31). It was obviously preached more widely, for it was familiar to Christians in Corinth (1 Cor. 4:20; 6:9), Galatia (Gal. 5:21), Colossae (Col. 1:13; 4:11), and Thessalonica (1 Thess. 2:12; 2 Thess. 1:5). We have already seen a reference to it in James 2:5.

The kingdom of God is verbally identified with peace in Paul's argument that Christians should refrain from exercising freedom in what they ate for the sake of weaker Christians who were not yet free: "For the kingdom of God is not food and drink but righteousness and peace and joy in the Holy Spirit" (Rom. 14:17).

More important than the references to the preaching of the kingdom was the hope for the kingdom that saturates the New Testament. It was this hope that enabled the apostolic church to be a subversively different community within the Roman Empire and to endure the suffering that came to it as a result.

Suffering

Jesus regarded his suffering, his "reverse fighting," as essential to his peacemaking ministry. The apostolic church likewise exercised its ministry through suffering.

Once Paul made a list of his own sufferings, including labors, imprisonments, floggings, often near death:

Five times I have received from the Jews the forty lashes minus one. Three times I was beaten with rods. Once I received a stoning. Three times I was shipwrecked; for a night and a day I was adrift at sea; on frequent journeys, in danger from rivers, danger from bandits, danger from my own people, danger from Gentiles, danger in the city, danger in the wilderness, danger at sea, danger from false brothers and sisters; in toil and hardship, through many a sleepless night, hungry and thirsty, often without food, cold and naked. And, besides other things, I am under daily pressure because of my anxiety for all the churches. Who is weak, and I am not weak? Who is made to stumble, and I am not indignant? (2 Cor. 11:24–29)

See also 2 Cor. 12:10; 2 Tim. 3:10–12.

More frequently Paul speaks for the apostolic band:

For I think that God has exhibited us apostles as last of all, as though sentenced to death, because we have become a spectacle to the world, to angels and to mortals. We are fools for the sake of Christ, but you are wise in Christ. We are weak, but you are strong. You are held in honor, but we in disrepute. To the present hour we are hungry and thirsty, we are poorly clothed and beaten and homeless, and we grow weary from the work of our own hands. . . . We have become like the rubbish of the world, the dregs of all things, to this very day. (1 Cor. 4:9–13)

We are afflicted in every way, but not crushed; perplexed, but not driven to despair; persecuted, but not forsaken; struck down, but not destroyed. (2 Cor. 4:8–9)

As servants of God we have commended ourselves in every way: through great endurance, in afflictions, hardships, calamities, beatings, imprisonments, riots, labors, sleepless nights, hunger . . . ; in honor and dishonor, in ill repute and good repute. We are treated as imposters, and yet are true; as unknown, and yet are well known; as dying, and see—we are alive; as punished, and yet not killed; as sorrowful, yet always rejoicing; as poor, yet making many rich; as having nothing, and yet possessing everything. (2 Cor. 6:4–5, 8–10)

It was not only the apostles who suffered. The rank and file of the church also suffered. The first letter of Peter was written to a suffering church, which is why, as we shall see, it has so much to say about Jesus as the Suffering Servant.

Even if you do suffer for doing what is right, you are blessed. Do not fear what they fear, and do not be intimidated, but in your hearts sanctify Christ as Lord. (1 Peter 3:14–15)

> Since therefore Christ suffered in the flesh, arm yourselves also with the same intention (for whoever has suffered in the flesh has finished with sin), so as to live for the rest of your earthly life no longer by human desires but by the will of God. (4:1–2)

> Beloved, do not be surprised at the fiery ordeal that is taking place among you to test you, as though something strange were happening to you. (4:12)

> After you have suffered for a little while, the God of all grace, who has called you to his eternal glory in Christ, will himself restore, support, strengthen, and establish you. (5:10)

The apostolic church rejoiced in and boasted of its suffering. Punished by the Jewish authorities, "they rejoiced that they were considered worthy to suffer dishonor for the sake of the name" (Acts 5:41). Driven out of Antioch in Pisidia, "the disciples were filled with joy and with the Holy Spirit" (13:52). Returning to places where they had suffered, "they strengthened the souls of the disciples and encouraged them to continue in the faith, saying, 'It is through many persecutions that we must enter the kingdom of God' " (14:22). Flogged and imprisoned, Paul and Silas sang hymns at midnight in jail (16:25). They considered it a high privilege to suffer for Christ (Phil. 1:29).

It was the apocalyptic hope for the coming of the kingdom in its fullness that enabled the apostolic church to boast and rejoice in suffering.

> We also boast in our sufferings, knowing that suffering produces endurance, and endurance produces character, and character produces hope, and hope does not disappoint us, because God's love has been poured into our hearts through the Holy Spirit that has been given to us. (Rom. 5:3–5)

> We are children of God, and if children, then heirs, heirs of God and joint heirs with Christ—if, in fact, we suffer with him so that we may also be glorified with him. I consider that the sufferings of this present time are not worth comparing with the glory about to be revealed to us. (Rom. 8:16–18)

Rejoice in this, even if now for a little while you have had to suffer various trials, so that the genuineness of your faith—being more precious than gold that, though perishable, is tested by fire—may be found to result in praise and glory and honor when Jesus Christ is revealed. (1 Peter 1:6–7)

Rejoice insofar as you are sharing Christ's sufferings, so that you may also be glad and shout for joy when his glory is revealed. (1 Peter 4:13)

It is evident that there is an almost mystical link between the suffering of Christians and the suffering of Christ:

We are . . . always carrying in the body the death of Jesus, so that the life of Jesus may also be made visible in our bodies. For while we live, we are always being given up to death for Jesus' sake, so that the life of Jesus may be made visible in our mortal flesh. So death is at work in us, but life in you. (2 Cor. 4:10–12)

I want to know Christ and the power of his resurrection and the sharing of his sufferings by becoming like him in his death, if somehow I may attain the resurrection from the dead. (Phil. 3:10–11)

I am now rejoicing in my sufferings for your sake, and in my flesh I am completing what is lacking in Christ's afflictions for the sake of his body, that is, the church. (Col. 1:24)

Clearly the apostolic church was more interested in enduring and understanding and using suffering than in dishing it out, either in self-defense or for revenge. It understood reverse fighting.[4]

The Battle Against the Demonic

The apostolic church may not have been as radical as Jesus in battling against the establishment,[5] but it clearly continued his battle against unclean spirits and demonic powers. We find records of exorcisms in Acts 5:16; 8:7; 16:18; and 19:12. Just as Jesus' more serious battle was with the strong one, with Beelzebul, the prince of demons, the ruler of this world, so the church's more serious battle was with the cosmic powers of darkness.

The church understood the cosmic powers as initially part of the good creation of God (Col. 1:15–17). But these powers shared in the fall. They now seek to separate us from the love of God (Rom. 8:38–39). They enslave us (Eph. 2:2; Col. 2:20; Gal. 4:3). Even so, God can continue to use them for God's purposes (Rom. 13:1).[6]

The very existence of the church is a sign that the sovereignty of these powers has been broken. And in order to continue to exist, to stand, the church must continually withstand the powers. It is not out to destroy the powers, but to avoid being seduced by them.[7] Thus we read:

> Finally, be strong in the Lord and in the strength of his power. Put on the whole armor of God, so that you may be able to stand against the wiles of the devil. For our struggle is not against enemies of blood and flesh, but against the rulers, against the authorities, against the cosmic powers of this present darkness, against the spiritual forces of evil in the heavenly places. Therefore take up the whole armor of God, so that you may be able to withstand on that evil day, and having done everything, to stand firm. Stand therefore, and fasten the belt of truth around your waist, and put on the breastplate of righteousness. As shoes for your feet put on whatever will make you ready to proclaim the gospel of peace. With all of these, take the shield of faith, with which you will be able to quench all the flaming arrows of the evil one. Take the helmet of salvation, and the sword of the Spirit, which is the word of God. (Eph. 6:10–17)[8]

When the writer speaks of "the whole armor of God," he surely has in mind the description of God's armor in Isaiah 59. There we read of "righteousness like a breastplate" and "a helmet of salvation" (Isa. 59:17), but there is a tremendous difference in the two pictures. Isaiah 59 belongs squarely in the old holy war tradition. Yahweh is displeased with the injustice that is rampant among the restoration community in Jerusalem (vs. 1–15). "The way of *shalom* they do not know, and there is no justice in their paths" (v. 8). Since no human being, no rod of the LORD's anger, appears to champion justice, Yahweh will do it in person (vs. 16–19). Yahweh will put on "garments of vengeance" and be clothed "in fury as in a mantle" (v.

17). Yahweh will wage warfare against people and nations that is both monergistic and antagonistic.

The writer to the Ephesians reclaims and transforms the holy war tradition. The followers of Jesus are to engage in warfare, and their armor includes the righteousness and salvation of God's armor. But there is no vengeance or fury. Instead, there is truth, faith, the word of God, and whatever makes them ready to proclaim the gospel of peace. And their enemies are not blood and flesh, but rulers, authorities, cosmic powers, spiritual forces of wickedness.

We said in chapter 9 that the New Testament idea of demons and demonic structures is passing strange to the modern mind. In this passage the animistic idea of "unclean spirits" that can invade individual human bodies and distort individual human spirits is not in view; but the idea of demonic systems and structures that exert enormous power in the world, that can invade the body politic and other human corporeities and dehumanize them, is what is at stake.

I have suggested elsewhere that value-free technology, the military-industrial complex, and narrow nationalism might be modern examples of such principalities and powers.[9] Hendrikus Berkhof suggests that human traditions, astrology, fixed religious rules, clans, public opinion, race, class, state, and *Volk* are among the powers.[10] Walter Wink sees the powers as the inner aspects of institutions, their "spirituality," the inner spirit or driving force that animates, legitimates, and regulates their outward manifestations.[11] They are "the invisible forces that determine human existence."[12] When such things dehumanize human life, thwart and distort the human spirit, block God's gift of *shalom,* the followers of Jesus are rallied for a new kind of holy war. In such a struggle the church continues the peacemaking ministry of Jesus.

Understanding Jesus

The apostolic church remembered Jesus' peacemaking commands and sought to continue Jesus' peacemaking ministry. It also rethought the meaning of Jesus for peacemaking, in the light of his death and resurrection. It moved beyond the faith *of* Jesus to its own faith *about* Jesus.

The Messiah

If we were correct in saying that Jesus more or less avoided the title "Messiah" and did not see himself as the fulfillment of prophecies of a just king who would manage and maintain *shalom*, then the early church made a radical reversal.

The climax of Peter's sermon on the Day of Pentecost is:

> Therefore let the entire house of Israel know with certainty that God has made him both Lord and Messiah, this Jesus whom you crucified. (Acts 2:36)

This was a constant theme of the early apostolic preaching: "And every day in the temple and at home they did not cease to teach and proclaim Jesus as the Messiah" (Acts 5:42; cf. 3:20; 4:10).

According to Acts, Paul's synagogue preaching had the same theme. He confounded the Jews who lived in Damascus by proving that Jesus was the Messiah (Acts 9:22). He did the same at Thessalonica (17:3) and Corinth (18:5).

In Paul's letters and the other New Testament letters, Jesus Christ (Jesus Messiah) and Christ Jesus (Messiah Jesus) became the ordinary way of speaking, so much so that many modern readers have thought of these expressions as Jesus' common name. This ordinary usage was so habitual that it may account for the seemingly careless way in which Christ is sometimes used in the Gospels.[13]

In his Gospel, Luke reclaims the Son of David theme. His infancy narrative goes to pains to state that Jesus was born in Bethlehem, the city of David (Luke 2:4, 11), of parents of the house and family of David (1:27; 2:4). The angel of the annunciation says that God will give Jesus "the throne of his ancestor David" (1:32). Zechariah sings of a mighty savior "in the house of his servant David" (v. 69). Matthew, in a different way, rehabilitates the Son of David title by associating it, not with warfare, but with healings

(Matt. 12:23; 15:22; 20:31; 21:9, 15).[14] Even Paul mentions Jesus' descent from David (Rom. 1:3).

In contrast, Jesus' chosen self-appellation, the Human One (Son of Man) scarcely appears outside the Gospels. Are we witnessing here a remilitarization of Jesus, a move from the Human One who receives the kingdom to a Son of David who wins it and maintains it by force of arms?

I think not. It is clear that the church is comfortable in calling Jesus the Messiah only after his death on the cross and his resurrection and exaltation. At this point he is no longer a prospective military conqueror like David. He is of no use to the Zealots.

The resurrection is Jesus' coronation. As the Risen One, he is now the king, fulfilling the functions of the promised Messiah, providing order and stability for the people of God, establishing and managing their *shalom*.

The Servant of the Lord

We have seen hints that during his ministry Jesus identified with the Servant of the Lord in Isaiah 40–55. The early church makes the identification explicit.

The Ethiopian eunuch is reading Isaiah 53:7–8 when Philip joins him in his chariot. "The eunuch asked Philip: 'About whom, may I ask you, does the prophet say this, about himself or about someone else?' Then Philip began to speak, and starting with this scripture, he proclaimed to him the good news about Jesus" (Acts 8:34–35).

Matthew sees the healing ministry of Jesus as the fulfillment of Isaiah 53:4 (Matt. 8:17) and his peaceful withdrawal in the face of threats, his desire for anonymity, as the fulfillment of Isaiah 42:1–4 (Matt. 12:15–21).

In the advice to slaves given in 1 Peter there is an amazing quotation from, and paraphrase of, Isaiah 53:

> For it is a credit to you if, being aware of God, you endure pain while suffering unjustly. If you endure when you are beaten for doing wrong, what credit is that? But if you endure when you do

right and suffer for it, you have God's approval. For to this you
have been called, because Christ also suffered for you, leaving you
an example, so that you should follow in his steps.

"He committed no sin,
and no deceit was found in his mouth."
When he was abused, he did not return abuse; when he suffered,
he did not threaten, but he entrusted himself to the one who judges
justly. He himself bore our sins in his body on the cross, so that,
free from sins, we might live for righteousness; by his wounds you
have been healed. For you were going astray like sheep, but now
you have returned to the shepherd and guardian of your souls. (1
Peter 2:19–25; cf. 3:14, 17–18; 4:1)

In a few passages, the New Testament applies the title "servant" to
Jesus. In the Greek record of the apostolic preaching, the word *pais*
(child) is used, emphasizing that the servant is beloved (cf. Isa. 42:1):

The God of Abraham, the God of Isaac, and the God of Jacob, the
God of our ancestors has glorified his servant (*pais*) Jesus, whom
you handed over and rejected in the presence of Pilate, though he
had decided to release him. (Acts 3:13)

For in this city, in fact, both Herod and Pontius Pilate, with the
Gentiles and the peoples of Israel, gathered together against your
holy servant (*pais*) Jesus, whom you anointed, to do whatever your
hand and your plan had predestined to take place. And now, Lord,
look at their threats, and grant to your servants to speak your word
with all boldness, while you stretch out your hand to heal, and
signs and wonders are performed through the name of your holy
servant (*pais*) Jesus. (Acts 4:27–30)

In the early Christian hymn quoted by Paul in Philippians, the
Greek word for slave (*doulos*) is used to emphasize the servant's
humiliation and suffering:

who, though he was in the form of God,
did not regard equality with God
as something to be exploited,
but emptied himself,
taking the form of a slave (*doulos*),

being born in human likeness.
And being found in human form,
   he humbled himself
   and became obedient to the point of death—
   even death on a cross.

(Phil. 2:6–8)

Jesus is *both* Messiah *and* Suffering Servant. What is astounding is not that these ideas lived quite separately in Jewish thought, but that the apostolic church put them together. Luke ventures to say that the church learned this from the risen Lord himself.

On the walk to Emmaus, Jesus says to the two disciples, "Oh, how foolish you are, and how slow of heart to believe all that the prophets have declared! Was it not necessary that the Messiah should suffer these things and then enter into his glory?" (Luke 24:25–26). And to the assembled disciples he says, "'These are my words that I spoke to you while I was still with you—that everything written about me in the law of Moses, the prophets, and the psalms must be fulfilled.' Then he opened their minds to understand the scriptures, and he said to them, 'Thus it is written, that the Messiah is to suffer'" (Luke 24:44–46).

The idea of a suffering Messiah is taken up in the apostolic preaching: "In this way God fulfilled what he had foretold through all the prophets, that his Messiah would suffer" (Acts 3:18). At Thessalonica, Paul, arguing from scripture, explains and proves "that it was necessary for the Messiah to suffer" (Acts 17:3). In his letters he speaks frequently of the suffering and death of Christ (the Messiah): Romans 3:24–25; 5:6, 8; 6:3, 8; 8:17, 34; 14:15; 15:3; 1 Corinthians 1:23; 2:2; 8:11; 15:3; 2 Corinthians 8:9; Galatians 2:19; 3:1, 13; 6:14; Philippians 3:10. The list could go on and on through most of the New Testament writings.

The Victor

The Servant/Messiah is not only the Victim, who "never said a mumblin' word," giving his back to those who strike him and his cheeks to those who pluck out his beard, led like a lamb to the slaughter; he is also the Victor in a life-and-death battle. It is a battle with those mysterious superhuman and/or subhuman forces that we have already met in our discussion of the whole armor of God in Ephesians 6.

There is a dramatic word in Colossians that Christ "disarmed the rulers and authorities and made a public example of them, triumphing over them in it [the cross]" (Col. 2:15).[15] The astounding paradox, or we might even call it, reverently, God's practical joke, is that it is precisely in offering himself as Victim that Christ becomes Victor. "Reverse fighting" wins! The helpless Suffering Servant divides spoil with the strong! The Stronger One overcomes the strong one through suffering! If the stupid rulers had understood this, they would never have crucified the Lord of glory (1 Cor. 2:8). The hour of Jesus' apparent defeat in death is the hour in which this world is judged and "the ruler of this world" will be driven out (John 12:31). "The Son of God was revealed for this purpose, to destroy the works of the devil" (1 John 3:8).

Interestingly, among the hostile powers defeated by Christ the Victor is the law, not the law as Torah, gracious instruction for the establishment and maintenance of *shalom*, but the law as commandments and ordinances, as a damning bill of particulars posted against us. Christ "erased the record that stood against us with its legal demands. He set this aside, nailing it to the cross" (Col. 2:14). Another hostile power is sin: "For God has done what the law, weakened by the flesh, could not do: by sending his own Son in the likeness of sinful flesh, and to deal with sin, he condemned sin in the flesh" (Rom. 8:3). As the hymn puts it, "He breaks the power of reigning sin and sets the prisoner free." Another is death: Christ "abolished death and brought life and immortality to light through the gospel" (2 Tim. 1:10).

The power of Christ's enemies is broken, but their defeat is not final. The battle goes on. A favorite text of the apostolic church was Psalm 110:1:

> The LORD says to my lord,
>   "Sit at my right hand
> until I make your enemies your footstool."

This passage is reflected in 1 Peter 3:22, where Christ "has gone into heaven and is at the right hand of God, with angels, authorities, and powers made subject to him." And in 1 Corinthians 15:24–26 we read, "Then comes the end, when he hands over the kingdom to God the Father, after he has destroyed every ruler and every authority and power. For he must reign until he has put all his enemies under his feet. The last enemy to be destroyed is death."[16]

The imperial title "Lord" is closely associated with Christ's victory over the powers. The rest of the Philippians hymn cited above reads:

> Therefore God also highly exalted him
>   and gave him the name
>   that is above every name,
> so that at the name of Jesus
>   every knee should bend,
>   in heaven and on earth and under the earth,
> and every tongue should confess
>   that Jesus Christ is Lord,
>   to the glory of God the Father.
>
>   (Phil. 2:9–11)

The knees that bend in heaven and under the earth are the knees of the unseen powers whom the Victor has conquered. The earliest Christian confession—"Jesus is Lord" (Rom. 10:9; 1 Cor. 12:3)—is a confession of that victory.

With the confession of Christ the Victor, Jesus the Lord, the apostolic church has reclaimed and transformed the ancient picture of the Divine Warrior. His warfare is not with people or nations, but with the powers that thwart and distort human life. "Lord Sabaoth his name, . . . And he must win the battle."[17]

The Reconciler/Peacemaker

As Messiah, Jesus was Prince of Peace (Isa. 9:6). As Suffering Servant, "the chastisement of our peace was upon him; and with his stripes we are healed" (Isa. 53:5, KJV). As Victor, he defeated the spiritual forces that work against peace. In short, Jesus not only practiced and taught and recommended peace, but in some profound way he brought about peace for us and for the world through his death and resurrection. He is the Peacemaker. The church wrestles with this arresting theological insight in the following passage:

> Therefore, since we are justified by faith, we have peace with God through our Lord Jesus Christ, through whom we have obtained access to this grace in which we stand; and we boast in our hope of sharing the glory of God. . . . God proves his love for us in that while we still were sinners Christ died for us. Much more surely then, now that we have been justified by his blood, will we be saved through him from the wrath of God. For if while we were enemies, we were reconciled to God through the death of his Son, much more surely, having been reconciled, will we be saved by his life. But more than that, we even boast in God through our Lord Jesus Christ, through whom we have now received reconciliation. (Rom. 5:1–2, 8–11)

We remember that one aspect of the Warrior God remained constant in the prophets and in the teaching of Jesus: God's antagonistic warfare against his rebellious and unfaithful people. The suffering and death of the Messiah is God's offer of a cease-fire in that war, God's offer of terms of peace. It proves that God's love is even stronger than God's wrath.

It opens the way for reconciliation, one of the most important and beautiful of all biblical words.[18] Theologians have often preferred to speak of "justification," and it is a precise, courtroom word. But "reconciliation" is a heart word, with the pain of estrangement and the joy of return written all over it. It is Hosea remarrying his wayward wife. It is Yahweh standing in the ruins of Jerusalem and the ruins of the old covenant, offering a new covenant written on the heart. It is the comfortable word to Jerusalem that her warfare is over. It is the father falling on the neck of the prodigal son. "Peace with God" (Rom. 5:1) and "reconciliation" (v. 11) are synonymous in this passage. Both offer a present reality—"this grace in which we stand" (v. 2), "the reconciliation now received" (v. 11), and both hold out a future hope—"of sharing the glory of God" (v. 2), of ultimate salvation (v. 10).

> So if anyone is in Christ, there is a new creation; everything old has passed away; see, everything has become new! All this is from God, who reconciled us to himself through Christ, and has given us the ministry of reconciliation; that is, in Christ God was reconciling the world to himself, not counting their trespasses against them, and entrusting the message of reconciliation to us. (2 Cor. 5:17–19)

The old warfare between God and the world is gone; everything is new! The initiative in reconciliation is from God. It is not that the Suffering Servant/Messiah persuades God to be reconciled. God sets Christ forth as the reconciliation. God is at work *in* Christ. The scope of reconciliation is not limited to Israel or to the church. The world is reconciled, including all those enemies of Israel and the church against which the antagonistic warfare of God was formerly directed.

> For in him [the beloved Son] all the fullness of God was pleased to dwell, and through him God was pleased to reconcile to himself all things, whether on earth or in heaven, by making peace through the blood of his cross.
> And you who were once estranged and hostile in mind, doing evil deeds, he has now reconciled in his fleshly body through death, so as to present you holy and blameless and irreproachable before him. (Col. 1:19–22)

Here once again reconciling and making peace are synonyms. Peacemaking is not peripheral to Christianity, but anchored at its center, at the cross. And it involves not only the Colossian believers, who were once estranged and hostile in mind, not only the world as in 2 Corinthians, but "all things, whether on earth or in heaven." By the cross not only are all earthly peoples and kingdoms reconciled to God, but peace is made with God's most formidable enemies, the heavenly powers, the things "invisible whether thrones or dominions or rulers or powers" (Col. 1:16)!

In the passages considered thus far, the reconciliation wrought through the Servant/Messiah is, if we may use a spatial metaphor, vertical. It is reconciliation between believers and God, between the world and God, between the heavenly powers and God. But this vertical reconciliation has horizontal effects. It brings about horizontal reconciliation between warring factions of humanity.

> So then, remember that at one time you Gentiles by birth, called "the uncircumcision" by those who are called "the circumcision"—a physical circumcision made in the flesh by human hands—remember that you were at that time without Christ, being aliens from the commonwealth of Israel, and strangers to the covenants of promise, having no hope and without God in the world. But now in Christ Jesus you who once were far off have been brought near by the blood of Christ. For he is our peace; in his flesh he has made both groups into one and has broken down the dividing wall, that is, the hostility between us. He has abolished the law with its commandments and ordinances, that he might create in himself one new humanity in place of the two, thus making peace, and might reconcile both groups to God in one body through the cross, thus putting to death that hostility through it. So he came and proclaimed peace to you who were far off and peace to those who were near; for through him both of us have access in one Spirit to the Father. So then you are no longer strangers and aliens, but you are citizens with the saints and also members of the household of God, built upon the foundation of the apostles and prophets, with Christ Jesus himself as the cornerstone. In him the whole structure is joined together and grows into a holy temple in the Lord; in whom you also are built together spiritually into a dwelling place for God. (Eph. 2:11–22)

In the view of the writer to the Ephesians the most serious division within humanity was the division between Jews and Gentiles. It was prototypical of all the other divisions that divide us. It was the astounding work of the Servant/Messiah to reconcile that division. This horizontal reconciliation was possible only when it coincided with the vertical reconciliation. "One new humanity in place of the two" was possible only when both groups were reconciled to God "in one body through the cross" (vs. 15–16). Conversely, vertical reconciliation is incomplete if it does not impel us to the horizontal. "Peace with God" and war with other human groups cannot well coexist. Since in this passage "reconciling" and "making peace" are again synonyms, peacemaking between warring human groups can never be peripheral. The horizontal, as well as the vertical, is anchored at the very center of Christianity, at the cross.

The New Testament presents two moving symbols for what was effected by the cross. One is this: "The curtain of the temple was torn in two, from top to bottom" (Matt. 27:51; Mark 15:38; Luke 23:45). This was the curtain that hung before the Holy of Holies, that sacred place where only the high priest might enter, and he only on the Day of Atonement, covered with the blood of sacrifice. The cross removed the barrier between a holy God and sinful human beings, made atonement, gave access into that grace in which we stand.

The other symbol is the wall of separation, a wall in the temple beyond which Gentiles might not go. A piece of that wall has been recovered, with the inscription: NO MAN OF ANOTHER NATION MAY ENTER THE FENCE AND ENCLOSURE OF THIS TEMPLE, AND IF HE IS CAUGHT, HE HAS ONLY HIMSELF TO BLAME IF HIS DEATH ENSUES. The cross broke down that dividing wall between Jews and Gentiles, creating one new humanity in the place of two, thus making peace.

Summary

The apostolic church, in reflecting on Jesus the Messiah, the Suffering Servant, the Victor, came to understand him preeminently as the Peacemaker between God and humanity and between the divisions within humanity. This was expressed in the story that angels sang at his birth of peace on earth (Luke 2:14). It was expressed in the summary of Jesus' ministry in the apostolic preaching: "You know the message [God] sent to the people of Israel, preaching peace by Jesus Christ" (Acts 10:36). It was expressed in the words "He is our peace" (Eph. 2:14). "Yahweh is peace," said

Gideon. "This one will be peace," said Micah. "He is our peace," said the apostolic church.

That church was caught up in the biblical ambiguity, as chapter 10 has evidenced.[19] But, as is the case with Jesus, it is easy to see where the weight falls. That church did not wage war. It was a subversively different community within the Roman Empire. As the pressures against it grew and persecution increased, it was the power of apocalyptic hope that enabled it to remain faithful.

12

An Ambiguous Apocalypse

Just as the Old Testament contains a full-blown apocalypse in the book of Daniel, so the New Testament contains a full-blown apocalypse in the Revelation to John.[1] In it the hope that sustained the church as a subversively different community is expressed in full-blown apocalyptic imagery. The Revelation is so typical of apocalyptic writing that it is often called *the* Apocalypse.

The setting of the book is evidently an apocalyptic situation. The writer is in exile for his faith (Rev. 1:9). Martyrs have died for the faith and more martyrdoms are expected (2:13; 6:9–11). The Roman state, which appeared in Acts and in Romans 13 as a protector of Christians, now threatens them with persecution; it is satanic, called up out of the human mass and set over it by the dragon, that ancient serpent who is called the devil and Satan, the deceiver of the whole earth (12:9, 18); it is a beast, like the beasts in Daniel (13:1–8); it is a whore (17:1–18). The state has become blasphemous, claiming what belongs only to God (13:1, 5–6). A second beast, the state religion, compels people to worship the beast (13:4, 8, 12, 15). There is no hope for deliverance within history. Hope must center on an act of God beyond history, which human action can neither hasten nor delay.[2]

Other typical features of apocalyptic writing follow from the situation. The bulk of the book is a series of visions (Revelation 1; 4–22). Angels abound, carrying out divine commands, and sometimes explaining the visions to the seer. The book is in a code which the persecutor will not understand, but the persecuted will, for example, Babylon = Rome. Indeed the key to the code is the Old Testament; the Apocalypse is saturated with Old Testament allusions. Numbers are prominent, numbers with hidden meanings (see the many series of seven: seven seals, seven trumpets, seven thunders, seven bowls; also the number of the beast in 13:18).[3]

The Apocalypse is not escapist literature or a guidebook for futurists. It is explicit political criticism.[4] It is protest literature.[5] It is a stark protest against all compromise, against the "that's the way the world is" attitude that we noted in chapter 10.[6] Its message is that in the struggle, God is not neutral.[7]

War in the Apocalypse

The Revelation to John is clearly the most warlike book in the New Testament. When the Lamb opens the scroll of human history (Revelation 5), out come the four horsemen of the Apocalypse (6:1–8). The rider on the white horse is a warrior with a bow and he comes out conquering and to conquer. The rider on the red horse is permitted to take peace from the earth, so that people will slaughter one another, and is given a great sword. The rider on the black horse brings inflation in the wake of war. And the rider on the pale green horse is Death: death by the sword, by famine, by disease. Human history is to be a history of wars.

Heaven itself is not exempt from war. There is war in heaven between Michael and his angels and the dragon and his angels (12:7). We are reminded of the heavenly army of Yahweh in ancient Israelite poetry, which battled most often against the enemies of Israel, but on occasion against the dragon of primeval chaos (see above, chapter 4). Michael and his forces win and the dragon and his forces are cast down to the earth (12:8–9). Unable to destroy the woman he has been pursuing (Israel? the church?), the dragon goes off to make war on the rest of her children (12:17).

The final conflict, which we met in Old Testament apocalyptic, is here again. Curiously, it is here twice. The beast and the kings of the earth with their armies gather to make war at Harmagedon (16:12–

16). The rider on the white horse whose name is The Word of God comes forth to meet them (19:11–16). The rider and his army win the battle, the beast and his false prophet are thrown alive into the lake of fire, and the army of the beast is slaughtered, making a great supper for the birds of the air (19:17–21). Then the devil is bound for a thousand years (20:1–6). After the thousand years the devil is released and a second final battle is fought. The devil rallies nations from the four corners of the earth (echoes of Gog and Magog in Ezekiel 38–39) and attacks the camp of the saints and the beloved city. This time fire comes down from heaven and consumes the army; the devil joins the beast and the false prophet in the lake of fire (Rev. 20:7–10).

In addition to these visions of warfare, the Apocalypse is filled with series of woes and calamities. The opening of the sixth seal brings a devastating earthquake plus commotion in the heavenly bodies (6:12–16). The first four trumpets bring the destruction of a third of the earth, a third of the sea, a third of the rivers, a third of the sun, moon, and stars (8:6–12). The fifth trumpet brings a plague of locusts, reminiscent of Joel (9:1–11). The sixth trumpet brings an angelic army with two hundred million cavalry, who kill a third of humankind (9:13–19). The first five bowls of God's wrath bring five plagues reminiscent of the plagues of Egypt in Exodus (16:1–10). Earthquakes come again and again, accompanied by thunder, lightning, smoke, fire, and hail (8:5; 11:13, 19; 16:18–21). In Isaiah 45:7, Yahweh says, "I make weal (*shalom*) and create woe." The emphasis in the Apocalypse falls on the woe. God seems to be at war with the whole earth. It is worth noting that the earthquakes and their accompaniments are echoes of various stories in the holy war tradition.

As the book moves to its climax, it becomes clear that the great object of God's wrath is Babylon = Rome. The lament over Babylon (18:1–19:4) calls to mind the lament over Nineveh in Nahum or over Tyre in Ezekiel 26–28. Interestingly, and in contrast to the Old Testament parallels, there is no vision of the warfare that will bring down "Babylon." We only have the metaphor of a big splash, a great millstone thrown into the sea (18:21). But the gloating over the enemy's fall is exactly like the gloating of the prophets in Old Testament taunt songs. Hallelujahs go up to God for God's vengeance on the great beast, the great whore.

What is perhaps most disturbing of all is the warlike picture of Jesus in the Apocalypse. In the initial vision that opens the book, Jesus has a sharp, two-edged sword coming out of his mouth (1:16; cf. 2:12, 16). The Son of David idea is revived (3:7; 22:16). In the great vision of the worship in heaven, we meet "the Lion of the tribe of Judah, the Root of David" (5:5). In another vision, the Human One has a sharp sickle in his hand with which he reaps the earth. When an angel also reaps, blood flows as high as a horse's bridle for a distance of two hundred miles (14:14–20). In the final battle the rider on the white horse is clearly the Messiah. His name is Faithful and True, the Word of God, King of kings and Lord of lords. His description resembles the initial vision: eyes like a flame of fire, a sharp sword coming out of his mouth. Allusions to the messianic prophecies and psalms abound. In righteousness he judges and makes war (19:11–16).

The ambiguity, of course, is that the most prominent name for Jesus in the Apocalypse is "the Lamb," often "the Lamb that was slaughtered" (5:6, 8, 12, 13; 6:1, 16; 7:9, 10, 14, 17; 12:11; 13:8; 14:1, 4, 10; 15:3; 17:14; 19:7, 9; 21:9, 14, 22, 23, 27; 22:1, 3). The reference to the Suffering Servant (Isa. 53:7) is clear enough. He is the one who conquers by "reverse fighting," by accepting suffering rather than by causing others to suffer. T. R. Hobbs, who sees the New Testament as "transforming" the holy war tradition of the Old, finds in the "helpless figure" of the slain Lamb, standing as the meaning of history, the completion of the transformation.[8]

Peace in the Apocalypse

This warlike book contains amazing visions of peace. They are of two kinds.

The first kind is visions of a peace that coexists with war and woe. It exists at the same time, but in a different place. Alongside the reality of human history with its strife and distress, there is another reality, the heavenly reality, where all is properly ordered and unceasing worship surrounds the throne. It is visions of that heavenly reality, brought back by the seer, that enable believers suffering the stress and hopelessness of history to remain faithful and endure to the end.

The seer is "in the Spirit on the Lord's day" (Rev. 1:10). He is aware of the worship taking place in the seven churches of Asia Minor. It is flawed worship in a world of violence and persecution. The churches have variously abandoned their first love (2:4), are facing imprisonment (v. 10), have embraced heresy (v. 15), are involved in fornication and idolatry (vs. 14, 20), are more dead than alive (3:1), have but little power (v. 8), are neither cold nor hot (v. 15). But then, on another level, it is given him to see the magnificent worship before the great throne in heaven (chs. 4–5). This worship is the hidden dimension of the tawdry earthly worship of the seven churches!

The series of the seven seals, as we have seen, reveals human history as a history of war and disaster, in which the martyrs cry out: "How long?" But the climax is another scene before the throne where those same martyrs join in the heavenly worship and are blessed with peace: shelter, no hunger, no thirst, no scorching heat. The Lamb will be their shepherd, leading them to springs of the water of life, "and God will wipe away every tear from their eyes" (7:17). This peace is the hidden dimension of human history with all its terrors!

The series of seven trumpets is similar. The first four bring unparalleled disasters, but then we are warned that the last three will be worse (8:13). The fifth and sixth are terrible indeed, but the seventh is a surprise: once again the curtain rises on the worship in heaven and Handel's "Hallelujah Chorus" is sung, declaring that "the kingdom of the world has become the kingdom of our Lord and of his Messiah, and he will reign forever and ever" (11:15).

Following the terrifying vision of the two beasts is a vision of the Lamb and the Lamb's elect, standing in safety and peace on Mount Zion (14:1–5).

The other kind of vision is the vision of final peace. Like the visions in Isaiah 65:17–25 and Zechariah 8:1–8, the vision of final peace in the Apocalypse centers on a city. The Apocalypse is a "tale of two cities": the earthly city of Babylon = Rome, which must be destroyed, and the heavenly city, the new Jerusalem, which in the end comes down to earth (21:1–22:5).[9]

There is peace between this city and God: no more antagonistic warfare, no more bowls of God's wrath. The covenant of peace so often promised in the Old Testament, and especially in Ezekiel—I will be your God, and you shall be my people—is realized in the new Jerusalem (21:3, 7). Its reality is signified by God's dwelling in the city (21:3); the throne of God and of the Lamb will be there, and the heavenly worship glimpsed throughout the book will now take place on earth in the new Jerusalem (22:3); God's servants in the city will see God's face and God's name will be on their foreheads (22:4). God and the Lamb will be the temple of the city (21:22), the light of the city (21:23; 22:5), the source of the city's water (21:6; 22:1).

In this city there will be no more tears, no more death, no more mourning and crying and pain (21:4), no more uncleanness (21:8, 27; 22:3), no more night (21:23; 22:5).

No longer will there be fear of hostile enemies: the city's gates will never be shut (21:25). One of the most remarkable statements is that "the kings of the earth will bring their glory into it" (21:24). "The kings of the earth" are big in Revelation. They are all over it. They are big and they are bad. They are cowards. When the Lamb opens the sixth seal and there is a great earthquake, the kings of the earth run and hide in caves from the face of God and the wrath of the Lamb (6:15–17). They are on the devil's side: the demons assemble them at Harmagedon to do battle with the Lamb (16:14, 16). Three times it is said that the kings of the earth commit fornication with the great harlot, the city of greed and lust (17:2; 18:3, 9). But in the end the kings of the earth bring their glory, their wealth and power, into the holy city. God has transformed enemies into friends and servants. Likewise "people will bring into it the glory and the honor of the nations" (21:26). Here is the ultimate extension of *shalom*. The nations, who have always been on the outside, no part of the people of God, are now on the inside.

The agricultural theme that marks so many visions of peace is not totally lost, for in the city there are trees on either side of the river that runs down the middle of the street. It is the tree of life, which we last saw in the Garden of Eden (Gen. 2:9; 3:22). It bears twelve kinds of fruit, one for each month, and its leaves are for the healing of the nations (Rev. 22:2).

The Role of God's People

At first glance it seems that the ambiguity regarding war and peace, which is so sharp in the Old Testament, has been resharpened in the Apocalypse. The ambiguity fades somewhat in the Gospels and epistles, but it returns with a vengeance in the Revelation to John. God creates more woe than weal. The Lamb makes war.

But there is no rallying cry here, as there was in the old days of holy war, for the people of God to come out and do battle. They are mainly spectators, not participants in the warfare.[10] Jesus' word to Peter in the garden (Matt. 26:52) is virtually repeated in Revelation 13:10, "If you kill with the sword, with the sword you must be killed."[11]

The people of God are not passive. They are urged to "conquer" (2:7, 11, 17, 26; 3:5, 12, 21), but they conquer, not by aggressive warfare, but by patient endurance, faithfulness, holding fast (1:9; 2:2–3, 10, 13, 19, 25; 3:10; 13:10; 14:12). They do indeed struggle with Satan, their accuser, but they conquer him "by the blood of the Lamb and by the word of their testimony, for they did not cling to life even in the face of death" (12:11). The fighting of the saints in the Revelation to John is "reverse fighting": enduring suffering, not inflicting it. That the Lamb that was slain opens the scroll means "that the cross and not the sword, suffering and not brute power determines the meaning of history."[12]

The Apocalypse, then, for all the din of battle in its pages, does not represent a turning back from the clear direction of the New Testament which we noted in chapter 11. There is remaining ambiguity here, to be sure. The angels, who are God's servants, send great suffering on the earth. The gates of the city are open, but the wicked are excluded. Alongside the new Jerusalem is the lake of fire. We have met the ineradicable ambiguity between God's wrath and love before. But the church's role is clear. Revelation expresses the faith that sustained the church in its faithfulness to Jesus' teaching. It expresses the hope that God's promises of victory are reliable no matter "how long" (6:9–11)[13] it takes for them to come true.

Conclusion

The Abolition of War

Neither shall they learn war any more.
(Micah 4:3)

The LORD makes wars cease to the end
of the earth.
(Ps. 46:9)

We do not wage war according to
human standards.
(2 Cor. 10:3)

I'm gonna lay down my sword and
shield
    down by the riverside. . . .
Ain't gonna study war no more.
(African American spiritual)

Conclusion: The Abolition of War

In trying to face honestly the painful ambiguity of the Bible regarding war and peace, we have made quite a pilgrimage. We started, not at the beginning, but at the center of scripture, and in chapters 1 and 2 we faced up to the ambiguity of Jesus in regard to this issue. The preponderance of the evidence, we said, indicates that Jesus taught and practiced the way of peace. Then we asked how he, nurtured and schooled in the Hebrew scriptures, could come to such a position. We spent chapters 3 through 8 on the considerable ambiguity that marks the Old Testament. In chapter 9 we decided that Jesus did not offer a Hegelian synthesis of the Old Testament thesis and antithesis; he made a clear choice, standing with the prophets, and especially with the prophetic picture of the Suffering Servant. In chapters 10 through 12 we noted that the apostolic church had it own ambiguities, but essentially stood with its Lord in the way of peace. The Apocalypse, for all its warlike passages, does not contradict this.

It remains for us to trace, in the barest outline form, the subsequent history of war/peace teaching and practice in the church, and to ask where we should go from here.

From Peace to Just War

The church of the first three centuries lived with the ambiguity of scripture as Jesus and the apostolic church had done: by making a clear choice. It was a peaceful, nonviolent church, whose members by and large did not engage in warfare.[1]

With the exception of Cornelius in the book of Acts, there is virtually no mention of Christians in the army until 170–180 C.E. Most Christians belonged to the underclasses and were not Roman citizens. They were not subject to the draft or even eligible to enlist. Christian writers of this early period mention war and peace in only the most general terms.

Beginning around 170–180 there are allusions to Christians in the army. There were more on the far eastern borders of the empire than in the near east, more in Rome than in North Africa. The numbers increased in the third century, but we have no way of knowing just how many there were. One thing we do know is that the Christian writers of this period were unanimous in condemning Christian participation in warfare. Some sanctioned peacetime service in the army, but all found killing forbidden by the law of love. Tertullian is typical with his saying: "The Lord, in disarming Peter, unbelted every soldier without exception."[2]

There was a crisis in the fourth century. Constantine emerged as a champion of the recently persecuted Christians. He claimed the help of the Christian God in defeating other claimants to the imperial throne, and many Christians cheered the military victories that consolidated his power. Once in power he chose Christianity as the religion that would unify his empire, and showered favors on the church. The church experienced rapid growth. Constantine placed the cross on army standards and many Christians flocked into the army. Meanwhile, barbarians threatened to destroy the empire which had maintained the Pax Romana. Many Christians began to see the situation as church and Rome versus barbarians and heathen. Augustine, who had been a severe critic of Rome's reliance on war and violence, came to feel that if the emperor was a Christian, Christians should fight in Rome's defense. To justify this, Augustine turned to the Old Testament wars. The side of scriptural ambiguity that Jesus and the early church had rejected was now chosen afresh. The people of God had once fought and they could fight again, but they must fight justly.

In framing the just war theory, Augustine drew, not only on the Old Testament but also on Cicero and other classical sources. He even drew on the love ethic of the New Testament, maintaining that

Christians could and should love their enemies, even in the act of killing them in battle. Just war could be ordered only by a Christian ruler. Its intent should be to restore peace and vindicate justice. Its conduct should be just: no breaking faith, looting, massacre, profanation of temples, conflagrations. Its mood should be somber, full of regret that such is necessary.

The just war theory was neither fish nor fowl. It was not a return to the holy war, which never spoke of loving enemies while killing them. And it was not a continuation of the choice made by Jesus and the apostolic church. That choice lived on in monasticism: the religious, those who seriously followed Christ, still could not fight.

Just war was further refined by Thomas Aquinas, who introduced such ideas as "proportionality" (the costs of war must be in reasonable proportion to the good that is to be achieved) and "discrimination" (war's destruction must not be directed against civilian populations or noncombatants). Just war is still the official position of Roman Catholicism and the major Protestant bodies. It has resulted in centuries of slaughter of Christians by Christians, not to mention crusades against Islam. The Reformation lost even the reminder of monastic pacifism and wrote just war into its creeds.[3] The ensuing religious wars almost destroyed Europe.

The bankruptcy of just war is evident. It has seldom prevented wars, because "Christian" nations always reason that their cause is just. Individual Christians who judge that a particular war is not just cannot be exempted from military service on that basis, even in nations that do exempt objectors to all war. Just war criteria have been contradicted by every war in this century. Nuclear war would only make clear what has already happened to proportionality and discrimination at Coventry, Dresden, the firebombing of Tokyo, the destruction of Baghdad, and "low-intensity warfare" in Central America.

The Abolition of War

If this is true, what should replace just war thinking? Does this particular attempt to face the Bible in all its ambiguity suggest a course of action in this day when it seems probable that warriors possess the power to end human history and reduce the planet to "a republic of insects and grass"?[4]

One alternative has just been mentioned: refusal to participate in any war. Most churches support individual members who take this position, usually called conscientious objection. Many nations assign such objectors alternate service under very severe limits. It is a costly and courageous witness. I would conclude from our study that, despite biblical ambiguity, it can claim biblical authority. Sadly, it leaves the war system intact.

Another alternative has roots in the radical wing of the Reformation and is powerfully articulated by Mennonite theologians in our own day. It involves individual conscientious objection, but goes on to make a corporate witness. Jesus threatened the corrupt society of his day, not by programs and goals, but by creating a new kind of community leading a radically new kind of life. Just so, the church in our day is called to witness, not by pronouncements and demonstrations, but by patient subordination and willing suffering as a peaceful community in a warring world.[5] As Vernard Eller expresses it, the church is called to be a rock in the whirlpool, simply by its existence deflecting the currents and changing the vectors of history.[6]

The position of Stanley Hauerwas and William H. Willimon in *Resident Aliens*[7] is strikingly similar. The post-Constantinian era began, Willimon wryly remarks, when the Fox Theater stayed open on Sunday evening in 1963 in Greenville, South Carolina. Since then the church can no longer see itself as part of the Empire, sharing power and even dictating policy. The church is rather a colony of aliens, confessing and practicing a different way of life.

There is much to ponder in this position. Certainly the era of Constantine is over and should have been over long ago. Certainly it is the height of hypocrisy for the church to try to clean up the state's act before it cleans up its own, and to rely on the state to make its own members behave, as in Sunday blue laws in Greenville, South Carolina. Certainly there is power in simply being the church.

Nevertheless, I think there is a step we can take beyond individual conscientious objection and corporate existence as an alien colony within the Empire. I think we can share a dream with the Empire. Those without status or portfolio can still dream, and their dreams can have strange power, like the dream of Martin Luther King, Jr. We can badger the Empire with that dream, refuse to be silent about it.

I would propose that our dream be the abolition of war. Not just the Nuclear Freeze or Reversing the Arms Race or a Comprehensive Test Ban, but the Abolition of War.[8]

The end of the cold war has not made this dream any less urgent. The dissolution of the Soviet Union and the dismantling of the Warsaw Pact have produced a false sense of security. As long as any nuclear arms remain, or as long as the knowledge of how to make them remains, and that is from now on, there is the clear and present danger that earthlings may destroy the earth. Nothing short of the abolition of war as a means for settling international disputes will effectively reduce that danger.

No Romanticism

When we propose the abolition of war as a substitute for just war, we are not proposing the total fulfillment of the Isaiah/Micah dream. The abolition of war would not be *shalom*. We know now that *shalom* is far wider and deeper than that. We know that only God can bring *shalom*. To achieve the abolition of war would not be to bring in the kingdom by human ingenuity. It would merely be a practical, imperfect step in honor of the kingdom, a distant approach to *shalom*.

It would not mean the beating of all swords into plowshares. Some weapons would remain. It would not mean the end of all force. Police force would remain. It would not mean the end of all fear, for the possible misuse and corruption of police force are to be feared. It would not mean the end of all oppression, for economic and political oppression can flourish even in the absence of war.

It would mean the end of soldiers' deaths; no more Vietnam monuments where grieving friends and relatives run their fingers over thousands of engraved names. It would mean the end of the slaughter of hundreds of thousands of civilians who are simply caught in "collateral damage." It would mean the end of the intentional conditioning of young men and women who are not naturally killers to kill. It would mean the end of the enormous financial burden of armaments, over a billion dollars a day, which bleeds the world's poor into perpetual and deepening poverty. It would mean the end of "national security states," of military dictatorships that thwart the hopes and dreams of newly freed nations in the developing world. It would mean the end of the control of industrialized nations by an unelected military-industrial complex, which effectively rules regardless of the party in power. And the end of much else.

Some Analogies

An analogy, of course, is the abolition of slavery. It did not bring in the kingdom of God. It did not mean the end of racism, which is alive and well all over the world today. It did not mean the end of segregation. And where segregation has legally ended, genuine equality of opportunity has not yet been achieved, nor is a genuinely multiracial society a reality, nor is there equal protection under the law.

But it did mean the end of human beings owning other human beings, with its dehumanizing effect on both owned and owner. It did mean the end of working for nothing. It did mean the end of the forced breakup and separation of families. It did mean the end of no protection under the law.

The institution of chattel slavery extended as far back into human history and prehistory as war. It was as unquestioned a part of life. The Bible is as ambiguous about slavery as it is about war. If anything, the texts supporting it are more numerous, and the texts opposing it are fewer in number. There were probably far more eloquent and learned sermons in defense of slavery, preached on biblical texts, than have ever been preached in defense of war. But the church, without rejecting scripture, made a choice. All humanity made a choice. And slavery, with a few exceptions (the slave labor of prisoners is one), is gone. The texts are still there, but I know of no one who is presently advocating a return to the "peculiar institution" on the basis of those texts.

In my lifetime many of those texts were dusted off and used in defense of segregation. I heard them all quoted on the floor of church courts, read them all again in church papers. But there were other texts in the blessed ambiguity of the Bible. The church of which I am a part made a choice, and the nation of which I am a part made a choice. Today only the far, far right of the Ku Klux Klan and the Aryan Nation is advocating a return to segregation based on those texts. They have been used in the defense of apartheid in South Africa, but apartheid seems on the verge of collapse.

The Bible is equally ambiguous about patriarchy, the uninhibited domination of females by males. Thanks to courageous women, the struggle against patriarchy is under way. Many churches have renounced it in word, if not in practice. Others cling to it, claiming biblical authority. In the secular arena much remains to be achieved. But the yeast which those women have mixed in the dough is rising! Once again the biblical ambiguity is going to be resolved by a choice.

Getting There

Returning to the abolition of war, can we map out a scenario for moving from the deeply entrenched war system to "studying war no more"? It would take another book, or series of books to enumerate the political, economic, religious, psychological, cultural steps that would need to be taken to get there. Such a book is beyond the bounds of this volume, beyond the bounds of any expertise I have. I suspect it is beyond the competence of those who are considered expert in such matters.

Some broad, idealistic strokes can perhaps be derived from the Isaiah/Micah vision with which this book began and which we analyzed in chapter 8. There will need to be *torah,* instruction, which when taken to heart will produce important psychological, religious, and cultural change. There will need to be *adjudication*, a way of settling disputes between strong nations without resorting to the arbitration of arms. There will need to be *conversion* of weapons of war to instruments of peace, conversion also of research and development for war to research and development for peace. There will need to be *economic justice*, land reform, the attempt to give more of the world's people access to the means of production and a stake in the commonwealth.

The practical difficulties are staggering. What is urged here is simply that the goal of abolishing war be seriously considered. That we cannot produce a blueprint or describe the process from beginning to end is no excuse for not taking the first steps. If this is a move, however distant and incomplete, toward God's *shalom*, we can trust God to shed light as we turn each corner in a long and circuitous route.

The Uses of Ambiguity

A basic reason why the church has not shared the dream of the abolition of war with the Empire, has spoken of it timidly if at all, is a sense, sometimes inarticulate but very real, of the enormous ambiguity of scripture. If our basic authority is so full of war, can we speak to the world, or even to ourselves about the abolition of war? On the other hand, if peace is so urgent in scripture, can we keep silent and just "be the church"? That is why I have attempted in this book to face that ambiguity head on.

Paul D. Hanson has argued that ambiguity, which he calls the diversity or polarity of scripture, is not a theological disadvantage, but a theological advantage.[9] It moves our focus from the Book to the God to whom the Book testifies. It shifts our vision from past events to God's great purpose that has marched through those events and marches into the future. Scripture does not give us the unchanging, cut-and-dried instructions for the problems of our day that we often desire. Because of its diversity and polarity, scripture questions us and demands of us decisions, much as the parables of Jesus questioned his hearers and demanded that they take a stand.

I find, and I hope my readers will find, that the ambiguity of the Bible regarding war and peace questions us and demands that we take a stand. We can no longer say, "Because there has always been war, there will always be war. Because Israel was a warlike people, fighting wars, we must be warlike and fight. Because God is reputed to have ordered them to fight, God must be ordering us to fight." The Bible is more ambiguous than that. The God of the Bible promises to do, and does "new things." We cannot claim the authority of scripture for saying that the abolition of war is impossible. It is certainly as possible and as scriptural as the abolition of slavery or the abolition of patriarchy.[10]

Living in the Meantime

The abolition of war will not take place next Tuesday. It may be a long time coming with many false steps and turnings along the way. As resident aliens we have little clout for bringing it about, no campaign plans, no carefully honed set of objectives, and no timetable. How shall we live in the meantime? The biblical ambiguity again questions us, demands a decision. Will we live out of the past with its wars and rumors of wars? Will we live by a prudential ethic, calculated to make survival as likely as possible? Or will we follow the prophets in saying that it is the future actions of God that must determine our present conduct? Without denying the importance, the historical truth, the literary power of the biblical war passages, we can choose to live from God's promises of the final victory of *shalom.*

God promises a world where weapons of war are converted into implements of peace, where research and development for war, military training camps and war colleges are no more, where war is abolished and people live in their homes and gardens without fear. Will we dare to live now as though that were already true? God promises the kingdom of God with its great reversal! Will we dare to live now as though things were already reversed? God promises the New Jerusalem with trees whose leaves are for the healing of the nations, where even the kings of the earth finally deposit their treasures, and where the gates are never shut. Will we dare to live now as though our cities could be that city?

The Sermon on the Mount has been called an eschatological ethic in the sense that it is totally impractical until Christ comes again and establishes his eternal kingdom. I am suggesting that it is an eschatological ethic in the sense that it calls us to live right now as though the kingdom of Christ were already established: to live in purity and faithfulness and honesty; to keep our good deeds secret; to rely on God for all we need; to be nonjudgmental, constant in prayer, hearing and doing the word of God; to live the disarmed, forgiving, nonviolent life.

Because the kingdom has not fully come, the disarmed, forgiving, nonviolent life seems impractical and highly risky. We shall be called fools. But who is to say that the armed, vengeful, violent life is more practical or less risky? Or that we can tolerate it, once we have caught a vision of *shalom?*

Notes

Introduction: Paralyzing Ambiguity

1. A full discussion of Micah 4:3–4 and its parallel in Isa. 2 will be found in chapter 8.

2. *The Challenge of Peace: God's Promise and Our Response* (Washington, D.C.: United States Catholic Conference, 1983).

3. *In Defense of Creation: The Nuclear Crisis and a Just Peace* (Nashville: Graded Press, 1986).

4. Not all evangelicals are in this camp. Among the most courageous voices for peace are those of evangelicals like Ronald J. Sider and Jim Wallis. See Sider's "An Evangelical Witness for Peace" in *Preaching on Peace*, which he edited with Darrel J. Brubacher (Philadelphia: Fortress Press, 1982), pp. 25–28; and Wallis's collection of articles from the magazine *Sojourners*, which he edits, entitled *Waging Peace* (San Francisco: Harper & Row, 1982).

5. For a penetrating analysis of the psychological and cultural reasons, see the writings of Sam Keen, particularly *Faces of the Enemy* (San Francisco: Harper & Row, 1986).

6. To say that scripture is ambiguous is not to slander it. Equivocation is saying two opposite things with intent to deceive; but ambiguity may arise out of the way words function and the way things are. The historical process is by nature ambiguous. The intention of the biblical writers is often ambiguous, like all human intentionality. The mystery of God's will remains ambiguous to our understanding.

7. One of the fairest and most rigorous wrestles with biblical ambiguity known to me is Willard M. Swartley's *Slavery, Sabbath, War and Women* (Scottdale, Pa.: Herald Press, 1983).

8. Paul D. Hanson, *The Dawn of Apocalyptic* (Philadelphia: Fortress Press, 1975), esp. pp. 411–413; *The Diversity of Scripture* (Philadelphia: Fortress Press, 1982).

9. Paul D. Hanson, "War and Peace in the Hebrew Bible," *Interpretation* 38 (1984): 347–362.

10. Jean Lasserre, *War and the Gospel* (Scottdale, Pa.: Herald Press, 1974), pp. 23–24.

11. T. R. Hobbs, *A Time for War* (Wilmington, Del.: Michael Glazier, 1989), pp. 222–233.

12. A good example of this is in Harry Emerson Fosdick, *A Guide to Understanding the Bible: The Development of Ideas Within the Old and New Testaments* (New York: Harper & Brothers, 1938), pp. 1–54.

13. Peter C. Craigie, *The Problem of War in the Old Testament* (Grand Rapids: Wm. B. Eerdmans Publishing Co., 1978), pp. 107–112.

14. Reinhold Niebuhr, *Moral Man and Immoral Society* (New York: Charles Scribner's Sons, 1932).

15. Here I am advocating a canonical approach on a practical basis: if we want a "level playing field" in debates about the Bible and war and peace, we need to start with a common definition of what constitutes the Bible, what can be quoted in the argument. There are, of course, more profound biblical and theological reasons for a canonical approach. See the work of Brevard S. Childs, notably *An Introduction to the Old Testament as Scripture* (1979); *The New Testament as Canon* (1984); *Old Testament Theology in a Canonical Context* (1986). See also the work of James A. Sanders, notably *Torah and Canon* (1972); *Canon and Community* (1984); *From Sacred Story to Sacred Text* (1987). All books cited here were published by Fortress Press in Philadelphia.

16. This is the method followed by Vernard Eller in *War and Peace from Genesis to Revelation* (Scottdale, Pa.: Herald Press, 1981). J. Carter Swaim in *War, Peace, and the Bible* (Maryknoll, N.Y.: Orbis Books, 1982) moves back and forth between the Testaments, but starts with the Old.

17. Lamar Williamson, Jr., agrees that Jesus is "the hermeneutical key" to the discrepancy between the Old and New Testaments. See "Jesus of the Gospels and the Christian Vision of Shalom," *Horizons in Biblical Theology* 6 (1984): 1–26.

18. Ulrich Mauser, *The Gospel of Peace* (Louisville, Ky.: Westminster/John Knox Press, 1991), p. 35.

1. Jesus: "Not Peace, but a Sword"

1. This, as much that is said in this chapter, is a "surface" interpretation, making the kind of case that peace through strength advocates would find congenial. For a deeper analysis and a defense of contemporary tax resistance, see Lamar Williamson, Jr., "Limits on a Christian's Obedience to the State" and George R. Edwards, "Biblical and Contemporary Aspects of War Tax Resistance" in *The Peacemaking Struggle: Militarism and Resistance,* ed. Ronald H. Stone and Dana W. Wilbanks (Lanham, Md.: University Press of America, 1985), pp. 103–122. Also Christopher Rowland, *Radical Christianity* (Maryknoll, N.Y.: Orbis Books, 1988), pp. 24–25. For an interpretation "from below," from the standpoint of the world's oppressed, see José Cardenas Pellares, *A Poor Man Called Jesus* (Maryknoll, N.Y.: Orbis Books, 1986), pp. 72–76.

2. John Howard Yoder suggests that the swords, while inadequate for defense, were essential to the fulfillment of prophecy. Two swords were enough to make Jesus formally guilty of attempted insurrection, the charge that led to his crucifixion. Thus "he was counted among the lawless." See *The Politics of Jesus* (Grand Rapids: Wm. B. Eerdmans Publishing Co., 1972), pp. 54, 56.

3. Pacifists have often been eager to explain these passages in ways that eliminate any compromise of Jesus with violence. See, for example, John Ferguson, *The Politics of Love* (Nyack, N.Y.: Fellowship Publications, 1979). I have preferred to accept genuine ambiguity as a part of Jesus' authentic humanity. Thus I have let the passages stand and admitted the possibility of nonpacifist interpretations.

4. Robert Eisler, IESOUS BASILEUS OU BASILEUSAS, 2 vols. (Heidelberg: Carl Winter, 1929–30).

5. S. G. F. Brandon, *Jesus and the Zealots: A Study of the Political Factor in Primitive Christianity* (New York: Charles Scribner's Sons, 1967).

6. George R. Edwards specifically and effectively refuted Brandon in *Jesus and the Politics of Violence* (New York: Harper & Row, 1972).

2. Jesus: "Put Away Your Sword"

1. Carol Frances Jegan points out that this was the last of Jesus' healing miracles, strangely omitted from the usual lists. More than any other it helps us comprehend something of Jesus' commitment to nonviolence and forgiveness of enemies. See her *Jesus the Peacemaker* (Kansas City, Mo.: Sheed & Ward, 1986), pp. 26–27.

2. This saying is missing in some of the most important ancient manuscripts.

3. Israel: Warlike People

1. The vexed question as to the historicity of the "conquest" will be discussed in chapter 4.

2. The problem of the historicity of Sennacherib's "defeat" will be discussed in chapter 4, note 3.

3. The Egyptian army was on its way, possibly to Carchemish, to assist the declining power of Assyria (Nineveh had already fallen) against the rising power of Babylon. See John Bright, *A History of Israel* (Philadelphia: Westminster Press, 1959), p. 303. Jeremiah, however, dates the battle of Carchemish later, in the fourth year of King Jehoiakim (Jer. 46:2).

4. T. R. Hobbs in *A Time for War* (Wilmington, Del.: Michael Glazier, 1989) half-humorously criticizes the title of a book by his fellow Canadian Peter C. Craigie, *The Problem of War in the Old Testament* (Grand Rapids: Wm. B. Eerdmans Publishing Co., 1978). War may be a problem to us, he says, but it was never a problem to the ancient Israelites. It was taken for granted as a part of life (see p. 17).

5. For example, Jonathan Schell, *The Fate of the Earth* (New York: Alfred A. Knopf, 1982).

4. Yahweh: Warrior God

1. It is difficult to determine the historical kernel, if any, in these stories. In them, the king of Israel is not named. With them should be compared a similar story in 2 Chronicles 20, which bears many marks of the Chronicler's invention. Historical or not, these stories preserve the ancient exodus faith, that the LORD can deliver the people without their fighting at all. Note particularly 2 Chronicles 20:17, "This battle is not for you to fight; take your position, stand still, and see the victory of the LORD on your behalf, O Judah and Jerusalem."

2. From "The Destruction of Sennacherib" by Lord Byron. The entire poem reveals a genuine understanding of what we have called monergistic war.

3. After Hezekiah bought off the invader with the temple treasures (2 Kings 18:14–16), did Sennacherib return on the same expedition and besiege Jerusalem? Or were there two expeditions, one in 701 B.C.E., and another sometime after 690? Or is the whole account of Sennacherib's

defeat a fiction? Brevard Childs in *Isaiah and the Assyrian Crisis* (Naperville, Ill.: Alec R. Allenson, 1967) has surveyed the Assyrian annals and made a form-critical analysis of all the relevant biblical passages. He concludes that the historical problem has no easy or conclusive solution.

4. Psalm 109 is so vengeful that the translators of the *NRSV* have added "They say" in verse 6 in order to remove the terrible words that follow from the psalmist's lips and place them on the lips of the enemy, but there is no basis in the original for "They say."

5. Walter Brueggemann, *The Message of the Psalms* (Minneapolis: Augsburg Publishing House, 1984), pp. 81–88.

6. These psalms in general fall into Brueggemann's classification, "psalms of disorientation," though some he would classify as "psalms of new orientation" (ibid.).

7. To this might be added the curse on Meroz in Judges 5:23. Lind, however, holds that Meroz was no part of Israel; its inhabitants were non-Israelites who lived among and were friendly with the Israelites. See Millard C. Lind, *Yahweh Is a Warrior* (Scottdale, Pa.: Herald Press, 1980), pp. 71–72.

8. See Patrick D. Miller, Jr., *The Divine Warrior in Early Israel* (Cambridge, Mass.: Harvard University Press, 1973), pp. 67, 98.

9. Lind argues convincingly that this is an ancient story, predating the work of the Deuteronomic historian. *Yahweh Is a Warrior*, pp. 96–97.

10. As Walter Brueggemann puts it, Yahweh and Yahweh alone equalizes the struggle between lightly armed David and heavily armed Goliath. See *David's Truth in Israel's Imagination and Memory* (Philadelphia: Fortress Press, 1985), p. 34.

11. Brueggemann would say that what was issued in this case was not a command, but a permit, a legitimization of the desire of the oppressed for freedom from oppression. Horses and chariots are the instruments of oppression and marginalized Israel is authorized to hamstring the horses and burn the chariots (Josh. 11:6). See *Revelation and Violence: A Study in Contextualization* (Milwaukee: Marquette University Press, 1986).

12. Albrecht Alt, "Erwägungen über die Landnahme der Israeliten in Palestina," 1939, in *Kleine Schriften zur Geschichte des Volkes Israel*, vol. 1 (Munich: C. H. Beck'sche Verlagsbuchhandlung, 1953), pp. 126–175; Martin Noth, *The History of Israel*, 2nd ed., revised E. T. (New York: Harper & Brothers, 1960), pp. 73ff.; Gerhard von Rad, *Der heilige Krieg im alten Israel* (Zurich: Zwingli Verlag, 1951), pp. 16ff.; see note 17 for English edition.

13. John Bright, *A History of Israel* (Philadelphia: Westminster Press, 1959), pp. 117–120.

14. See George E. Mendenhall, "The Hebrew Conquest of Palestine," *The Biblical Archaeologist* 25 (1962), and Norman K. Gottwald, *The Tribes of Yahweh* (Maryknoll, N.Y.: Orbis Books, 1979).

15. For a helpful discussion of how "the Deuteronomic Ideology" made the *herem* a standard element of the conquest, turned a human vow into a divine command, and assigned a new purpose to the *herem* (to avoid syncretism), see Patrick D. Miller, Jr.'s commentary *Deuteronomy* in the Interpretation series (Louisville, Ky.: John Knox Press, 1990), p. 41.

16. A similar set of secular wars is ascribed to Saul in 1 Sam. 14:47–48. The stories in 1 Sam. 15; 17; 18:30; 19:8 elaborate on the brief summary.

17. Von Rad, *Der heilige Krieg im alten Israel* (1951). This seminal piece was finally published in English in 1991: *Holy War in Ancient Israel* (Grand Rapids: Wm. B. Eerdmans Publishing Co.). The English version has a splendid introduction by Ben C. Ollenburger and a fine bibliography.

18. Ibid., p. 29 (German); p. 52 (English).

19. Ibid., pp. 56–62 (German); pp. 100–108 (English).

20. Gerhard von Rad, *Old Testament Theology*, vol. 2 (New York: Harper & Row, 1965), pp. 155–169.

21. Rudolf Smend, *Yahweh War and Tribal Confederation* (Nashville: Abingdon Press, 1970).

22. The various scholars who agree with Smend on this point are reviewed by Peter C. Craigie in *The Problem of War in the Old Testament* (Grand Rapids: Wm. B. Eerdmans Publishing Co., 1978), p. 49.

23. This devastating critique was delivered by Norman Gottwald in "War, Holy" in *The Interpreter's Dictionary of the Bible, Supplementary Volume,* ed. Keith Crim et al. (Nashville: Abingdon Press, 1976), pp. 942–944. See also Fritz Stolz, *Jahwehs und Israels Krieg* (Zurich: Theologischer Verlag, 1972), and esp. G. H. Jones, "Holy War or Jahweh War?" *Vetus Testamentum* 25 (1975): 642–658.

24. Miller, *The Divine Warrior in Early Israel*, p. 2.

25. Millard C. Lind, *Yahweh Is a Warrior* (Scottdale, Pa.: Herald Press, 1980).

26. Von Rad groups it with Pss. 105 and 135 in his *Holy War in Ancient Israel*, p. 82, n. 136 (German); p. 131, n. 5 (English).

27. This is supported by David Noel Freedman and Frank M. Cross, Jr., in several articles. See, for example, their joint article "The Song of

Miriam," *Journal of Near Eastern Studies* 14 (1955): 237–250; also Cross, "The Song of the Sea and Canaanite Myth" in his *Canaanite Myth and Hebrew Epic* (Cambridge, Mass.: Harvard University Press, 1973). Interestingly, Patrick D. Miller, Jr., embraces an early date for this poem, even though he persists in agreeing with von Rad that holy war was always synergistic. *The Divine Warrior in Early Israel*, pp. 113–117, 156.

28. This thesis is set forth in a very clear and simple form in a book for children written by one of Lind's disciples: Lois Barrett, *The Way God Fights* (Scottdale, Pa.: Herald Press, 1987).

29. See Lind, *Yahweh Is a Warrior*, pp. 110–111.

30. Lord Byron, "The Destruction of Sennacherib."

31. Miller, *The Divine Warrior in Ancient Israel* (Cambridge, Mass.: Harvard University Press, 1973).

32. By careful reconstruction and exegesis, Miller finds references to the cosmic army in additional verses in these ancient songs. I have cited those where the references may be easily recognized by English readers.

33. Miller sees this in Ps. 68:22; Hab. 3:8–15; and elsewhere.

34. G. Ernest Wright, *The Old Testament and Theology*, the Sprunt Lectures for 1968 (New York: Harper & Row, 1969).

35. Ibid., pp. 130–131.

5. Yahweh: Giver of *Shalom*

1. For an excellent introduction to the breadth of the meaning of *shalom*, see Donald E. Gowan, *Shalom: A Study of the Biblical Concept of Peace* (1984), available from the Kerygma Program, 300 Mt. Lebanon Boulevard, Suite 205, Pittsburgh, PA 15234.

2. As Gowan points out, the more usual Hebrew expression for the absence of war is "rest," as in Josh. 23:1. *Shalom*, p. 10.

3. Walter Brueggemann, *Living Toward a Vision: Biblical Reflections on Shalom*, rev. ed. (New York: United Church Press, 1982), p. 16.

4. Ibid., pp. 17–20.

5. Ibid., pp. 27–36.

6. Paul D. Hanson, "War and Peace in the Hebrew Bible," *Interpretation* 38 (1984): 341.

7. This is a point which Gerhard von Rad makes with great emphasis in his article "Shalom in the Old Testament," *Theological Dictionary of the New Testament*, ed. G. Kittel and G. Friedrich (Grand Rapids: Wm. B. Eerdmans Publishing Co., 1964–1976), 2:402–406. A survey of all the

occurrences of *shalom* bears him out. The one possible exception, which he also noted, is Lamentations 3:17.

8. For a full discussion of this blessing, which is older than the P document in which it is found, see Patrick D. Miller, Jr., "The Blessing of God," *Interpretation* 29 (1975): 240–251.

9. Hanson, "War and Peace in the Hebrew Bible," p. 347.

10. Walter Brueggemann, *The Land* (Philadelphia: Fortress Press, 1977), pp. 3, 2.

11. *Ibid.,* p. 51. Walter Harrelson, *From Fertility Cult to Worship* (Garden City, N.Y.: Doubleday & Co., 1969), pp. 12–13.

12. Brueggemann, *The Land,* pp. 60–61.

13. Ibid., p. 64.

14. See Ruth 4:7. It has been fashionable to make Ruth a postexilic writing, reacting to the chauvinism of Ezra and Nehemiah. However, Edward F. Campbell in *Ruth,* Anchor Bible, vol. 7 (Garden City, N.Y.: Doubleday & Co., 1975), argues for an early ninth-century date.

15. Ruth is a beautifully written, multivalent story. Recent discussions emphasize Ruth's risk-taking initiative and self-assertion in the heavily patriarchal society of Bethlehem. This is an important reading of the story. See, for example, Phyllis Trible, *God and the Rhetoric of Sexuality* (Philadelphia: Fortress Press, 1978), ch. 6; Johanna W. H. Bos, *Ruth, Esther, Jonah,* Knox Preaching Guides (Atlanta: John Knox Press, 1986); Danna Nolan Fewell and David Miller Gunn, *Compromising Redemption: Relating Characters in the Book of Ruth* (Louisville, Ky.: Westminster/John Knox Press, 1990). But the relation of the Ruth story to the *shalom* legislation of Leviticus and Deuteronomy should not be overlooked. Only in a setting where the poor and the alien have a right to the produce of the fields and where laws regarding land and family were designed to prevent the rise of a permanent underclass could Ruth's initiative have been exercised with any effect at all.

6. The Prophets: Champions of *Shalom*

1. See George E. Mendenhall, *The Tenth Generation* (Baltimore: Johns Hopkins University Press, 1973).

2. The connection between *shalom* and justice is reflected in the word itself. The verbal form of the same root, especially in the piel, means "to restore a lost thing, to repay a debt, to make reparation, to reward good with good or evil with evil." Related nouns *shillem* and *shillum* mean "requital, recompense, retribution."

3. See David Peterson, ed. *Prophecy in Israel* (Philadelphia: Fortress Press, 1987), pp. 8–10.

4. See Vernard Eller, *War and Peace from Genesis to Revelation* (Scottdale, Pa.: Herald Press, 1981), ch. 4.

5. Even though the promise to Abraham, often forgotten, moves in a different direction: "In you all the families of the earth shall be blessed" (Gen. 12:3).

7. Predictions of War

1. See Gerhard von Rad, *Old Testament Theology*, vol. 2 (New York: Harper & Row, 1965), pp. 116–119.

2. See Walter Brueggemann, "At the Mercy of Babylon: A Subversive Rereading of the Empire," *Journal of Biblical Literature* 110 (1991): 3ff.

3. Donald E. Gowan cites a number of examples of this in Ezekiel. See *Eschatology in the Old Testament* (Philadelphia: Fortress Press, 1986), p. 50.

4. I follow here the discussions by Paul D. Hanson in *The Dawn of Apocalyptic* (Philadelphia: Fortress Press, 1975) and *Old Testament Apocalyptic* (Nashville: Abingdon Press, 1987). This leads necessarily to the rejection of Gerhard von Rad's view that the term "apocalyptic" should be limited to Daniel and the apocalypses in the Pseudepigrapha, and that there is no vital connection between prophecy and apocalyptic. Von Rad sees apocalyptic as the child of the wisdom movement. See his *Old Testament Theology*, vol. 2, pp. 301–308.

5. See the helpful discussion in von Rad, *Old Testament Theology*, vol. 2, pp. 49–50.

6. Most scholars regard these "predictions" as predictions after the fact. They date Daniel in the Greek period and believe the writer is relating the history of the Middle East from Nebuchadnezzar to Antiochus Epiphanes under the form of "predictions." The genuine predictions are the final ones which picture the end of human kingdoms and the coming of God's kingdom.

8. Promises of Peace

1. This is a fundamental point in Jürgen Moltmann's *Theology of Hope* (New York: Harper & Row, 1975). See pp. 42–43, 95–106, 124–133.

2. Biblical scholars date this sermon as early as the reign of Hezekiah or as late as the time of Ezekiel.

3. Deuteronomy, of course, is dated during the reign of Josiah, but

there is evidence that a litany of blessings and curses was a part of Israel's liturgy before the monarchy. See Deuteronomy 27 and Joshua 8:30–35.

4. See Rosemary Radford Ruether's incisive essay "The Biblical Vision of the Ecological Crisis" in *Teaching and Preaching Stewardship*, ed. Norden C. Murphy (New York: Commission on Stewardship of the National Council of Churches, 1985), pp. 202–209.

5. Compare Donald E. Gowan, *Eschatology in the Old Testament* (Philadelphia: Fortress Press, 1986), pp. 32–37.

6. For the strange hold of David on the imagination of Israel, see Walter Brueggemann, *David's Truth in Israel's Imagination and Memory* (Philadelphia: Fortress Press, 1985).

7. Von Rad interprets this line to signify a rejection of the current line of David, a call to start over with another royal line. See his *Old Testament Theology*, vol. 2 (New York: Harper & Row, 1965), pp. 169–175.

8. Some critics attribute Isaiah 32:1–8 to the writers of wisdom literature and see 33:17–22 as postexilic, as late as the time of the Maccabees. I see nothing that prohibits locating these passages in the time of Isaiah, when Israel was on its land.

9. Von Rad, *Old Testament Theology*, vol. 2, pp. 169–175, sees the Micah prophecy as a strong counterstatement to the royal psalms.

10. Compare Gowan, *Eschatology in the Old Testament*, pp. 24–27.

11. I follow here the reconstruction of Paul D. Hanson in *The Dawn of Apocalyptic* (Philadelphia: Fortress Press, 1975).

12. Isaiah 4:2–6, which may also belong to the postexilic community in Jerusalem, makes a similar move from field to city. See also Isaiah 33:17–24; Ezekiel 48:35.

13. The one new note is the serpent, eating dust. It could be part of the peaceful picture: the serpent no longer bites other animals. As NRSV translates it, it seems an interruption in the peaceful picture, a gibe aimed at enemies for whom the serpent is an apt symbol. Paul Hanson, in his reconstruction of the struggle in the restoration community in Jerusalem between the dominant Zadokite priests and the followers of Second Isaiah, who were the authors of Isaiah 56–66, calls attention to the remarkable series of contrasts in Isaiah 65:13–15. "My servants" are the oppressed prophetic party and "you" are the Zadokite priests. It is my surmise that the serpent in v. 25 of the same chapter is another reference to the Zadokite priests, who will not share the idyllic peace of the new heavens, the new earth, the new Jerusalem.

14. Hanson in *The Dawn of Apocalyptic*, pp. 299–316, finds Zechariah

9 comparable to Exodus 15 and Judges 5, to many of the royal psalms, and to similar hymns in Second Isaiah.

15. Hanson, ibid., does not regard Zechariah 9:9–10 as an interruption, but makes nothing of the king's humility, nor of his disarming, not of enemies, but of his own people—of Judah and Ephraim, who in v. 13 are the two instruments of war in the Divine Warrior's hands. I cannot see vs. 9–10 as in any way applicable to the Divine Warrior of the rest of the poem.

16. In 1 Kings 4:20–28 there is an exuberant description of peace in the time of Solomon. There was "peace on all sides," and "Judah and Israel lived in safety, from Dan even to Beer-sheba, all of them under their vines and fig trees." Walter Brueggemann makes the adventurous proposal that this is a piece of irony on the part of the historian. Actually, Solomon's military bureaucracy did not fulfill the dream of all sitting under their own vines and under their own fig trees (Micah 4:4). It was rather a nightmare in which the peasantry were drafted away from vines and fig trees into the army or taxed out of the possession of their small farms in order to support the Solomonic magnificence. See his article "Vine and Fig Tree: A Case Study in Imagination and Criticism," *Catholic Biblical Quarterly* 43 (1981): 188–204.

9. Jesus Revisited

1. Le Chambon is the little village that sheltered Jews in Vichy France during World War II. See the account of this amazing example of nonviolent resistance in Philip P. Halle, *Lest Innocent Blood Be Shed* (New York: Harper & Row, 1979).

2. See André Trocmé, *Jesus-Christ et la revolution non-violente* (Geneva: Labor et Fides, 1961). (E.T., *Jesus and the Nonviolent Revolution*, trans. Michel Shenk; Scottdale, Pa.: Herald Press, 1974.) This is summarized in John Howard Yoder, *The Politics of Jesus* (Grand Rapids: Wm. B. Eerdmans Publishing Co., 1972), pp. 36–38, 64.

3. Compare the even more exclusive remark in Matthew 10:5–6.

4. Many scholars regard these detailed predictions in Luke as "prophecies after the fact."

5. Jesus' prediction of the destruction of the temple may be indirectly reflected in Matthew 26:60; Mark 14:58; and John 2:19.

6. This parable has obviously been reworked by the early church into an allegory. This is most evident in Matthew 21:43, where, following the crucifixion, the kingdom of God will be taken away from "you" (= the Jewish religious leaders) and given to "a people that produces the fruits of

the kingdom" (= the church). The sending of the "beloved son" fits church theology more easily than other sayings of Jesus about himself. In its original form, this parable possibly predicted God's punishment of Israel for their persecution of the prophets (cf. Matt. 5:12; 23:29–34, 37; Luke 6:23; 11:47–49; 13:33–34). The instrument of this punishment would be a disastrous war.

7. Ever since the publication of Johannes Weiss's *Die Predigt Jesu vom Reich Gottes* in 1892, a growing number of New Testament scholars have seen Jesus as a "thorough-going eschatologist" (Albert Schweitzer's term), deeply influenced by Jewish apocalyptic writings.

8. Did Jesus expect the final conflict and the final end within the generation then living? Mark 13:30 would indicate that he did, and most New Testament scholars take that view. But Mark 13:32 is a disavowal of any knowledge of a timetable, and the extensive scenario would have to be exceedingly compressed to fit into a single generation. What did happen within that generation was the fall of Jerusalem in 70 C.E.

9. See John Bright, *The Kingdom of God* (Nashville: Abingdon Press, 1953), for a powerful development of the centrality of the kingdom.

10. This is a major emphasis in Millard Lind, *Yahweh Is a Warrior* (Scottdale, Pa.: Herald Press, 1980). See pp. 31–32, 51–53, 64, 89, 108, 167–168, 170.

11. The presence of vs. 23–24 in Ezekiel 34 shows that the idea of a restored Davidic kingdom just would not die. According to commentators, e.g., G. Herbert May in *The Interpreter's Bible*, vol. 6, (ed. George A. Buttrick et al.; Nashville: Abingdon Press, 1956), this is an insertion by a later editor.

12. See the discussion of Zechariah 9:9–10 in chapter 8.

13. I still find the arguments of John Wick Bowman in *The Intention of Jesus* (Philadelphia: Westminster Press, 1943) very convincing. He states his thesis on pp. 1 and 2.

14. See Walter Wink's discussion of demons in *Unmasking the Powers* (Philadelphia: Fortress Press, 1984), pp. 41–68.

15. Ulrich Mauser sees the saying as one of a series of "I have come" statements and believes that the context of strife and division aroused by the Christian mission (Matt. 10:35f.) was added later. See *The Gospel of Peace* (Louisville, Ky.: Westminster/John Knox Press, 1991), pp. 38–42.

16. Wink, *Unmasking the Powers,* pp. 41–42.

17. Ched Myers, *Binding the Strong Man: A Political Reading of Mark's Story of Jesus* (Maryknoll, N.Y.: Orbis Books, 1988). The title is drawn, of

course, from Jesus' parable cited earlier in this chapter. The Markan version speaks specifically of "tying up" the strong man.

18. Ched Myers makes the interesting but complicated suggestion that the war against the establishment and the war against the demons are two aspects of a single war. He sees the demons as somehow representatives of the establishment. Thus in the first exorcism (Mark 1:21–28) Myers stresses that Jesus has invaded the space (synagogue) and time (Sabbath) of the scribes. His teaching is declared by the people to have more authority (*exousia*) than that of the scribes. At this point the man with the unclean spirit cries out, "What have you to do with us, Jesus of Nazareth? Have you come to destroy us?" The "us," says Myers, indicates that the demoniac is pleading on behalf of the scribal aristocracy, which Jesus is threatening. *Binding the Strong Man*, pp. 141–142.

19. Yoder, *The Politics of Jesus*, p. 57.

20. Ibid., p. 61.

10. The Church: Part of a Violent World

1. Ulrich Mauser find another reference in the word of the Philippian jailer in Acts 16:36. Indeed, "the concept of peace in the book of Acts is engaged in silent dialogue with the ideal of Roman Peace." *The Gospel of Peace* (Louisville, Ky.: Westminster/John Knox Press, 1991), pp. 84–85. For a fuller study, see Klaus Wengst, *Pax Romana and the Peace of Jesus Christ* (Philadelphia: Fortress Press, 1987).

2. Romans 13:1–7 is not as simple as its translation in the NRSV might lead readers to believe. There has been voluminous debate as to whether the word *exousiai* in verse 1 means "governing authorities," or the cosmic powers that were widely understood in the Greco-Roman world to stand behind various human authorities. See the thorough discussion in Clinton D. Morrison, *The Powers That Be* (Naperville, Ill.: Alec R. Allenson, 1960). The practical import—that Christians should be respectful of, and subject to the state—remains, no matter how the exegetical question is resolved. There are, however, limits on that respect and subjection. The power of earthly rulers is not inherent in their position. It is derived from God, whether directly or through angelic "authorities" that stand behind them. If they forget the source of their power, if they rebel against God, if they no longer act as God's deputies, if instead of rewarding good conduct and punishing evil conduct they do the reverse, they must be resisted. We shall see in chapter 12 how the church came to that position regarding Rome. For a thorough discussion of this passage from a pacifist point of view, see

John Howard Yoder, *The Politics of Jesus* (Grand Rapids: Wm. B. Eerdmans Publishing Co., 1972), ch. 10.

3. Howard Thurman has written movingly of the way in which Jesus had an appeal for his ex-slave grandmother that Paul could never have. Jesus was totally marginal; Paul had a foothold in the structures of power, and he exercised it. See *Jesus and the Disinherited* (Nashville: Abingdon Press, 1949; repr. Richmond, Ind.: Friends United Press, 1976), pp. 30–34.

11. The Church: Christ's Peaceful People

1. Here I side with John Howard Yoder against the view prevalent among social ethicists today that the early church found Jesus' sociopolitical ethics, including his teaching on peace, irrelevant and was interested in his life, death, and resurrection only as the basis for justification by faith; that whatever ethics the church taught was drawn from Hellenistic culture, particularly Stoicism. See *The Politics of Jesus* (Grand Rapids: Wm. B. Eerdmans Publishing Co., 1972), pp. 15–21, 163–192.

2. It is an interesting question whether we should include here the constant use of "peace" at the beginning and ending of the letters that went back and forth between Christians of the first generation. The standard greeting was "Grace to you and peace" (Rom. 1:7; 1 Cor. 1:3; 2 Cor. 1:2; Gal. 1:3; Eph. 1:2; Phil. 1:2; Col. 1:2; 1 Thess. 1:1; 2 Thess. 1:2; 1 Tim. 1:2; 2 Tim. 1:2; Titus 1:4; Philemon 1:3; 1 Peter 1:2; 2 Peter 1:2; 2 John 3). "Peace" also figures at the close of several letters (Rom. 15:13, 33; 16:20; 2 Cor. 13:11; Gal. 6:16; Eph. 6:23; Phil. 4:9; 1 Thess. 5:23; 2 Thess. 3:16; Heb. 13:20; 1 Peter 5:14; 3 John 15). Were these conventional greetings? Not in the Greek culture of the first century. However, among Jews *shalom* had become something of a customary greeting. The distinctively Christian element was the designation of God the Father and Jesus the Messiah as twin sources of grace and peace.

3. Based on important manuscripts, the NRSV translates that the two groups were Jews and Hellenists (Greek-speaking Jews). This would scarcely have been noteworthy, since those two groups coexisted in the Jerusalem church (Acts 6:1). Moreover we have the firsthand testimony of Paul that the table fellowship of Jews and Gentiles at Antioch had disturbed the Jerusalem church (Gal. 2:11–14).

4. John Howard Yoder makes the interesting point that the *imitatio Christi* practiced and urged by the apostolic church is confined to suffering, to "reverse fighting." There is no duty to imitate his itinerancy, his celibacy, his self-support as an artisan, his rural ethos. "Only at one point, only on one

subject—but then consistently, universally—is Jesus our example: in his cross." *The Politics of Jesus,* pp. 96–97; see also p. 134.

5. This is the position of Christopher Rowland in *Radical Christianity* (Maryknoll, N.Y.: Orbis Books, 1988), pp. 34–45. See our discussion in chapter 10.

6. See Hendrikus Berkhof, *Christ and the Powers* (Scottdale, Pa.: Herald Press, 1962). Yoder, *The Politics of Jesus,* ch. 8, follows Berkhof.

7. Yoder, *The Politics of Jesus,* p. 153.

8. Two earlier Pauline passages may have suggested a discourse on the weapons of Christian warfare: 2 Corinthians 6:6–7 and 10:3–5.

9. In *Christ the Peacemaker: Studies in Colossians* (Atlanta: General Assembly Mission Board, Presbyterian Church in the United States, 1982), pp. 58–65. My remarks there were based on an address by Bruce Rigdon to a group of American and Russian church leaders, entitled "Taming the Principalities and Powers."

10. Berkhof, *Christ and the Powers,* pp. 22, 25, 27.

11. See Walter Wink, *Naming the Powers* (Philadelphia: Fortress Press, 1984), p. 5 and passim.

12. Walter Wink, *Unmasking the Powers* (Philadelphia: Fortress Press, 1986), title page.

13. See chapter 11, section "The Messiah."

14. This has been noted by Christoph Burger in *Jesus als Davidssohn* (Göttingen: Vandenhoeck & Ruprecht, 1970) and by Ulrich Mauser in *The Gospel of Peace* (Louisville, Ky.: Westminster/John Knox Press, 1991), pp. 50–53.

15. Berkhof, *Christ and the Powers,* pp. 30ff., gives a profound analysis of this text. See also Wink, *Naming the Powers,* pp. 55–60.

16. Wink, *Naming the Powers,* pp. 50–55, suggests that Christ will "neutralize" rather than destroy the powers.

17. The understanding of Christ as Victor was brought forcibly to the attention of the theological world by Gustaf Aulén's *Christus Victor* in 1931 (English translation reprinted many times by SPCK in London). Interestingly, as far as I can tell, Aulén made no use of the Old Testament on this point.

18. The central theme of the Confession of 1967 of the Presbyterian Church (U.S.A.) is reconciliation: "God's reconciling work in Jesus Christ and the mission of reconciliation to which he has called his church are the heart of the gospel in any age."

19. For a very balanced discussion of the ambiguity of the New Testa-

ment church, see Christopher Rowland, *Christian Origins* (Minneapolis: Augsburg Publishing House, 1985), pp. 272–285.

12. An Ambiguous Apocalypse

1. There is, of course, an extensive Jewish and Christian apocalyptic literature outside of the canon, including such works as 1 Enoch, 2 Esdras, the Apocalypse of Baruch, the Apocalypse of Peter, and others. Josephine Massyngberde Ford in *Revelation,* Anchor Bible, vol. 38 (Garden City, N.Y.: Doubleday & Co., 1975), suggests that Revelation is essentially a Jewish apocalypse, originating in the school of John the Baptist, to which Christian additions have been made in chs. 1–3; 21–22. This has not commanded wide agreement, but it emphasizes the kinship between Jewish and Christian apocalypses.

2. The Apocalypse is best understood by oppressed people who find themselves in an actual apocalyptic situation. This is why Allan Boesak's *Comfort and Protest: The Apocalypse from a South African Perspective* (Philadelphia: Westminster Press, 1987) speaks with such authority. Fashionable millennial speculations by well-to-do Christians will always miss the point.

3. For a brief discussion of the typical features of apocalyptic writing, see the article "Apocalypticism" by Martin Rist in *The Interpreter's Dictionary of the Bible,* ed. George A. Buttrick et al. (Nashville: Abingdon Press, 1962), vol. 1, pp. 157–161. Adela Yarbro Collins summarizes the results of more recent study of apocalyptic writings in general and of Revelation in particular in "Reading the Book of Revelation in the Twentieth Century," *Interpretation* 40 (1986): 229–242.

4. Boesak, *Comfort and Protest,* p. 17.

5. Ibid., p. 38.

6. In agreement with Christopher Rowland and Mark Corner in *Liberating Exegesis: The Challenge of Liberation Theology to Biblical Studies* (Louisville, Ky.: Westminster/John Knox Press, 1989), pp. 146–153.

7. Boesak, *Comfort and Protest,* p. 84.

8. T. R. Hobbs, *A Time for War* (Wilmington, Del.: Michael Glazier, 1989), p. 233.

9. I am obviously not persuaded by those who see in Rev. 21–22 two Jerusalems, one earthly during the millennium, the other heavenly. See R. H. Charles, *Apocrypha and Pseudepigrapha of the Old Testament* (Oxford: Clarendon Press, 1913), 2:140–226, and P. Gaechter in *Theological Studies* 10 (1949): 485–521. Ford in *Revelation* in the Anchor Bible takes the same position.

10. "Revelation does not authorize violence and militarism. It is true that this book draws upon ancient combat myths which depict struggles between good and evil. It is true that militant images are employed to portray the victory of God over every evil force in creation. However, the battle is God's, in behalf of the beleaguered and oppressed faithful. Nowhere does the writer call upon the Christians to take up arms against Rome or other victimizing powers." Fred B. Craddock, "Preaching the Book of Revelation," *Interpretation* 40 (1986): 272.

11. "It seems to me that an illustrative sample of quietist or pacifist apocalyptic writing is the Revelation of John. Here I believe we have an outstanding example of the Divine Warrior motif and the *complete* absense of a call to arms on the part of human beings." Josephine Massyngberde Ford, "Shalom in the Johannine Corpus," *Horizons in Biblical Theology* 6 (1984): 67.

12. John Howard Yoder, *The Politics of Jesus* (Grand Rapids: Wm. B. Eerdmans Publishing Co., 1972), p. 238.

13. Compare Martin Luther King, Jr.'s speech on the State House steps in Montgomery: "How long? Not long. Because the arm of the moral universe is long, but it bends toward justice." James Melvin Watson, ed., *A Testament of Hope: The Essential Writings of Martin Luther King, Jr.* (San Francisco: Harper & Row, 1986), p. 230.

Conclusion: The Abolition of War

1. The following account is substantiated by Roland H. Bainton in *Christian Attitudes Toward War and Peace* (Nashville: Abingdon Press, 1960), pp. 66–84; John Ferguson, *The Politics of Love* (Nyack, N.Y.: Fellowship Publications, 1979), pp. 53–65; Knut William Ruyter, "Pacifism and Military Service in the Early Church" in *Crosscurrents* 32 (1982–83): 54–70; Liza Sowle Cahill, "Nonresistance, Defense, Violence, and the Kingdom in Christian Tradition," *Interpretation* 38 (1984): 380–397.

2. Tertullian, *On Idolatry*, in *Ante-Nicene Fathers*, ed. Alexander Roberts and James Donaldson (Grand Rapids: Wm. B. Eerdmans Publishing Co., 1965), 3:73.

3. Some examples: Augsburg Confession: "Christians may without sin . . . engage in just wars." Second Helvetic Confession: "And if it is necessary to preserve the safety of the people by war, let [the magistrate] wage war in the name of God; provided he has first sought peace by all means possible, and cannot save his people in any other way except by war. And when the magistrate does these things in faith, he serves God by those very works

which are truly good, and receives a blessing from the Lord." Westminster Confession of Faith: "[Christian magistrates] may lawfully, now under the New Testament, wage war upon just and necessary occasions."

4. See Jonathan Schell, *The Fate of the Earth* (New York: Alfred A. Knopf, 1982), and any number of other books dealing with the nuclear threat.

5. This is the argument of John Howard Yoder's helpful book *The Politics of Jesus* (Grand Rapids: Wm. B. Eerdmans Publishing Co., 1972; repr. 1985).

6. Vernard Eller, *War and Peace from Genesis to Revelation* (Scottdale, Pa.: Herald Press, 1981), pp. 160–163.

7. Stanley Hauerwas and William Willimon, *Resident Aliens: A Provocative Christian Assessment of Culture and Ministry for People Who Know That Something Is Wrong* (Nashville: Abingdon Press, 1989).

8. As I was writing this I was informed that the American Peace Network is currently helping to rewrite the New Abolitionist Covenant (a 1979 call for the abolition of nuclear arms) to make it a covenant for the abolition of war.

9. Paul D. Hanson, *The Diversity of Scripture* (Philadelphia: Fortress Press, 1982).

10. This point was made powerfully by Clinton M. Marsh in his sermon ". . . And the Time Is Now." See *Church and Society* 71, no. 1 (1990): 77–84.

Index of Scripture References

Index of Names